CAMBRIDGE
UNIVERSITY PRESS

UNIVERSITY *of* CAMBRIDGE
ESOL Examinations

Cambridge English

Objective
Key

Student's Book
with answers

Annette Capel   Wendy Sharp

Second Edition

CAMBRIDGE UNIVERSITY PRESS

Cambridge, New York, Melbourne, Madrid, Cape Town,
Singapore, São Paulo, Delhi, Mexico City

Cambridge University Press
The Edinburgh Building, Cambridge CB2 8RU, UK

www.cambridge.org
Information on this title: www.cambridge.org/9781107627246

First published 2005

Printed in Italy by L.E.G.O. S.p.A.

A catalogue record for this book is available from the British Library

ISBN 978-1-107-62724-6 Student's Book with Answers with CD-ROM
ISBN 978-1-107-66282-7 Student's Book without Answers with CD-ROM
ISBN 978-1-107-64204-1 Teacher's Book with Teacher's Resources Audio CD/CD-ROM
ISBN 978-1-107-69008-0 Class Audio CDs (2)
ISBN 978-1-107-64676-6 Workbook with Answers
ISBN 978-1-107-69921-2 Workbook without Answers
ISBN 978-1-107-66893-5 Student's Book Pack (Student's Book with Answers with CD-ROM and Class Audio CDs (2))
ISBN 978-1-107-60561-9 For Schools Practice Test Booklet with Answers with Audio CD
ISBN 978-1-107-69445-3 For Schools Pack without Answers (Student's Book with CD-ROM and Practice Test Booklet)

Additional resources for this publication at www.cambridge.org/elt/objectivekey

Map of Objective Key Student's Book

TOPIC	EXAM SKILLS	GRAMMAR	VOCABULARY	PRONUNCIATION (P) AND SPELLING (S)
Unit 1 Friends 8–11 1.1 Friends for ever 1.2 Borrow this!	Paper 2 Listening: Part 1	Present simple: *be, have* Questions in the present tense	Personal possessions Adjectives	(P) The alphabet
Exam folder 1 12–13	Paper 2 Listening: Part 1 Short conversations			
Unit 2 Shopping 14–17 2.1 For sale 2.2 Shopping from home	Paper 1: Part 1 (Reading) Paper 2 Listening: Part 3	*How much ...?* *How many ...?* *some* and *any*	Shopping and shops	(P) /ɑː/ *car*, /eɪ/ *face*, /æ/ *apple* (S) Plurals
Exam folder 2 18–19	Paper 1 Reading and Writing: Part 1 (Reading) Notices			
Unit 3 Food and drink 20–23 3.1 Breakfast, lunch and dinner 3.2 Food at festivals	Paper 2 Listening: Part 5 Paper 1: Part 4 (Reading) Paper 1: Part 9 (Writing)	Present simple Telling the time Adverbs of frequency	Food and drink Celebrations Dates (day and month)	(S) Contractions (P) /ɪ/ *chicken*, /iː/ *cheese*
Writing folder 1 24–25	Paper 1 Reading and Writing: Part 6 (Writing) Spelling words			
Unit 4 The past 26–29 4.1 A real adventure 4.2 A mini-adventure	Paper 1: Part 4 (Reading) Paper 2 Listening: Part 5	Past simple Past simple: short answers Past simple + *ago*	Nationalities	(S) Regular verbs in the past simple (P) Regular past simple endings
Units 1–4 Revision 30–31				
Unit 5 Animals 32–35 5.1 Going to the zoo 5.2 An amazing animal	Paper 1: Part 6 (Writing) Paper 2 Listening: Part 3 Paper 1: Part 5 (Reading)	Lists with *and* Conjunctions *and, but, or, because*	Animals Collocations with *do, make, take* and *spend*	(P) List intonation (S) *their, there, they're*
Exam folder 3 36–37	Paper 1 Reading and Writing: Part 2 (Reading): Multiple choice Paper 1 Reading and Writing: Part 5 (Reading): Mulitple-choice cloze			
Unit 6 Leisure and hobbies 38–41 6.1 Theme park fun 6.2 Free time	Paper 3 Speaking: Part 2 Paper 3 Speaking: Part 1 Paper 2 Listening: Part 4 Paper 1: Part 9 (Writing) Paper 1: Part 2 (Reading)	Comparative and superlative adjectives Comparative adverbs	Leisure activities Descriptive adjectives and adverbs	(S) Comparative and superlative adjectives (P) /ə/ *camera*
Exam folder 4 42–43	Paper 2 Listening: Parts 4 and 5 Gap-fill			
Unit 7 Clothes 44–47 7.1 The latest fashion 7.2 Your clothes	Paper 1: Part 4 (Reading) Listening for information Paper 1: Part 3 (Reading)	Simple and continuous tenses	Clothes Adjectives to describe clothes	(S) *-ing* form (P) The last letters of the alphabet: w, x, y, z
Writing folder 2 48–49	Paper 1 Reading and Writing: Part 7 (Writing) Open cloze			
Unit 8 Entertainment 50–53 8.1 A great movie 8.2 Cool sounds	Paper 1: Part 5 (Reading) Paper 2 Listening: Part 1	Modal verbs 1: *must, have/had to, may, can, could*	Films, music	(P) Short questions (S) Mistakes with vowels
Units 5–8 Revision 54–55				

TOPIC	EXAM SKILLS	GRAMMAR	VOCABULARY	PRONUNCIATION (P) AND SPELLING (S)
Unit 9 Travel 56–59 9.1 Holiday plans 9.2 Looking into the future	Listening for information Paper 1: Part 3 (Reading) Paper 1: Part 7 (Writing)	The future with *going to* and *will*	Travel	(P) /h/ *hand* (S) Words ending in *-y*
Exam folder 5 60–61	Paper 3 Speaking: Parts 1 and 2			
Unit 10 Places and buildings 62–65 10.1 Inside the home 10.2 Famous buildings	Paper 2 Listening: Part 2 Paper 1: Part 2 (Reading)	The passive – present and past simple	Furniture, rooms Colours, materials Opposites	(S) Words ending in *-f* and *-fe* (P) Dates (years)
Exam folder 6 66–67	Paper 1 Reading and Writing: Part 4 (Reading) Right, Wrong, Doesn't say			
Unit 11 Sport 68–71 11.1 Living for sport 11.2 Keeping fit	Paper 1: Part 4 (Reading) Paper 2 Listening: Part 5 Paper 1: Part 6 (Writing)	Word order in questions Verbs in the *-ing* form	Sport and sports equipment Fitness	(P) /b/ *basketball*, /v/ *volleyball* (S) *gu-, qu-*
Writing folder 3 72–73	Paper 1 Reading and Writing: Part 9 (Writing) Short message			
Unit 12 The family 74–77 12.1 Family tree 12.2 Large and small	Paper 2 Listening: Part 3 Paper 1: Part 4 (Reading)	Possessive adjectives and pronouns Subject, object and reflexive pronouns *everything, something, anything,* etc.	People in a family	(P) /aʊ/ *cow*, /ɔː/ *draw* (S) Words ending in *-le*
Units 9–12 Revision 78–79				
Unit 13 The weather 80–83 13.1 Sun, rain or snow? 13.2 Weather problems	Paper 2 Listening: Part 2 Paper 1: Part 5 (Reading)	*(not) as ... as* *enough* and *too*	Weather	(P) Unstressed words with /ə/ (S) *to, too* and *two*
Exam folder 7 84–85	Paper 2 Listening: Part 2 Multiple matching			
Unit 14 Books and studying 86–89 14.1 Something good to read 14.2 Learn something new!	Paper 1: Part 4 (Reading) Paper 2 Listening: Part 4 Paper 1: Part 3 (Reading)	Position of adjectives *I prefer / I'd like*	Books School subjects, education	(P) Silent consonants (S) Words which are often confused
Exam folder 8 90–91	Paper 1 Reading and Writing: Part 3 (Reading) Multiple choice			
Unit 15 The world of work 92–95 15.1 Working hours 15.2 Part-time jobs	Paper 1: Part 4 (Reading) Paper 2 Listening: Part 3	Present perfect *just* and *yet*	Work, jobs	(S) Words ending in *-er* and *-or* (P) /ð/ *clothes*, /θ/ *thirsty*
Writing folder 4 96–97	Paper 1 Reading and Writing: Part 8 (Writing) Information transfer			
Unit 16 Transport 98–101 16.1 Journeys 16.2 A day out	Paper 3 Speaking: Part 2 Paper 2 Listening: Part 1	Modal verbs 2: *must, mustn't, don't have to, should, need to, needn't*	Transport Collocations with transport Free-time activities Directions	(P) Weak and strong forms (S) *i* or *e*?
Units 13–16 Revision 102–103				
Unit 17 Science and technology 104–107 17.1 Totally Techno 17.2 New ideas	Paper 1: Part 5 (Reading) Paper 2 Listening: Part 3	Infinitive of purpose The infinitive with and without *to*	Technology Collocations with *get, give, have, make, see, watch*	(P) Contractions (S) Correcting mistakes

TOPIC	EXAM SKILLS	GRAMMAR	VOCABULARY	PRONUNCIATION (P) AND SPELLING (S)
Exam folder 9 108–109	Paper 2 Listening: Part 3 Multiple choice			
Unit 18 Health and well-being 110–113 18.1 Keeping well! 18.2 A long and happy life	Paper 1: Part 6 (Writing) Paper 1: Parts 3 and 4 (Reading) Paper 2 Listening: Part 5 Paper 1: Part 9 (Writing)	Word order of time phrases First conditional	Parts of the body Health	(P) Linking sounds (S) Words which don't double their last letter
Exam folder 10 114–117	Paper 1 Reading and Writing: Part 4 (Reading) Multiple choice			
Unit 19 Language and communication 118–121 19.1 Let's communicate! 19.2 Different languages	Paper 2 Listening: Part 2 Paper 1: Part 7 (Writing) Paper 1: Part 5 (Reading)	Prepositions of place Prepositions of time	Communicating Countries, languages, nationalities	(P) Word stress (S) Spellings of the sound /iː/
Writing folder 5 122–123	Paper 1 Reading and Writing: Part 9 (Writing) Short message			
Unit 20 People 124–127 20.1 Famous people 20.2 Lucky people	Paper 1: Part 4 (Reading) Paper 2 Listening: Part 4 Paper 3 Speaking: Part 2 Paper 1: Part 6 (Writing) Paper 1: Part 2 (Reading)	Review of tenses	Describing people	(P) Sentence stress (S) ck or k?
Units 17–20 Revision 128–129				
Extra material 130–135				
Grammar folder 136–148				
Vocabulary folder 149–153				
Practice for Key Writing Part 6 154–158				
List of irregular verbs 159				
Answers and recording scripts 161				
Acknowledgements 199				

Content of Cambridge English: Key

The Cambridge English: Key (and Key for Schools) examination is at A2 level of the Common European Framework. There are three papers – Paper 1 Reading and Writing, Paper 2 Listening and Paper 3 Speaking.

There are five grades: Pass with Merit (about 85% of the total marks) and Pass (about 70% of the total marks) are passing grades at A2 level. An additional grade of Pass with Distinction records a pass at B1 level. A Narrow Fail (about 5% below the pass mark) records A1 level achievement. For this and the Fail grade, the results slip will show the papers which had particularly low marks.

Paper 1 Reading and Writing 1 hour 10 minutes   (50% of the total marks)

There are nine parts in this paper and they are always in the same order. Parts 1–5 test a range of reading skills and Parts 6–9 test basic writing skills. You write all your answers on the answer sheet.

Part	Task type	Number of questions	Task format	Objective Exam folder
Reading Part 1	Matching	5	You match five sentences to eight notices.	EF 2
Reading Part 2	Multiple choice (A, B or C)	5	You choose the right words to complete five sentences.	EF 3
Reading Part 3	Multiple choice (A, B or C) AND Matching	5	You choose the right answer to complete short conversational exchanges.	EF 8
Reading Part 4	Right / Wrong / Doesn't say OR	7	You answer seven questions on a text. OR	EF 6
	Multiple choice (A, B or C)	7	You read a text and choose the right answer to seven questions.	EF 10
Reading Part 5	Multiple choice (A, B or C)	8	You choose the right words to complete eight spaces in a short text.	EF 3
Writing Part 6	Word completion	5	You decide which words go with five definitions and spell them correctly.	WF 1
Writing Part 7	Open cloze	10	You fill ten spaces in a text such as a postcard with single words, spelled correctly.	WF 2
Writing Part 8	Information transfer	5	You complete a set of notes or a form with information from one or two texts.	WF 4
Writing Part 9	Short message	1	You write a short message, such as a note, an email or a postcard (25–35 words), which includes three pieces of information.	WF 3, WF 5

Paper 2 Listening about 30 minutes (including 8 minutes to transfer answers)   (25% of the total marks)

There are five parts in this paper and they are always in the same order. You hear each recording twice. You write your answers on the answer sheet at the end of the test.

Part	Task type	Number of Questions	Task format	Objective Exam folder
Listening Part 1	Multiple choice (A, B or C)	5	You answer five questions by choosing the correct picture, word or number. There are two speakers in each short conversation.	EF 1
Listening Part 2	Matching	5	You match five questions with eight possible answers. There are two speakers.	EF 7
Listening Part 3	Multiple choice (A, B or C)	5	You answer five questions about a conversation between two speakers.	EF 9
Listening Part 4	Gap-fill	5	You complete five spaces in a set of notes. There are two speakers.	EF 4
Listening Part 5	Gap-fill	5	You complete five spaces in a set of notes. There is one speaker.	EF 4

Paper 3 Speaking 8–10 minutes for a pair of students   (25% of the total marks)

There are two parts to the test and they are always in the same order. There are two candidates and two examiners. Only one of the examiners asks the questions.

Part	Task type	Time	Task format	Objective Exam folder
Speaking Part 1	The examiner asks both candidates some questions.	5–6 minutes	You must give information about yourself.	EF 5
Speaking Part 2	The candidates talk together to find out information.	3–4 minutes	You are given some material to help you ask and answer questions.	EF 5

New for the second edition of Objective Key

In this second edition, there are new texts, pictures and exercises, as well as new audio recordings. There is also extra A2 level vocabulary from the English Vocabulary Profile (see below). A new CD-ROM and free website material provide more practice.

 ## English Vocabulary Profile

The English Vocabulary Profile is an online resource with information about the words and phrases that learners of English know at each of the six levels of the Common European Framework – A1 to C2. For important A2 vocabulary, see the Key words boxes in the units, the Vocabulary folder and the Practice for *Key* Writing Part 6.

 ## CD-ROM

A CD-ROM provides many interactive activities, including grammar, vocabulary, listening and reading and writing. Games make practising the language fun. All the extra activities are linked to topics in the Student's Book.

Website www.cambridge.org/elt/objectivekey
The website contains further grammar and vocabulary practice for students.

1.1 Friends for ever

1 Here are some reasons why friends are important. Look at them together. Which are true for you? Which is the best reason? Write three more reasons together.

Twelve reasons why friends are great!

1 Friends are always there for you.

2 It isn't fun to watch television alone.

3 You get funny text messages from them.

4 They don't tell you lies.

5 You have someone to go shopping with.

6 Friends don't forget your birthday.

7 It's great to go on the PlayStation together.

8 You can chat about football for hours.

9 Your best friend has your favourite ice cream in the fridge.

10 They help you with your homework.

11 Parties without your friends aren't good!

12 Friends make you laugh.

be and have

2 Copy and complete the verb boxes. Some words are in exercise 1.

The verb *be*
I *am*, I'm, I'm not
you
he, she, it
we
they

The verb *have*
I
you
he, she, it
we
they

Pronunciation

3 **1 02** Spelling is important in the Key exam. Listen and write down the letters you hear. What famous names do the letters spell?

1 _ _ _ _ _   _ _ _ _ _ _ _ _
(a tennis player)

2 _ _ _ _ _ _ _ _   _ _ _ _
(a film star)

3 _ _ _ _   _ _ _ _ _ _ _
(a boy in a cartoon)

4 _ _ _ _   _ _ _ _ _
(a footballer)

5 _ _ _   _ _ _ _ _ _
(a popular film)

6 _ _ _   _ _ _   _ _ _ _ _ _ _ _
(an American band)

Listening

4 **1 03** Listen to Maria asking four teenagers about their best friends. Complete the information.

1 Matt

Best friend is _____ Jonny _____
How old is he? _____
What do they do together? _____

2 Elena

Best friend is _____
When do they meet? _____

3 Kelly-Anne

Best friend is _____
Why is she special? _____
How old is Kelly-Anne? _____

4 Tom

Best friend is _____
Where do they go together? _____

5 **1 04** Listen and write short answers to Maria's questions.

1 What's your best friend called?
2 Can you spell that?
3 How old is he or she?
4 When do you meet?
5 Where do you go together?
6 What do you do together?
7 Why is your friend special?

6 Now ask and answer questions 1–7 from exercise 5 in pairs. Use some of this language from the recording.

OK ... can you spell that?

It's M-A-R-T-A.

Right, and why is Marta special?

Well, because she ...

Key speaking

asking	answering
OK ...	Well ...
Right ...	That's easy.
So ...	That's difficult.
And ...	That's right.

1.2 Borrow this!

1 What things do you lend your friends? Do they always give them back? Use these words to help you.

2 Read the photo story with another student. Why is Sam angry at the beginning? Why isn't he angry at the end?

Key words

books   clothes   computer games   DVDs   magazines   make-up   money

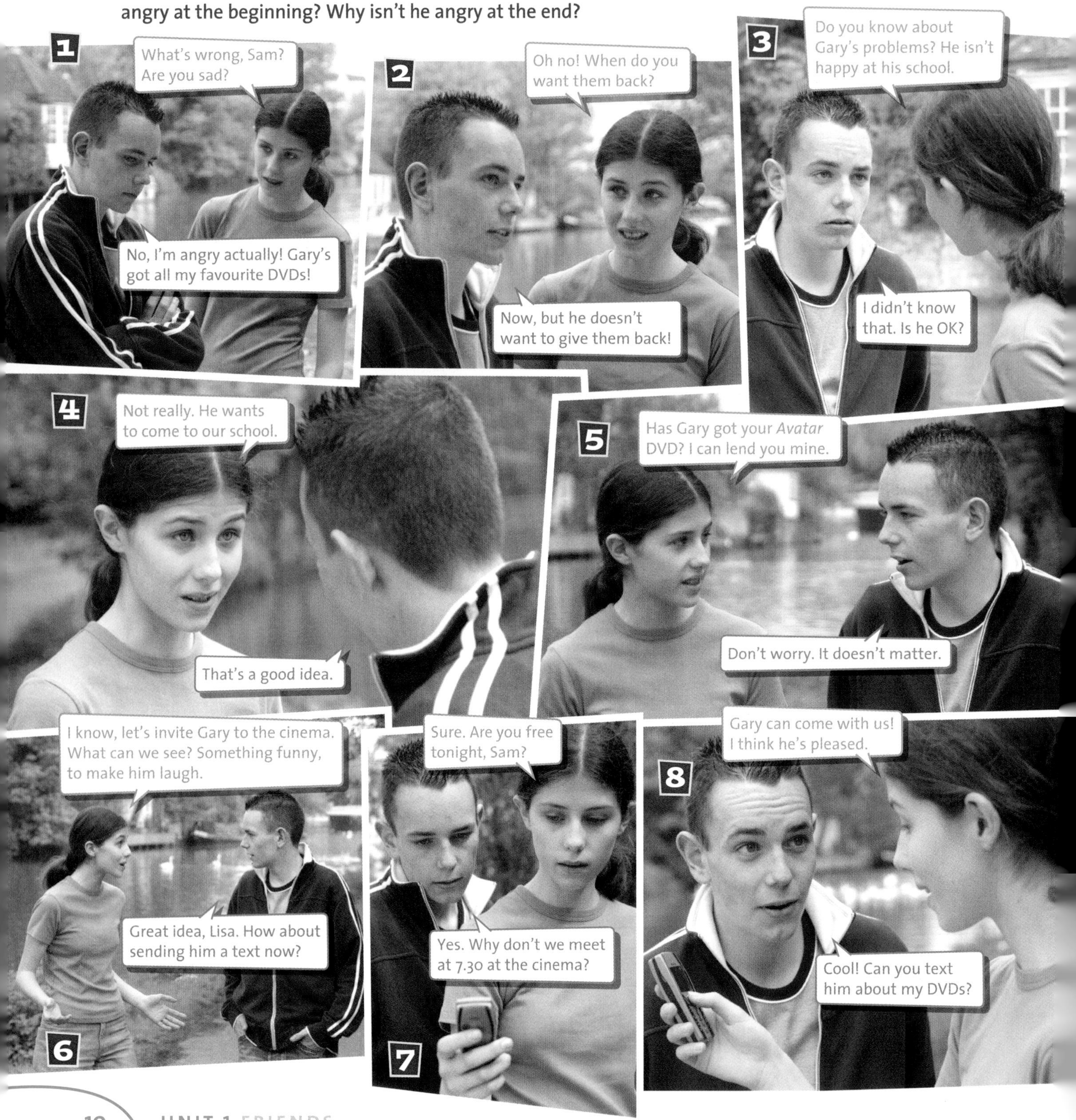

1
What's wrong, Sam? Are you sad?

No, I'm angry actually! Gary's got all my favourite DVDs!

2
Oh no! When do you want them back?

Now, but he doesn't want to give them back!

3
Do you know about Gary's problems? He isn't happy at his school.

I didn't know that. Is he OK?

4
Not really. He wants to come to our school.

That's a good idea.

5
Has Gary got your *Avatar* DVD? I can lend you mine.

Don't worry. It doesn't matter.

6
I know, let's invite Gary to the cinema. What can we see? Something funny, to make him laugh.

Great idea, Lisa. How about sending him a text now?

7
Sure. Are you free tonight, Sam?

Yes. Why don't we meet at 7.30 at the cinema?

8
Gary can come with us! I think he's pleased.

Cool! Can you text him about my DVDs?

Grammar Asking questions

3 Read the photo story again and find:
- a *Yes/No* question like this one: *Are you sad?*
- a *Wh-* question like this one: *What's wrong, Sam?*

Look carefully at the order of the words in the questions. Then read the grammar rules and add an example question for each one.

Yes/No questions in the present tense

- Questions with *have got*: Has Gary got your *Avatar* DVD?
  The verb *have* always comes first and *got* comes after the subject.
  EXAMPLE: ....

- Questions with *be*: Are you free tonight, Sam?
  The verb also comes first.
  EXAMPLE: ....

- Questions with *can*: Can you text him about my DVDs?
  This verb comes first and the main verb comes after the subject.
  EXAMPLE: ....

- Questions with *other verbs*: Do you know about Gary's problems?
  The question starts with *Do* or *Does* and the main verb comes after the subject.
  EXAMPLE: ....

Wh- questions in the present tense

- Questions with *be* and *have got*: What is wrong, Sam?
  The verb comes after the question word.
  EXAMPLE: ....

- Questions with *can*: What can we see?
  This verb comes after the question word and the main verb comes after the subject.
  EXAMPLE: ....

- Questions with *other verbs*: When do you want them back?
  The verb form *do* or *does* comes after the question word, then the subject and then the main verb.
  EXAMPLE: ....

Suggesting things

You can use *How about ... +ing?* and *Why don't/doesn't ...?* to suggest things:
EXAMPLE: ....
EXAMPLE: ....

G → page 136

4 Correct the mistakes that exam candidates made with questions. Two are correct.
1 When you want to come here?
2 Where you are now?
3 How about meet me at 7 o'clock?
4 Why don't we meet at the station?
5 Why you think it is interesting?
6 What do you want to buy?
7 Who he does like?

5 Ask and answer questions.
1 Why / you / happy?
   A: *Why are you happy?*   B: *Because it's sunny!*
2 Where / you / live?
3 What / your dad's / first name?
4 When / this lesson / finish?
5 Who / special friend?
6 How / lending me ...?

Vocabulary

6 Complete the sentences with an adjective from the box. There is one extra adjective. Then find three more adjectives in the sentences.

Key words

amazing   free   horrible   ~~lucky~~
pleased   popular   sick   true   worried

1 Maria's so ___lucky___ – she's got two tickets for tonight's rock concert!
2 My mum's .... – she's in bed with flu.
3 Are you .... tonight? Let's go out!
4 This sweet is really ....! Can I have a different one?
5 I'm really .... to see you. How are you?
6 Don't look so .... – I'm not angry!
7 Your new phone is ....! I want one.
8 Why is this cartoon so ....? I think it's really boring!

Activity

Questionnaires

- Look at page 130. Ask questions to complete the questionnaire about your partner. Ask him/her to spell difficult words!

- Tell the class about your partner.

Exam folder 1

Listening Part 1 Short conversations

In Part 1 of the Listening paper, you will hear five short conversations on different topics. There are always two speakers (usually a man and a woman). There is an example and five questions. You must choose the correct answer from options A, B or C. These options can be pictures, words or numbers.

Note: Write your answers on the question paper during the test. **You do not transfer any answers to the answer sheet until the end of the test.**

Here is an example of the answer sheet for Part 1. You must write your answers in pencil.

Part 1			
1	A	B	C
2	A	B	C
3	A	B	C
4	A	B	C
5	A	B	C

Here is an example question. Read the question and the recording script. Match the parts in colour to pictures A, B or C. Then look at the other words in the recording script and decide on the correct answer.

What did David do after school?

A	B	C

Mother You're late, David. Did you work in the library after your lessons finished?

David Mum, it was too sunny to be inside! I watched the football team with some of my friends. They won the match! I can go to the library another afternoon.

Mother I suppose so. Well, why don't you go on the PlayStation with your sister before dinner?

David She's busy with her homework.

EXAM ADVICE

Before you listen
- Read the questions and look at the choices to help you understand the topic.
- Underline the important words in each question.

First listening
- Listen out for language that matches the words you have underlined. In the example above, *after school* is in the question, and *after your lessons finished* is on the recording.
- Remember to listen carefully for the tense (e.g. present simple, present perfect) and person (e.g. *he, she, they*) used in the question.
- Mark your answer in pencil on the question paper.

Second listening
- Check your choice of answer is correct and answer any questions you couldn't answer the first time.

Part 1

Questions 1–5

You will hear five short conversations.
You will hear each conversation twice.
There is one question for each conversation.
For questions **1–5**, put a tick (✓) under the right answer.

1 What is the man buying for his lunch?

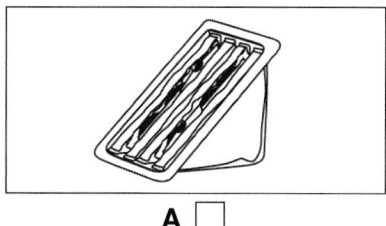      

A ☐   B ☐   C ☐

2 When is Maria's party?

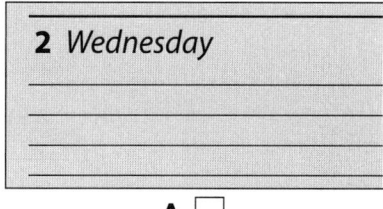   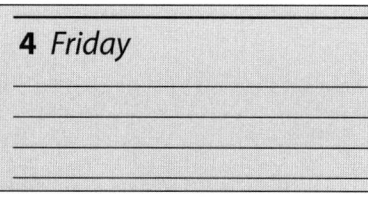   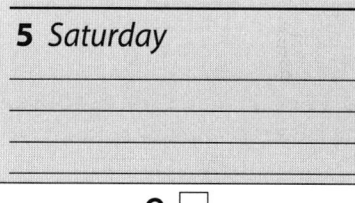

A ☐   B ☐   C ☐

3 Which postcard does the woman choose?

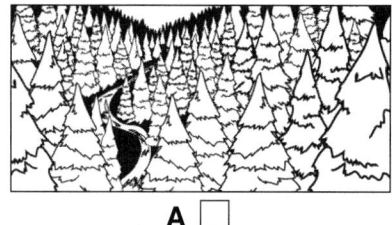   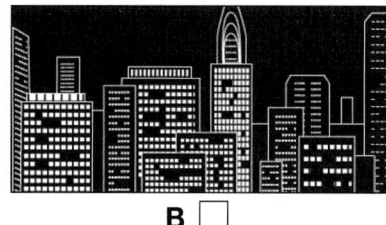   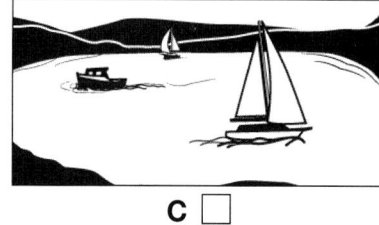

A ☐   B ☐   C ☐

4 How much does the woman pay for the DVD?

£9.50   £10.50   £19.50

A ☐   B ☐   C ☐

5 What did the girl leave at Ben's flat?

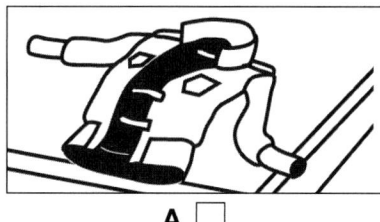      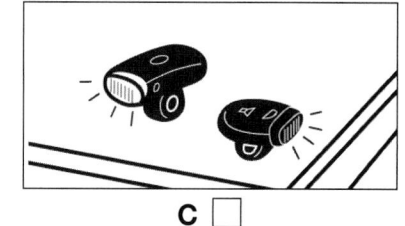

A ☐   B ☐   C ☐

2.1 For sale

Vocabulary

1 Name the things in the pictures. Where can you buy them? Match each group of things to a place in the box.

Key words

> bookshop   chemist   department store
> market   sports shop

Key words → page 149

2 What else can you buy in each place? Make lists.

3 How much shopping do you do? Answer these questions.

  1 How much chocolate do you buy every week?
  2 How many magazines do you get each month?
  3 How much money do you spend on sweets?
  4 How many pairs of trainers do you have?
  5 How many T-shirts did you buy last year?

Grammar extra

How much ...? How many ...?

- Use *How much ...?* with uncountable nouns (e.g. *shopping, chocolate, money*).
- Use *How many ...?* with countable nouns (e.g. *magazines, DVDs, T-shirts*).

4 Ask and answer questions using *How much ...?* or *How many ...?* with these nouns.

> books   clothes   DVDs   ice cream
> make-up   shampoo   shoes

Reading

A ND WASH IN COLD WATER

B P rking is free for customers

C de of 100% leather

D sta dishes all £7.95 with lad & mineral water

E RROTS 1.60P/ KILO

F TURDAY 5 SEPT, 21.00 CKETS £15 & £20

G MERAS HALF PRICE – LE ENDS TOMORROW!

H VERT: mes for PlayStation ly £10 each one: 01956 823001

5 Look quickly at texts A–H. Where can you see them?

EXAMPLE: *You can see A on a sweater.*

6 Read the texts more carefully. What letters are missing?

7 Which text (A–H) says this (1–5)?
  1 Things are cheaper than usual today.
  2 You get a drink with this meal.
  3 Call the number if you are interested in any of these.
  4 It costs nothing to leave your car if you are shopping here.
  5 Do not put this in a machine.

a: eı æ

8 1 06 **Listen and repeat.**
Underline the letters that make the sounds /ɑː/, /eɪ/ and /æ/.

/ɑː/
car
supermarket
artist
department store

/eɪ/
face
sale
PlayStation
email

/æ/
apple
map
carrot
advert

9 Look at exercise 6 again and find more words for the three lists in exercise 8. Say them first and then write them down.

2.2 Shopping from home

1 What are these ways of shopping? Do you do any shopping like this? Is it better than going into shops? Why? / Why not?

Listening

2 Read the conversation. Don't worry about the spaces at the moment. What is the conversation about?

Kevin Good morning. Sportswear, Kevin speaking. How can I help you?

Sally Hi. I've got your catalogue here, but I can't find the price list. Can you give me some prices?

Kevin Of course. Please tell me the page number you're looking at.

Sally OK. The first thing is on page (**1**) .... and it's the football shirt, the blue and red one.

Kevin OK. The small and medium sizes are £22.65 and large and extra large are (**2**) £ ....

Sally Right. I'd like to order one, please, size small.

Kevin Fine. Have you got any more things to order?

Sally Yes, I'd like some trainers. They're on page (**3**) .... How much are the black and purple ones at the top of the page?

Kevin Well, they *were* £49.50 but they're in the sale now, so they're only (**4**) £ .... But we don't have any left in small sizes. What shoe size are you?

Sally I'm a (**5**) ....

Kevin Let me check. Wow, you're lucky! We've got one pair in that size.

Sally Great. Well, that's all I need. My name and address is ...

3 **1 07** Now listen to the conversation and write the missing numbers.

Grammar _some_ and _any_

4 Look at these sentences from page 16.

1 I'd like some trainers.
2 I'd like some information.
3 Have you got any more things to order?
4 We don't have any left in small sizes.
5 Can you give me some prices?

Complete rules a–e with _some_ or _any_ and match them to sentences 1–5.

a We use ___some___ with uncountable nouns in affirmative sentences. ☑2

b We always use _____ in negative sentences. ☐

c We use _____ with countable nouns in affirmative sentences. ☐

d We use _____ for a request. ☐

e We usually use _____ in questions. ☐

G → page 137

Spelling sp●t

Plurals

Countable nouns usually have different singular and plural forms, e.g. _car, cars._

With uncountable nouns, there is only one form of the word, e.g. _rice._

To make a plural …

a we usually add -_s_:
one book   some books

b When the noun ends in -_sh_, -_ch_, -_ss_, -_s_ or -_x_, we add -_es_:
dish   dishes   bus   buses
glass   glasses   box   boxes

c When the noun ends in -_o_ after a consonant, we also add -_es_:
tomato   tomatoes

d When the noun ends in -_y_ after a **vowel**, we add -_s_:
toy   toys

e When the noun ends in -_y_ after a **consonant**, we change _y_ to _i_ and add -_es_:
story   stories

f Some nouns have irregular plurals, for example:
woman   women   fish   fish
child   children   foot   feet

6 Make these words plural. Which group (a–f) do they belong to?

baby   coach   dress   monkey
potato   tooth   window

5 Complete the sentences with _some_ or _any._

1 I can't find ___any___ sunglasses I like here.
2 There are _____ nice jackets in the shops at the moment.
3 Are there _____ yellow surfing T-shirts in the sale?
4 I want to buy _____ trainers, please.
5 Mum, can you lend me _____ money?
6 Let's get _____ sandwiches.
7 Has that website got _____ special prices?
8 Why don't we buy _____ new DVDs?
9 There isn't _____ bread left – can you get _____ in town?

Activity

Picture puzzle

- Look at the pictures. Write the singular and plural forms of the word under each picture.

1	2	3	4
map	....	....	....
maps	....	....	....

5	6	7
....	....	....
....	....	....

8	9	10	11
....	....	....	....
....	....	....	....

12	13	14	15
....	....	....	....
....	....	....	....

- Now write the last letter of each singular form in the boxes below. They make four words. What do the words say?

1 2 3 4   5 6 7   8 9 10 11   12 13 14 15
☐P☐☐☐ ☐☐☐ ☐☐☐☐ ☐☐☐☐

Exam folder 2

Reading Part 1 Notices

Part 1 of the Reading and Writing paper is a matching task. There is an example and five questions. You must choose the correct answer from eight notices (A–H).

1 These language areas are often tested in Part 1. Add another example to each one.

1 modal verbs *you can* ....

2 comparison *older* ....

3 imperatives *don't forget* ....

4 prepositions with times and days of the week ... *until 5 p.m.* ....

5 prepositions with places *next to the restaurant* ....

2 Look at the exam task opposite and underline examples of the language areas 1–5 above in different colours.

Look at the exam task opposite and underline examples of the language areas 1–5 above in different colours.

EXAM ADVICE

- Look at the eight notices first to see what the topics are.
- Read the example sentence and its notice.
- Cross out the example letter, so that you don't choose it again by accident.
- Read each sentence carefully and underline the key words.
- Look for notices that have similar language.
- Don't just match a word or number in the sentence and notice – this may not be the right answer.
- Check your answers when you transfer them to your answer sheet. Below is an example of the answer sheet for Part 1.

Part 1							
1	A	B	C	D	E	F	G	H
2	A	B	C	D	E	F	G	H
3	A	B	C	D	E	F	G	H
4	A	B	C	D	E	F	G	H
5	A	B	C	D	E	F	G	H

Part 1

Questions 1–5

Which notice (**A–H**) says this (**1–5**)?

For questions **1–5**, mark the correct letter **A–H** on your answer sheet.

Example:

0 Do not leave any suitcases on the floor.   *Answer:* | **0** | A B C D̅ E F G H |

---

1 It is possible to swim later in the evening now.

2 This is cheaper because it isn't new.

3 All our prices are lower for a short time.

4 You can pay for your journey in a different way if necessary.

5 If you are 15 or younger, you may win some money.

A

> Buy train tickets at machine when office is closed

B

> FOR SALE
> Boy's bike, only 2 months old
> Half usual price

C

> TICKETS FOR TONIGHT'S CONCERT ARE ON SALE HERE
> FROM 7 PM

D

> PLEASE PUT ALL LUGGAGE ABOVE YOUR SEAT

E

> SALE ENDS NEXT TUESDAY –
> 15% OFF EVERYTHING UNTIL THEN

F

> UNDER 16s GOLF COMPETITION
> **FIRST PRIZE £30!**

G

> SPEND £50 AND GET A
> **FREE** SPORTS BAG

H

> POOL OPENING HOURS NOW LONGER:
> 7 am – 10 pm (was 8.45 pm)

3.1 Breakfast, lunch and dinner

Vocabulary

1 Look at the photos. Tell your partner what you see, then complete the puzzle below to find the word in the yellow squares.

```
¹G _ _ _ _ _
²A _ _ _ E
  ³F _ H
⁴T _ O
⁵C _ _ _ E
    ⁶B _ R
    ⁷O _ E
    ⁸S _ D
  ⁹S _ H
   ¹⁰S _ K
```

Key words → page 149

Pronunciation

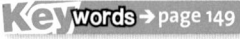

2 **1 08** Listen and repeat these words. Then write them in group 1 or group 2 below.

beans	bin	biscuit	chips	dinner	eat
feel	fill	fish	leave	live	meal	meat
seat	sit	tea			

group 1 /ɪ/ *chicken*	group 2 /iː/ *cheese*

1 09 Listen to check your answers.

3 What do you like? What don't you like? Talk about the food and drink in 1–7 using the sentences below.

1	apples	grapes	bananas
2	potatoes	pasta	bread
3	eggs	chicken	fish
4	pizza	curry	chilli
5	ice cream	yogurt	chocolate
6	lemonade	coffee	milk
7	salad	carrots	mushrooms

EXAMPLE: *I hate grapes, but I quite like bananas.*

Key speaking

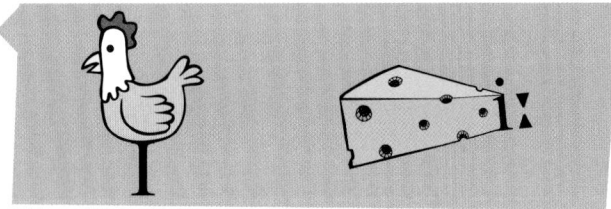

I love .... 😊

I like .... best. / I prefer .... 😊

I quite like .... 🙂

.... is/are OK. 😐

I don't like .... very much. 🙁

I hate .... 😠

I think .... taste(s) horrible. 😠

Listening

4 🔊 10 Listen to Jack and Katie talking about food and drink. Write J for Jack and K for Katie. Who ...

1 always has a big breakfast?
2 buys a cake for a snack?
3 has chips or pizza for lunch?
4 thinks salad is good for you?
5 prefers water to juice?
6 doesn't like coffee or tea?
7 loves chocolate?
8 doesn't like ice cream?

5 Find out what four people in your class like and don't like. Write down their answers.

EXAMPLE: Ask: *Sergio, what do you like?*
Write: *Sergio likes steak best and he doesn't like fish.*

Grammar Present simple

6 Complete this table with *like*.

affirmative	I/You/We/They .... chocolate.
	He/She/It .... milk.
negative	I/You/We/They .... fish.
	He/She/It .... fruit.
question	.... I/you/we/they .... apples?
	.... he/she/it .... water?

G → page 137

Spelling spot

Contractions

7 Complete the table.

| does + not = *doesn't* |
| do + not = |
| has + not = |
| have + not = |
| is + not = |
| are + not = |

8 Katie says *My mum makes breakfast at seven o'clock.* We sometimes talk about the time when we talk about meals. Match the times with the clocks.

1 seven forty-five; quarter to eight
2 one forty-two; eighteen minutes to two
3 four o'clock
4 two fifteen; quarter past two
5 eight minutes past three
6 five thirty; half past five

G → page 137

9 🔊 11 Listen to Harry talking about his day. Complete the notes.

Breakfast	Lunch	Dinner
(0) *8.00 a.m.*	(2) .... p.m.	(4) .... p.m.
tea	salad	chicken or
toast	a cake	(5) ....
(1)	(3)	rice or pasta
		(6) ....

Activity

Talk about your day

• Ask three people in your class about their day and complete the questionnaire on page 130.

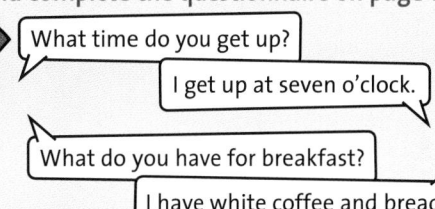

What time do you get up?
I get up at seven o'clock.
What do you have for breakfast?
I have white coffee and bread.

• Now ask another student about the people in his/her questionnaire.

What time does Paolo have lunch?
He has lunch at one o'clock.

• Which food is the most popular in your class for breakfast/lunch/dinner?

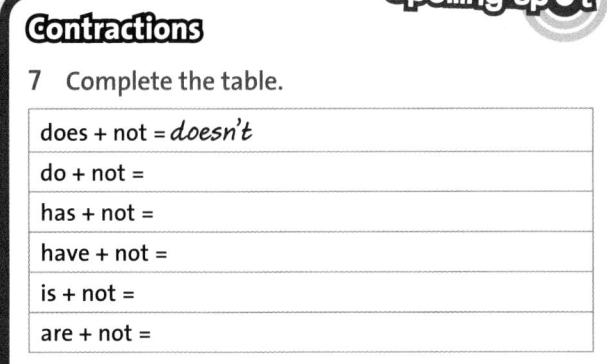

3.2 Food at festivals

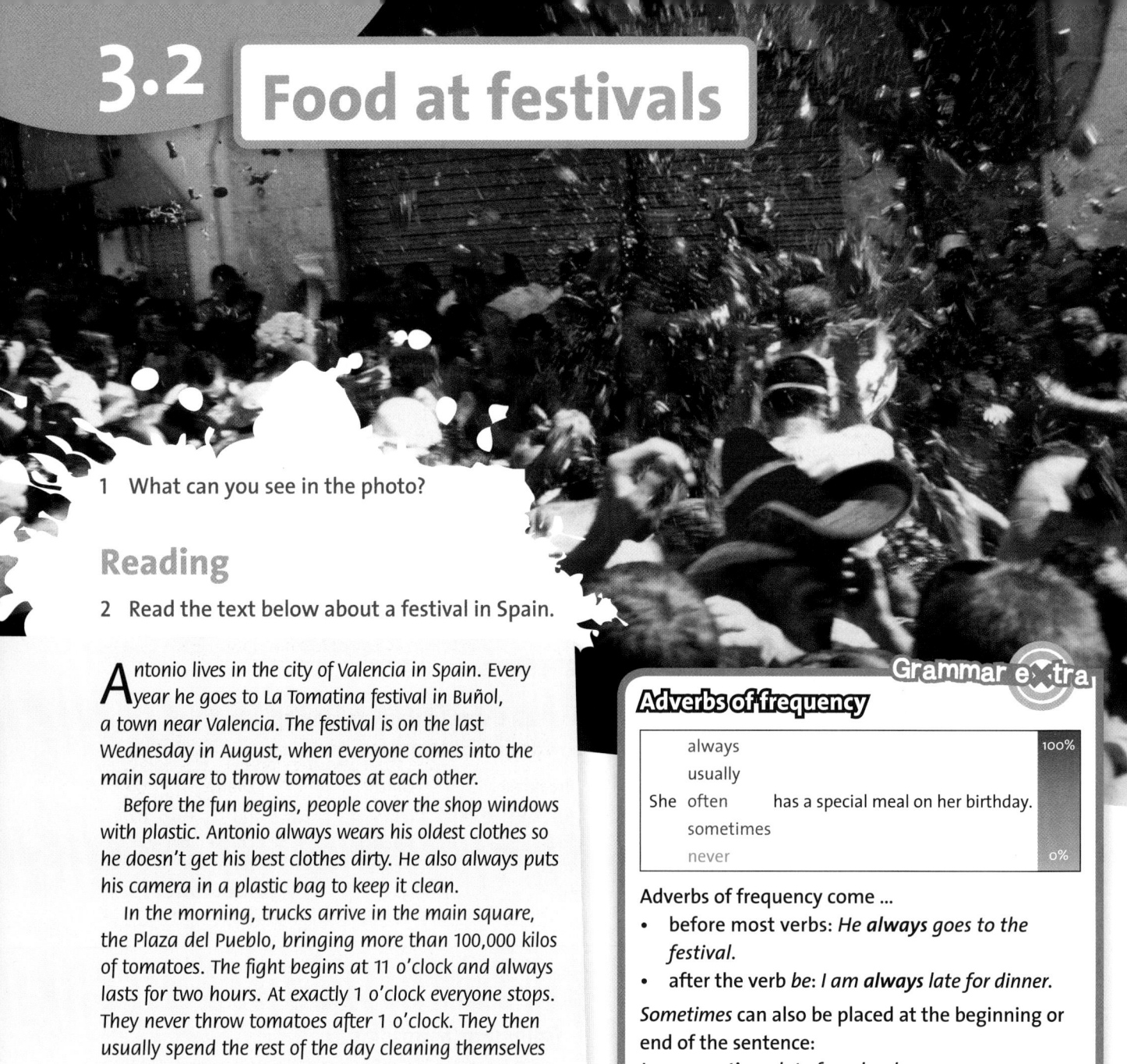

1 What can you see in the photo?

Reading

2 Read the text below about a festival in Spain.

Antonio lives in the city of Valencia in Spain. Every year he goes to La Tomatina festival in Buñol, a town near Valencia. The festival is on the last Wednesday in August, when everyone comes into the main square to throw tomatoes at each other.

Before the fun begins, people cover the shop windows with plastic. Antonio always wears his oldest clothes so he doesn't get his best clothes dirty. He also always puts his camera in a plastic bag to keep it clean.

In the morning, trucks arrive in the main square, the Plaza del Pueblo, bringing more than 100,000 kilos of tomatoes. The fight begins at 11 o'clock and always lasts for two hours. At exactly 1 o'clock everyone stops. They never throw tomatoes after 1 o'clock. They then usually spend the rest of the day cleaning themselves and the town! In the evening, Antonio usually watches the fireworks, eats the local food and sometimes joins in the dancing.

Are these sentences right or wrong? Underline the part of the text with the answer.

1 Antonio comes from Buñol.
2 The festival is at the beginning of August.
3 Antonio never wears his best clothes at the festival.
4 Everyone buys tomatoes from a local shop.
5 The fight usually lasts for more than two hours.
6 The next day everyone cleans the streets.
7 Antonio always watches the fireworks.
8 Antonio sometimes dances.

Grammar eXtra

Adverbs of frequency

	always		100%
	usually		
She	often	has a special meal on her birthday.	
	sometimes		
	never		0%

Adverbs of frequency come …
- before most verbs: *He **always** goes to the festival.*
- after the verb *be*: *I am **always** late for dinner.*

Sometimes can also be placed at the beginning or end of the sentence:
*I am **sometimes** late for school.*
***Sometimes** I am late for school.*
*I am late for school **sometimes**.*

3 Complete these sentences with *always, often, usually, sometimes* or *never*.

1 I get up at 9 o'clock. (100%)
   I always get up at 9 o'clock.
2 My mum makes cakes on Tuesdays. (75%)
3 I am hungry at lunch time. (100%)
4 I am late for dinner. (55%)
5 Pete has a party on his birthday. (100%)
6 We have fireworks on New Year's Eve. (25%)
7 Sam meets his friends on New Year's Eve. (90%)
8 You eat spaghetti with a knife. (0%)

Grammar

4 Read about Santa Lucia Day in Sweden. Fill each space with the verb in the correct form.

My name is Klara and I (**0**) ...... *come* ...... (come) from Sweden. On December 13th every year we (**1**) .... (have) a festival called *Santa Lucia*. Lucia brings light in the dark winter.

The oldest daughter in each house is Santa Lucia for the day. In the morning all the children go to their parents while they are sleeping. They (**2**) .... (wear) white clothes and they (**3**) .... (carry) candles. The girl who is Santa Lucia (**4**) .... (wear) a crown with candles on her head. She (**5**) .... (wake) her parents with coffee and special yellow cakes called *Lussekattor*. Her sisters and brothers (**6**) .... (help) her. People (**7**) .... (often ask) me if the candles on the crown are real. Now they (**8**) .... (be not) real, they are electric. Boys (**9**) .... (not wear) candles, they have a tall hat instead.

At school we (**10**) .... (choose) a girl to be Santa Lucia for the day. We all (**11**) .... (sing) a special song. I (**12**) .... (like) Santa Lucia day because my school (**13**) .... (always close) early on that day.

5 Ask your partner about his/her special days. Talk about what you do, what you eat and drink, what presents you give or get, etc.

What do you do on your birthday?

I usually have a party.

What happens when there is a public holiday in your town?

My family and I go out to a restaurant.

What do you do at New Year?

We often have fireworks.

6 Write a note to a friend about a festival in your town/country.

Say:
- when the festival is
- what you do at the festival
- what you eat.

Activity

When's your birthday?

- Make groups of four to six students.

- Then everyone in the group must stand in the order of the date of their birthday.

- The winners are the team who get in the right order first. Everyone must be able to say the date of their birthday in English. If they can't, the team is out.

Writing folder 1

Writing Part 6
Spelling words

In Part 6 of the Reading and Writing paper there is an example and five questions (**36–40**). Each question is a sentence which gives a description of a word. You must write the word, spelling it correctly. The first letter of the word is always given to you.

Here are some ways to practise spelling.

1 Match the first part of the word in A to the second part in B. The words are all about food and drink.

EXAMPLE: *meat*

A	B
1 me	ple
2 but	ce
3 wait	ket
4 di	rot
5 jui	ta
6 mar	at
7 pas	ato
8 tom	ter
9 car	ress
10 ap	sh

2 Exam candidates find some words difficult to spell. Find the word which is spelled wrongly in each group and correct the spelling.

1	favourite	diferent	disappointed	traditional	*different*
2	actor	nurse	painter	pilat	
3	pink	white	yello	grey	
4	bath	chair	bed	mirrer	
5	husband	mother	daughter	unkle	
6	beatiful	famous	rich	single	
7	television	telephon	cooker	camera	
8	cloudy	sunney	stormy	windy	
9	wich	who	that	when	
10	nice	friendly	comfortable	intresting	
11	hope	know	think	belive	
12	hospital	airport	library	appartment	
13	motobike	plane	train	coach	
14	becouse	except	while	before	
15	entrance	upstairs	adress	gate	
16	ambulance	scooter	bycicle	helicopter	

3 Write a description for these words.

1 a dining room   *I eat in this room.*
2 pizza
3 a waiter
4 a café
5 breakfast
6 a snack
7 a kitchen
8 a fridge
9 fruit
10 ice cream

4 Think of your own descriptions and ask your partner what the answer is.

EXAMPLE: A: *This is brown and it's very sweet. What is it?*
B: *Chocolate.*

- Read each sentence carefully.
- Count the number of spaces to find out how many letters the word has.
- Decide if the word needs to be plural or not (look for words like *this* or *these*).
- Write your answer on the question paper first.
- Check you have used the right number of letters.
- Write your answer on your answer sheet. Opposite is an example of the answer sheet for Part 6.

Part 6		Do not write here
36		1 ⌐ 36 2 ⌐
37		1 ⌐ 37 2 ⌐
38		1 ⌐ 38 2 ⌐
39		1 ⌐ 39 2 ⌐
40		1 ⌐ 40 2 ⌐

Part 6

Questions 36–40

Read the descriptions (**36–40**) of some things you can eat or drink.

What is the word for each one?

The first letter is already there. There is one space for each other letter in the word.

For questions **36–40**, write the words on your answer sheet.

Example:

0 This is a popular fast food that you can eat with chips. b _ _ _ _ _

Answer:	**0**	*burger*

36 It is good to drink this when the weather is hot. l _ _ _ _ _ _ _

37 These are red and you find them on pizza. t _ _ _ _ _ _ _

38 This fruit is round and has lots of juice. o _ _ _ _ _

39 This makes food sweet. s _ _ _ _

40 You often eat these on a picnic. s _ _ _ _ _ _ _ _

4.1 A real adventure

1 What do you know about gold? Are these sentences right or wrong?

  1 You can eat gold.
  2 Olympic gold medals are only made from gold.
  3 Most gold today comes from South Africa.
  4 There is gold in some Formula 1 racing cars.
  5 You can make clothes from gold.

Now read the rest of the story and then answer the questions below.

Reading

2 Read the information about Skookum Jim below. Are the sentences right or wrong? If there is no information, write 'Doesn't say'. You should read each sentence carefully and then find information in the text which gives you an answer. Underline this information. If you can't find any information to underline, then the answer will be 'Doesn't say'.

First study the example sentences and text.

EXAMPLES:

o   Skookum Jim came from Canada. *Right*
oo   Jim liked the name 'Skookum'. *Doesn't say*
ooo Skookum Jim worked in a city. *Wrong*

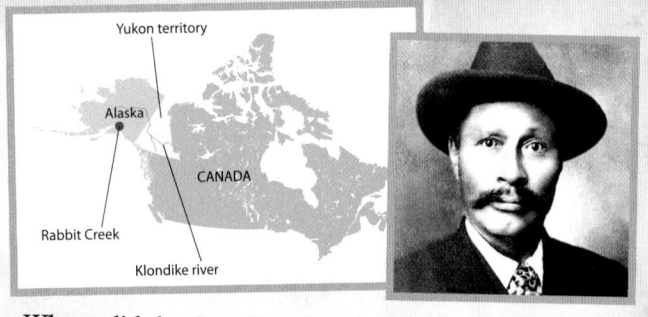

Where did the <u>Canadian Skookum Jim</u> find gold? Well, in August 1896, he found it in a place called Rabbit Creek, a small river near the Klondike River in Canada and became very rich. Skookum – his name means 'big and strong' – worked for men who wanted to find gold in Alaska. He and his horses carried their <u>bags over the mountains and showed them where to look for gold.</u>

Skookum Jim was with his cousin and sister when he found gold for himself. One day, the family decided to go on a fishing trip and Skookum Jim was in the Creek when he saw something in the water. He picked it up. Immediately, he knew that it was gold and he was very happy!

When people found out about the gold, they all wanted to come to Rabbit Creek. Men travelled from all over the world by ship and by train. They sold their farms and left their homes and families to look for gold. Many people built boats to take them down the rivers to Rabbit Creek.

It was a dangerous journey as the boats were full of the food the people needed. But some people didn't go only for the gold, they went for the adventure too.

Skookum Jim became very rich. He built a large house for his wife and daughter and they stayed at home while he spent the winters hunting bears and other wild animals in the forests.

1 Skookum Jim found some gold inside a fish.
2 People came from everywhere to Rabbit Creek to find gold.
3 The men brought their wives and children with them.
4 The boats were built of wood from the forest.
5 Some people only wanted to go for the adventure.
6 Skookum Jim gave some money to everyone in his family.
7 In winter Skookum Jim preferred going on hunting trips to staying at home.

Grammar Past simple

3 Look at the story about Skookum Jim. Find the past simple form of these verbs.

regular verbs

1 want ....
2 work ....

irregular verbs

3 find ....
4 become ....
5 be .... (two forms)

Now complete these sentences.

Making a question:

Where .... the Canadian Skookum Jim .... gold?

Making a negative:

But some people .... only for the gold, they went for the adventure too.

Ⓖ → page 138

Ⓖ → page 138

Spelling sp⊙t

Regular verbs in the past simple

Regular verbs in the past simple end in *-ed*. For example ask – asked, fill – filled

verb ends in ...	rule	example
-e decide	add *-d*	One day, the family decided to go on a fishing trip.
consonant + vowel + consonant *travel*	double last letter and add *-ed*	People travelled from all over the world by ship and by train.
consonant + *y* *carry*	*y* becomes *ied*	He carried their bags over the mountains.
vowel + *y* *stay*	add *-ed*	They stayed at home.
more than one consonant *pick*	add *-ed*	He picked it up.

4 What is the past simple of the following verbs?

1 arrive	5 use	9 study
2 stop	6 return	10 chat
3 help	7 like	
4 look	8 play	

Pronunciation

5 There are three ways to pronounce a regular verb in the past simple: /t/, /d/ and /ɪd/. Underline all the regular verbs in the story about Skookum Jim and decide which column, /t/, /d/ or /ɪd/, to put them in.

/t/	/d/	/ɪd/

🔊 1 12 Listen to check your answers. Then repeat the words.

6 Read the Skookum Jim story again to find the past simple of these irregular verbs. (You can find more irregular verbs on page 159.)

Key words

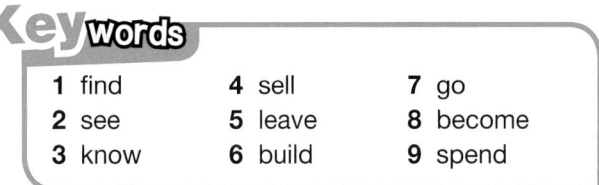

1 find	4 sell	7 go
2 see	5 leave	8 become
3 know	6 build	9 spend

Activity

Who is it?

- 🔊 1 13 Listen to two students playing *Who is it?* Who is the famous person?

- Now you play. Player A thinks of a famous person from the past. Player B asks up to twelve questions to find out the name of the person.

EXAMPLE: B: *Were you a man?*
A: *Yes, I was. / No, I wasn't.*
B: *Did you paint pictures?*
A: *Yes, I did. / No, I didn't.*

4.2 A mini-adventure

1 Match the question form with the right verb(s). Ask your partner questions about an interesting place that he or she visited last year.

EXAMPLE: A: *Where did you go?*
B: *I went to an art gallery / to a museum / to London.*

Where did you	buy?
When did you	see?
How much did it	go?
How did you	go with?
What did you	stay?
Who did you	travel?
How long did you	come home?
	feel?
	cost?
	do?

Listening

2 ●1 14 Listen to a girl called Melanie talking about a school trip to Paris. Choose the correct answer.

1 Number of days in Paris: *2 / 5*
2 Coach left school at: *5.00 / 5.30* a.m.
3 Cost of trip: *£340 / £314*
4 Name of hotel in Paris:
 BERRI / VERRY
5 Enjoyed *shopping / boat trip* best.

3 ●1 14 Now listen to Melanie again and answer with short answers.

1 Did the students arrive at school late?
 No, they didn't.
2 Did Melanie like the coach journey?
3 Did it take eight hours to go from London to Paris?
4 Did they stay at a new hotel?
5 Did Melanie speak French all the time?
6 Did she take lots of photos?
7 Did they arrive back in London late?

Past simple + *ago*

| When did Melanie go on the school trip to Paris? |
| Two years **ago**. |
| When did you last see a film? |
| A week **ago**. |

4 Ask and answer with a partner. Answer using *ago* or one of the expressions in the box below.

EXAMPLE: brush hair
A: *When did you last brush your hair?*
B: *I brushed my hair two weeks ago.*

| last night/week/Saturday/month/year |
| this morning/afternoon |
| yesterday |
| in the summer/winter/spring/autumn |
| at breakfast/lunch/dinner time |
| at the weekend |

1 eat some chocolate
2 email a friend
3 read a magazine
4 listen to music
5 go to the cinema
6 play football
7 do some homework
8 go to an art gallery
9 buy some clothes
10 eat pizza

5 Correct the mistakes that exam candidates made with the past simple. There is one correct sentence.

1 You didn't came home at six o'clock.
2 Who you went to London with?
3 I laught a lot during the game.
4 I dance with Louise last night.
5 I plaied football with my brother on Saturday.
6 I stay with my friend yesterday.
7 I buy it because I love green.
8 Pablo visited a museum two weeks ago.
9 How much costed the trip?
10 Last Monday, the school tell us about the new holiday.

Activity

Word puzzle

• Find ten verbs in the past simple in the word square. (Look ↓ and →.) The first one has been done for you.

w	e	n	t	b	s	d	e	t	s
l	d	w	t	a	t	a	t	e	t
i	d	d	a	t	k	r	y	u	a
k	s	u	r	o	j	r	j	k	y
e	a	n	g	o	k	i	s	w	e
d	b	t	f	k	t	v	a	d	d
p	u	i	h	f	c	e	w	i	c
b	e	g	a	n	s	d	r	v	x
o	z	a	d	p	d	a	t	u	i
l	t	r	a	v	e	l	l	e	d

• Write a short paragraph about a trip you made. Use five of the verbs you found in the puzzle.

EXAMPLE: *Last summer was great because I went on a very exciting trip …*

Units 1–4 Revision

Speaking

1 Read these sentences with a partner. Say if each sentence is true for you and give some extra information.

EXAMPLE: My friends like the same things as I do.

No, not true. My friends are all very different. My best friend likes listening to bands. Some of my other friends like skateboarding and one prefers to play computer games.

1 I had a great party for my birthday.
2 I prefer to have a lot of friends, not just one best friend.
3 I spend a lot of money on clothes and DVDs.
4 I don't care about fashion.
5 I love chocolate.
6 I think people eat too much nowadays.
7 My best friend never makes me angry.
8 I like going on trips with my parents more than I do with my school.

Vocabulary

2 Circle the odd one out.

1	sad	happy	pleased	(green)
2	nice	small	boring	funny
3	interesting	popular	friend	strong
4	shop	store	house	market
5	fish	meat	coffee	biscuits
6	onion	orange	apple	bananas
7	river	chemist	mountain	forest
8	shampoo	clothes	make-up	soap

3 Put the letters in the right order to spell things you can eat and drink.

1 o m t t o a	7 s h f i
2 c k a n s	8 r r c t a o
3 t e a m	9 r b g r e u
4 k l m i	10 o c o h l t a c e
5 c e j i u	11 o t p a o t
6 p e g a r	12 n c e k h i c

Writing

4 Read the descriptions of different places where you can buy things. What is the word for each one? The first letter is already there.

1 People can buy fruit and vegetables here.

   m _ _ _ _ _

2 This shop sells clothes, shoes, toys and lots of other things.

   d _ _ _ _ _ _ _ _ _   s _ _ _ _

3 This shop sells medicines.

   c _ _ _ _ _ _

4 If you go here, you can buy most things.

   s _ _ _ _ _ _ _ _ _ _

5 You can buy trainers here.

   s _ _ _ _ _   _ _ _ _

Grammar

5 Choose the correct word.

1 Can I have *any / some* cake, please?
2 How *much / many* money do you have in your pocket?
3 How much *is / are* the pair of blue trainers?
4 I haven't got *any / some* food.
5 *Does / Do* he like eating at restaurants?
6 *Sometimes / Always* I go to a party on New Year's Eve.
7 Lisa *doesn't / don't* make a special cake for her birthday.
8 I didn't *went / go* shopping at the weekend.
9 *Did / Have* Skookum Jim find gold?
10 When did he *return / returned* to Rabbit Creek?

6 Read this article about Chinese New Year. Choose the correct word for 1–10.

Chinese New Year (**1**) *starts / start* with the new moon on the first day of the New Year and ends on the full moon 15 days later. Chinese New Year is on (**2**) *a / the* different date each year. New Year's Eve and New Year's Day are when families celebrate together.

People (**3**) *make / makes* large amounts of food for (**4**) *his / their* family and friends. On New Year's Day they (**5**) *ate / eat* a dish of vegetables, called jai. Other foods include a whole fish, chicken and noodles. For (**6**) *some / any* people in South China the favourite dish is sweet rice.

People clean their houses before New Year's Day. On New Year's Eve there are fireworks and (**7**) *at / on* midnight everyone opens every door and window in their house to say goodbye to the old year. (**8**) *Many / Much* people (**9**) *wear / wearing* red clothes at New Year because it (**10**) *is / has* lucky. Children receive little red envelopes with money inside.

7 Write the past simple of these irregular verbs.

1 know
2 come
3 find
4 sell
5 take
6 tell
7 become
8 leave
9 go
10 build

8 Read this conversation and put the verbs into the correct tense.

Jenny Hi Sam! How (**1**) ____*are*____ (be) you?

Sam I (**2**) _____ (be) fine, thanks, Jenny. I (**3**) _____ (telephone) you yesterday. Where (**4**) _____ (be) you?

Jenny I (**5**) _____ (need) some new shoes so I (**6**) _____ (go) shopping in town.

Sam (**7**) _____ (you / get) any?

Jenny Yes, look. What (**8**) _____ (you / think) of them?

Sam Oh, I (**9**) _____ (not be) sure that I (**10**) _____ (like) the colour. (**11**) _____ (be) they blue?

Jenny No, they (**12**) _____ (be) green! They (**13**) _____ (look) blue inside the shop, but when I (**14**) _____ (take) them outside the shop I (**15**) _____ (see) that they (**16**) _____ (be) green.

Sam (**17**) _____ (be) they expensive? They (**18**) _____ (look) very expensive to me.

Jenny No, I (**19**) _____ (get) them in the sale.

Sam You (**20**) _____ (be) lucky!

5.1 Going to the zoo

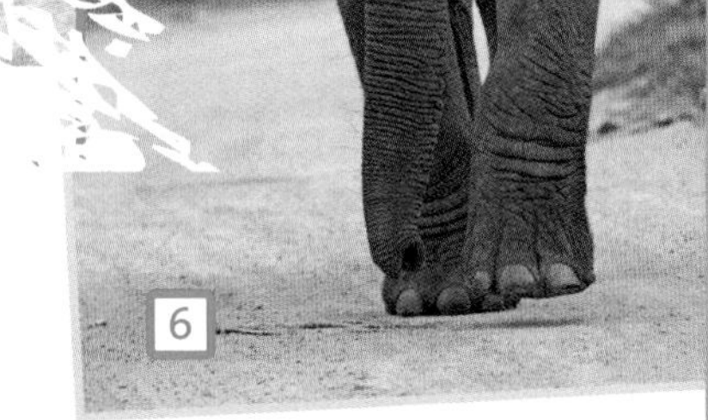

Vocabulary

1 Spell the names of the animals – they are all in the pictures above.

1 This animal can be black, white or brown. b _ _ _
2 You often see this animal sleeping. c _ _
3 You can take this animal for a walk. d _ _
4 Some people say that this animal never forgets. e _ _ _ _ _ _ _
5 You can ride this animal. h _ _ _ _
6 You can see this animal in the sea. f _ _ _
7 This animal likes bananas. m _ _ _ _ _
8 People call this animal the 'king of the animals'. l _ _ _

2 What's your favourite animal? Which animals are useful to people? Give a reason using *because*.

I like chickens because they give you eggs to eat.

I think monkeys are wonderful because they are so friendly.

Key words → page 150

Listening

3 🔵 15 Listen to Mark talking to Natalie about visiting their local zoo. Tick each word when you hear it. They are in the order you hear them.

1 zoo ✓   6 laugh
2 Sunday   7 drive
3 students   8 train
4 homework   9 four
5 camera   10 great

4 🔵 16 Look at the example and then listen to the first part of the conversation again.

EXAMPLE: *When will Mark and Natalie go to the zoo?*
          A Saturday
          B Sunday
          C Thursday

The answer is C. Natalie is busy on Saturday and Sunday.

5 ▸**1** **17** Read through the questions and then listen to the rest of the conversation and answer the questions.

1 Each zoo ticket will cost them
A £14.50.
B £17.50.
C £18.00.

2 Who is Mark going to take photos for?
A his mother
B his friend
C his teacher

3 Mark is going to photograph
A bears.
B monkeys.
C lions.

4 How will Mark and Natalie get to the zoo?
A by bus
B by train
C by car

5 The zoo closes at
A 4.30.
B 5.30.
C 6.30.

6 Ask and answer these questions with a partner. When did you last go to a zoo? What did you see? Do you like zoos?

Grammar extra

and

- Look at how we use a comma (,) and *and* when we make a list.
  I like horses, dogs and cats.
  The bear was large, hungry and dangerous.
  We swam, played volleyball and ate ice cream.
- *And* is less common with adjectives before a noun. We normally just use a comma.
  a big, yellow fish
- When we use *and* we often don't write words instead of repeating them.
  Nicole goes shopping and ~~she goes~~ swimming at the weekend.
  The monkeys and ~~the~~ birds were up in the trees.

7 Correct the mistakes that exam candidates made with *and*.

1 I saw a nice and colourful parrot at the zoo.
2 Yesterday we went to the zoo and yesterday we went to the museum.
3 Susanna went out yesterday and Susanna took her dog for a walk.
4 There are many cats, dogs, horses at the farm.
5 Some sheep were at the farm and some cows were at the farm.

Vocabulary

8 There are many words in English that go together. In the recording in exercise 4 Mark says *I've got to take some photographs of the animals* and *I don't want to spend too much money.*

Put the words below in the right column. Sometimes there is more than one answer. Use an English–English dictionary to help you.

do	make	take	spend
		photographs	*money*

> an appointment   a cake   the cooking
> the dog for a walk   an exam   homework
> nothing   a phone call   the shopping   time

9 Choose the correct word.

1 Natalie *made / spent* some time looking at the penguins.
2 Natalie *did / made* her homework when she got home from the zoo.
3 Mark *did / took* some shopping for his mum.
4 Natalie said, 'Can you wait a minute? I need to *make / do* a phone call.'
5 Mark *took / made* his exams last week.

10 Ask and answer these questions.

> When do you do your homework?

> I usually do it when I get home from school. I do it on the kitchen table. I hate it when my teacher gives me lots to do.

1 Do you know how to make a cake?
2 Do you ever do nothing all day?
3 How much money do you spend on magazines?
4 Do you help to do the food shopping at home?
5 Do you ever do the cooking for your family?

5.2 An amazing animal

1 Do this quiz with a partner before you read the article about polar bears.

1 Polar bears live in
a) the Arctic.
b) Antarctica.

2 Polar bears have
a) white skin.
b) black skin.

3 Polar bears usually eat
a) fish.
b) people.

4 Polar bears are about
a) three metres long.
b) six metres long.

5 Polar bears are the size of
a) a car.
b) a bus.

6 Polar bears usually have
a) one baby.
b) two babies.

7 Polar bears have their cubs every
a) two years.
b) three years.

8 Polar bears usually live
a) in family groups.
b) alone.

9 Polar bears are
a) in danger.
b) not in danger.

Reading

2 Read the article to see if you were right. Don't worry about the spaces for now.

IN DANGER

The polar bear got its name <u>because</u> it spends most of its time in the Arctic. It is also called by other names, for example, white bear or ice bear. It is very cold where polar bears live. The temperature is very often as low as –45°C.

The polar bear is the largest meat-eating animal on land. The male weighs from 350 to 650 kg <u>and</u> he is two and a half to three metres long – almost as long as a car. A polar bear's skin is black <u>but</u> its fur has no colour – it looks white when the sun shines on the ice. It has big feet so it can stand easily on the ice. It is a very good swimmer. When a polar bear gets out of the sea, it shakes water from its fur like a dog <u>or</u> it removes the water by rolling on the ice.

The polar bear likes to live alone. It walks long distances, sometimes 30 km a day, (1) .... it needs to find food. The bear eats fish (2) .... it also enjoys seal meat. It goes swimming (3) .... lies in the sun when it isn't looking for food!

The female bear usually has two babies once every three years. The babies, or cubs, are born in November. Sometimes the cubs die in their first year (4) .... they have an accident (5) .... they don't get enough food to eat. If they live, they stay with their mother for nearly two years (6) .... then they must leave her to go and live alone on the ice.

There are only about 20,000 polar bears alive today. The area where you find them has many problems (7) .... the ice is becoming thinner or disappearing. Polar bears need your help!

Grammar Conjunctions

3 Look at the underlined words in paragraphs 1 and 2 in the article about the polar bear. These words are called 'conjunctions'. Then complete the grammar explanation.

- We use *because* , ... , ...
  and .... to make one long sentence.
  1 We use .... to say 'why' things happen.
  2 We use .... when there is a choice or an alternative idea.
  3 We use .... when we want to add an idea.
  4 We use .... when there is a contrast.

G → page 139

4 Read the article again and fill the spaces with A, B or C.

1 **A** but	**B** because	**C** or
2 **A** and	**B** or	**C** because
3 **A** or	**B** but	**C** because
4 **A** but	**B** because	**C** and
5 **A** or	**B** but	**C** because
6 **A** or	**B** because	**C** but
7 **A** because	**B** but	**C** or

5 Below are some sentences about Paul, a zoo keeper (a person who looks after the animals in a zoo). Join the sentences together using *and*, *or*, *but* or *because*. There is sometimes more than one answer.

1 Paul looks after the elephants at a zoo. He also helps with the monkeys sometimes.
2 Paul studied in the evenings. He needed to learn about animals.
3 He takes the elephants for a walk every day. He never rides them.
4 Sometimes the elephants play with each other. Sometimes they like to lie in the sun.
5 Paul takes the elephants to the lake. The elephants like swimming there.

their, there, they're

Their, *there* and *they're* all sound the same but they have different spelling.

- *There are not many polar bears in the Arctic any more.*
- *Polar bears spend most of **their** life on the ice.*
- *When **they're** small, the polar bear cubs stay with **their** mother.*

6 Fill the spaces with *their*, *there* or *they're*.

I have two dogs, called Wolfie and Sammy. (**1**) .... quite small dogs. I take them for a walk in the park every day. They love it (**2**) .... because they can play with (**3**) .... ball and run around having fun. (**4**) .... favourite game is chasing the ducks into the lake. (**5**) .... always happy to go (**6**) ....

7 Write an email to a friend about a visit you made to a zoo.

Say:
- where the zoo is
- who you went with
- which animal you liked best.

Pronunciation

8 **1 18** Listen to Paul, the zoo keeper, saying which animals he likes. Listen to how his voice goes up and down. Repeat the sentences. Practise doing this when you do the Activity below.

I like lions, bears, monkeys and elephants.

And I like horses, dogs and cats.

Activity

Memory game

- Play this game. The first person says: *I went to the zoo and I saw a lion.*
- The next person continues: *I went to the zoo and I saw a lion and a tiger.*
- Continue, adding an animal each time.

Exam folder 3

Reading Part 2 Multiple choice

Part 2 of the Reading and Writing paper tests vocabulary. There is an example and five multiple-choice questions (**6–10**). The sentences are about a topic or story. You must choose the word which best fits in the space.

Here are some examples of the types of word which are tested. Which word in each group is wrong?
verbs – *go, made, carry, horse*
nouns – *left, house, dog, teacher*
adjectives – *happy, sun, nice, friendly*
adverbs – *hard, slowly, want, carefully*
words which go together – *have breakfast, make your homework, take a trip*

Part 2			
6	A	B	C
7	A	B	C
8	A	B	C
9	A	B	C
10	A	B	C

EXAM ADVICE

- Always read the instructions and the example sentence. This will tell you what the topic is.
- Before you answer the questions, read all the sentences quickly. Together they make a short story.
- Read each sentence carefully before you decide on your answer.
- When you choose your answer, think about the meaning of the sentence.
- Read the sentence with the answer to check that the grammar is correct.
- Remember to transfer your answers to your answer sheet.

Part 2

Questions 6–10

Read the sentences about visiting a farm.

Choose the best word (**A**, **B** or **C**) for each space.

For questions **6–10**, mark **A**, **B** or **C** on the answer sheet.

Example:

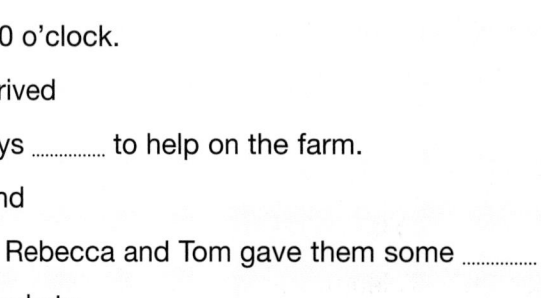

0   Rebecca and Tom .... visiting their uncle's farm.

   A want   **B** enjoy   **C** agree   *Answer:*

---

6   They .... their dad to take them there on Saturday.

   A asked   **B** said   **C** talked

7   They left home .... on Saturday morning.

   A well   **B** early   **C** ever

8   They .... at the farm at 10 o'clock.

   A got   **B** came   **C** arrived

9   Rebecca and Tom are always .... to help on the farm.

   A good   **B** happy   **C** kind

10   The horses were hungry so Rebecca and Tom gave them some ....

   A food   **B** water   **C** blankets

Reading Part 5 Multiple-choice cloze

Part 5 of the Reading and Writing paper tests grammar. There is a text with an example and eight multiple-choice questions (**28–35**). Here are some examples of the type of words which are tested.

Match the parts of speech (1–7) with the example words (a–g).

1	conjunctions	**a**	*few, several, many*
2	verb forms	**b**	*where, when, why*
3	articles	**c**	*and, but, because*
4	prepositions	**d**	*does, making, had*
5	pronouns	**e**	*a, the*
6	determiners	**f**	*in, at, on*
7	question words	**g**	*he, hers, somebody*

Part 5	
28	A B C
29	A B C
30	A B C
31	A B C
32	A B C
33	A B C
34	A B C
35	A B C

Part 5

Questions 28–35

Read the article about a girl and a dolphin.

Choose the best word (**A**, **B** or **C**) for each space.

For questions **28–35**, mark **A**, **B** or **C** on the answer sheet.

The helpful dolphin

One summer I went to Florida in the USA (**0**) .... holiday. I said goodbye to my family at the airport in London (**28**) .... I flew to Miami. I stayed with my friend Maria. Her grandfather had a boat and we (**29**) .... to go sailing. We had (**30**) .... lovely time sailing! One morning I decided to sit on the side of the boat. Suddenly, I fell off into the sea. I didn't know how to swim (**31**) .... well and I began to shout. Then, (**32**) .... a minute I felt (**33**) .... push me nearer the boat. (**34**) .... was a dolphin and he was trying to help me! Maria heard me shout and her grandfather pulled me back on the boat. After that I (**35**) .... to swim and I will always love dolphins!

Example:

0	**A** on	**B** at	**C** in	*Answer:*	**0** A B C

28	**A** but	**B** or	**C** and
29	**A** wanted	**B** wanting	**C** want
30	**A** one	**B** a	**C** the
31	**A** very	**B** such	**C** enough
32	**A** before	**B** after	**C** since
33	**A** something	**B** anything	**C** nothing
34	**A** Him	**B** I	**C** It
35	**A** learned	**B** learning	**C** learn

Theme park fun

Speaking

1 Look at the photos of rides at different theme parks. Which one would you like to go on? Why? Is there a theme park near where you live? What is it called?

2 Read the information below about two theme parks called Magic Land and Space Adventure. Decide which one you'd like to go to.

Magic Land
* Opened in 2008
* 20 different rides
* Opening dates: 5th April – 2nd December
* Opening hours: 8.30–21.00
* 4.8 million visitors a year
* Hotel: 900 rooms
* Price: Family ticket 180 euros

Space Adventure
* Opened in 1987
* 35 different rides
* Opening dates: 1st March – 30th November
* Opening hours: 10.00–22.00
* 10.8 million visitors a year
* Hotel: 1,200 rooms
* Price: Family ticket: 220 euros

3 In Part 2 of the Speaking test you will need to ask and answer questions. Student A: Ask Student B questions about Magic Land. Student B: Ask Student A questions about Space Adventure.

EXAMPLE: When / first open?
Student A: *When did Magic Land first open?*
Student B: *It first opened in 2008.*
1 How many rides / have?
2 Which dates / open?
3 What / opening hours?
4 How many visitors?
5 How many hotel rooms?
6 How much / cost?

4 Choose the correct information.
1 Magic Land is *older / newer* than Space Adventure.
2 At Space Adventure the opening hours are *longer / shorter* than at Magic Land.
3 Magic Land has a *bigger / smaller* hotel than Space Adventure.
4 Space Adventure is *more / less* expensive than Magic Land.
5 Space Adventure has *more / fewer* visitors than Magic Land.
6 I think Space Adventure is a *better / worse* theme park than Magic Land because it has more rides.
7 You can spend *more / less* time at Space Adventure than you can at Magic Land.

Grammar Comparative forms

5 Look at the sentences in exercise 4 and complete the information below.

- Short adjectives usually end in -er, e.g. (1) .... , (2) ....
- Long adjectives usually have *more* or *less* in front of them, e.g. (3) ....
- Some adjectives change completely in the comparative form, e.g. *good* and *bad* become (4) .... and (5) ....
- Comparative adjectives are often followed by the word (6) ....
- We can also use (7) .... and *fewer* or *less* with nouns; we use (8) .... with countable nouns and *less* with uncountable nouns.
- See the Spelling spot for the spelling rules.

G → page 140

Reading

6 Read the information below about theme parks.

The biggest *and the* best!

The first amusement park in the world was Bakken in Denmark. It opened in 1583! It had simple rides and also dancing and fireworks. <u>The largest</u> amusement park in the world today is probably Walt Disney World Resort in Florida, USA. It has four theme parks and two water parks. One of these, The Magic Kingdom, is <u>the most popular</u> theme park in the world, with 17 million visitors a year.

Kingda Ka in Six Flags Great Adventure theme park, New Jersey, USA, drops visitors from a height of 139 metres! It can carry up to 1,400 riders per hour and the ride lasts for 28 seconds. It's taller than any other ride in the world.

Formula Rossa at Ferrari World in Abu Dhabi has a roller coaster that travels at 240 km per hour. It is faster than any other roller coaster. People who went on it said that it felt like being in a rocket!

Grammar Superlative adjectives

Look at the words underlined in the text about theme parks. These are superlative adjectives.

- We form a superlative by adding -*est* to the end of short words and putting *the* before it.
  <u>The largest</u> amusement park in the world is Disney World Resort in Florida, USA.
- Longer adjectives have *the most* or *the least* in front of them.
  The Magic Kingdom is <u>the most popular</u> theme park in the world.

7 Complete these sentences.

1 Denmark has .... in the world.
2 Kingda Ka is .... in the world.
3 Formula Rossa has .... in the world.

G → page 140

Spelling spot

Comparative and superlative adjectives

- Adjectives ending in -*y* become -*ier* in the comparative and -*iest* in the superlative.
  easy   easier   the easiest
- Short adjectives ending in a vowel + consonant double the last letter.
  hot   hotter   the hottest

8 Complete this chart.

adjective	comparative	superlative
modern		
comfortable		
fit		
horrible		
angry		
attractive		
bright		
tidy		

6.2 Free time

Speaking

1. How often do you go shopping?
   When do you listen to music?
   What computer games do you play?
   When do you see your friends?
   How often do you go swimming or go to the cinema?
   Look at the pictures and tell your partner what other things you do in your free time.

Key words → page 150

Listening

2. You will hear a girl asking for information about Aqua Park, a water park where you can go swimming. Before you listen, read through the questions carefully and, with a partner, talk about what kind of words you think the answers will be.

   EXAMPLE: *I think the answer to 1 will be a time.*

   1 19 Listen and complete the notes.

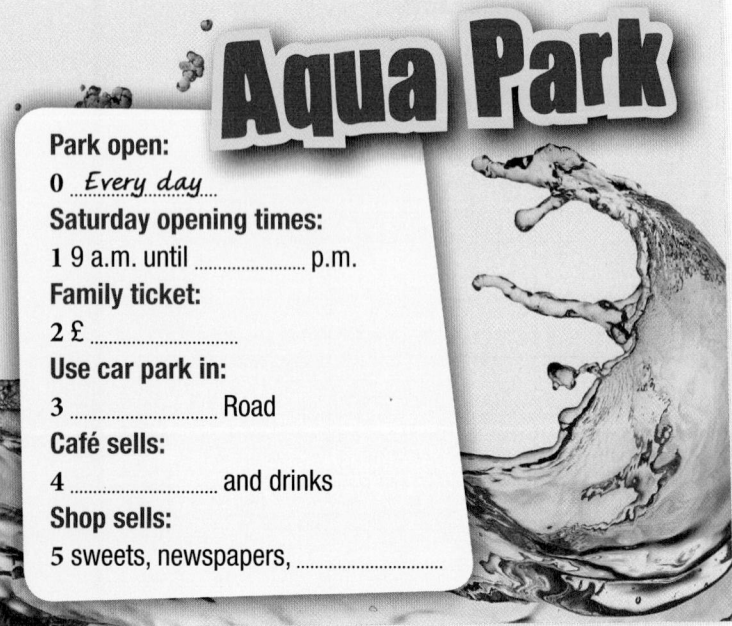

Aqua Park

Park open:
0 *Every day*
Saturday opening times:
1 9 a.m. until .... p.m.
Family ticket:
2 £ ....
Use car park in:
3 .... Road
Café sells:
4 .... and drinks
Shop sells:
5 sweets, newspapers, ...

Grammar extra

Comparative adverbs

- Most comparative adverbs are made with *more*. *You can get in more cheaply with a family ticket.*

- Adverbs that look the same as their adjectives, for example *fast, early, hard, long, high* and a few others, for example *late, soon* use -er and -est. *On Saturdays we close much later, at ten.*

- Irregular adverbs: *well – better, badly – worse*

3. Complete the sentences with the comparative of the adverb in brackets.

   1. I reached the park .... (soon) than I expected.
   2. Angela worked .... (hard) than anyone else in the class.
   3. Could you talk .... (quietly) please? I'm on the phone.
   4. Pete arrived at the party .... (early) than I did.
   5. The journey took .... (long) this time because of the traffic.
   6. Jan did .... (well) in his swimming exam than Carol.
   7. She read the letter again .... (carefully).

4 Read this note a candidate wrote in the exam. There are six spelling mistakes. Can you find them and correct them?

Dear Tom,
Last Saturday I went to Aqua Park with my freind Peter. It was a beatiful day becouse the sun was shining. The Park was very intresting and their were many things wich we could do. Next time you can come with me.
Simon

Reading

5 Do you ever go to parties with your friends? What are they like? What do you wear?

Read these sentences about having a party with friends. Choose the best word (A, B or C) for each space and say why the other words are wrong.

EXAMPLES:

0 Paul has lots of .... friends.
   (A special) **B** sure **C** own

The word 'special' can be used with people and things; 'sure' is not used before a noun; you need to have 'his' for 'own' to be correct.

00 Paul and his college friends .... to have a party on Saturday night.
   (A decided) **B** invited **C** thought
   decide + to do something
   invite + *someone* + to do something
   think + *about* + doing something

1 It doesn't .... a lot to have a party.
   A pay **B** spend **C** cost
2 Paul and his friends like listening to .... music.
   A friendly **B** good **C** excited
3 Paul is a .... of hip-hop music.
   A dancer **B** band **C** fan
4 Paul never thinks parties are ....
   A negative **B** boring **C** upset
5 Paul and his friends .... jeans to their party.
   A wore **B** put **C** dressed

Pronunciation

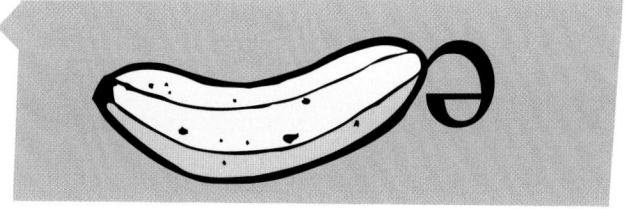

6 🔊 **1 20** Listen and repeat. All the words have the /ə/ sound, which is very common in English.

shorter   mother   alone   camera   banana
computer

7 Complete the crossword. All the words contain the /ə/ sound.

Across
1 by yourself
6 This has a keyboard.
9 the opposite of boring
10 Canada, the USA and Mexico are in North ....

Down
2 You do this with music.
3 You use this to take photographs.
4 the opposite of shorter
5 your dad
7 You see films there.
8 You get one in the post.

Activity

Questionnaires

· In pairs, A and B, ask questions to complete the questionnaires on page 131.

· When you finish asking questions, report back to the rest of the class using comparatives and superlatives.

Most people watch TV at the weekend.

The least favourite free-time activity is swimming.

Exam folder 4

Listening Parts 4 and 5 Gap-fill

In Parts 4 and 5 of the Listening paper you must write down some information.

In Part 4 there are always two speakers. Part 5 always has only one speaker. In both Part 4 and Part 5 there is an example and five questions (**16–20** and **21–25**). You must write down the words, letters or numbers that you hear.

Give the following information to your partner. Your partner should write down what you say. Spell out the words if necessary.

1 your telephone number
2 your full address
3 your favourite colour
4 your favourite day of the week
5 your birthday
6 the time you have breakfast
7 your height
8 the cost of going to the cinema

Part 4	
16	
17	
18	
19	
20	

Part 5	
21	
22	
23	
24	
25	

EXAM ADVICE

Before listening
- Read through the questions carefully.

First listening
- Don't write down the first thing you hear. Make sure you answer the question.
- Write your answer.

Second listening
- Check you are correct.
- Always write something, even if you are not sure your answer is right.
- At the end of the Listening test, write your answers in pencil on your answer sheet carefully. Check your spelling. Words that are spelled on the recording and words which are used quite often, for example, *red* or *bus*, must be spelled correctly. Opposite are examples of the answer sheet for Parts 4 and 5.

Part 4

Questions 16–20

You will hear a woman asking about a guitar for sale.

Listen and complete questions **16–20**.

You will hear the conversation twice.

Guitar for Sale		
Make of guitar:		Fender
Age of guitar:	**16**	.... months old
Price:	**17**	£
Address:	**18**	60 .... Road
Bus number:	**19**	
Best time to visit:	**20**	after ....

Part 5

Questions 21–25

You will hear some information about an activity centre.

Listen and complete questions **21–25**.

You will hear the information twice.

High Cross Activity Centre		
Open:		March to October
Possible to do:	**21**	football, climbing, ...
Cost of one week:	**22**	£
Size of largest group:	**23**	.... people
Name of manager:	**24**	Pete ....
Office telephone number:	**25**	

7.1 The latest fashion

1 Which of these do you wear? Talk about your own or the ones in the pictures.

On the front, it's got a picture of / it says …
On the back, there's a …
I bought it in …
My oldest / newest / most unusual one/pair is …

Reading

2 Which are the oldest – T-shirts, Converse boots or baseball caps? Check the dates in the three articles to find out when each was first worn.

3 Now read the articles and answer questions 1–7.

For each question, choose the answer A, B or C.

A = the T-shirt
B = Converse boots
C = the baseball cap

EXAMPLE:

0 Which of these is the oldest?   *B*

1 Which of these were first seen in films?
2 Which of these is useful in hot weather?
3 Which of these became well-known because of a sports person?
4 Which of these is sometimes worn in a different way?
5 Which of these was only available in two colours until the 1960s?
6 Which of these was used as an advertisement for a drink?
7 Which of these belongs to another company now?

The T-shirt

White cotton T-shirts were first worn by the US Navy in the 1940s but it was Hollywood movies that made them popular. Actors Marlon Brando and James Dean wore classic white T-shirts in films they made in 1954 and 1955. After this, every young man wanted to wear one. Women began to wear T-shirts from 1959, when the American actor Jean Seberg wore one in a French film. From the mid-1960s, companies like Coca-Cola used T-shirts to improve sales, putting logos or pictures on the front.

Converse boots

Marquis Mills Converse started his shoe company in 1908 but it wasn't until 1917 that he started making basketball boots. Then, in 1921, a basketball player called Chuck Taylor got a sales job with Converse. Chuck made the All-Star basketball boot famous, and in 1923 his name was included on the boot. For many years, 'Chucks' were only available in black but in 1947 a white boot was made. In 1966, the company started making boots and shoes in other colours. Nike bought Converse in 2003.

The baseball cap

The modern baseball cap was born in 1954, when a company developed the '59Fifty' for Major League baseball players to wear. These caps are worn by all kinds of people now, from famous film stars to rap singers – and probably by you as well. They are comfortable and help to keep the sun out of your eyes – unless you wear them back to front, like many tennis players!

Grammar Simple and continuous tenses

4 Complete the timeline with years from the text.

1 Marlon Brando's film came out.	2 More and more men were wearing T-shirts (but women weren't).	3 Jean Seberg wore a T-shirt in a film.	4 Men and women were both wearing T-shirts.

.... > ....–1958 > .... > 1960

5 Which tenses are used in the underlined verbs? Why are two different tenses used in 3?

1 Hannah <u>is wearing</u> jeans today.
2 Hannah <u>wears</u> jeans nearly every day.
3 Luckily, Hannah <u>was wearing</u> jeans when she <u>fell</u> off her bike.

G→ page 140

6 You saw a friend in a clothes shop yesterday. What was your friend doing? Make affirmative and negative sentences using these verbs.

EXAMPLE: *He was looking at some jeans.*
He wasn't wearing a coat.

buy   choose   look at   pay for   put on   try on   wear

7 Put the verbs in this timeline in the correct past tense. Then complete the story.

My friend .... (look at) clothes.

10.20 >>>>>>>>>>>>>>>>>>>>>>>>>>> 10.45

10.35 I .... (see) my friend.	10.45 The fire alarm .... (start).	10.46 We both .... (leave).

Yesterday morning I (**1**) ...*was walking*... (walk) around town when I (**2**) .... (see) my friend through a clothes shop window. He (**3**) .... (try on) a leather jacket, so I (**4**) .... (decide) to go inside the shop. I (**5**) .... (say) 'Hi' to my friend and then I (**6**) .... (go) to look at some jeans. I (**7**) .... (find) some really nice ones and I (**8**) .... (wait) to pay for them when the fire alarm (**9**) .... (start). We both (**10**) .... (leave) the shop immediately.

8 Complete each sentence using the correct past tense.

1 They .... (sell) beautiful T-shirts in the market last week.
2 I .... (buy) a really nice pair of boots in that shop.
3 Kelly .... (watch) TV when I .... (ring) her last night.
4 Yesterday morning I .... (wear) shorts, but when the sun .... (stop) shining I .... (change) into some jeans.
5 I .... (wait) for the bus when Jack .... (drive) past and .... (give) me a lift.
6 Tino .... (live) in Perugia when I last .... (hear) from him.

Spelling spot

-ing form

- Verbs ending in -*e* lose this letter:
  drive → driving
  I was driving beside the river when I saw a bear.
  hope → hoping
  Mike was hoping to meet you last weekend.

- Verbs ending in consonant + vowel + consonant usually double the last letter:
  begin → beginning
  Women were beginning to wear shorter skirts in 1963.

- Verbs ending in -*y* or -*w* do not double the last letter:
  pay → paying
  I was paying for the jeans when I heard the alarm.

9 Write the -*ing* form of these verbs.

break   make   stay   sit
leave   throw   lend   win

7.2 Your clothes

Vocabulary

1 Name the clothes and jewellery in 1–20.

Key words → page 150

2 Picture 1 shows *a pair of boots*. Picture 2 shows *a couple of hats*. What is the difference between these phrases? Which other pictures show a *pair* of something?

3 Choose a picture and use some of the words below to describe it, but don't say the word. Guess what your partner is describing.

EXAMPLE: *This pair has got two pockets. The material looks quite light.*
(Answer: *trousers – picture 16*)

Key words

adjectives	nouns
short/long	button
old/new	material
large/small	pair
dirty/clean	pocket
cheap/expensive	size
heavy/light	
leather/cotton/wool	leather/cotton/wool
gold/silver	gold/silver

Listening

4 ▶ 1 23 Listen to some English teenagers talking about the last clothes they bought. Who bought what? Tick the table.

	1 Ben	2 Louisa	3 Chris
cap			
jacket			
jeans			
shirt			
shorts			
T-shirt			
trousers			

5 🎧 **1 24** Listen again to Ben and fill the spaces with the missing words. Then repeat the sentences and phrases.

1 I .... as a .... on .... evenings

2 .... I saw this pair of .... cotton shorts

3 they looked ....

4 with a couple of .... T-shirts

6 🎧 **1 25** Now write down the words you hear. They begin with *w-*, *y-*, *z-* or *ex-*. The number of letters is given.

1 _ _ _
2 _ _ _ _
3 _ _ _ _ _
4 _ _ _ _ _ _ _
5 _ _ _ _
6 _ _ _ _ _
7 _ _ _ _
8 _ _ _ _ _ _ _ _ _
9 _ _ _ _ _
10 _ _ _ _ _
11 _ _ _ _
12 _ _ _ _ _

Reading

7 Choose A, B or C to complete these conversations.

1 Do you have this dress in a smaller size?
A You can tell.
B Let me check.
C No, it doesn't.

2 You're wearing your T-shirt back to front!
A Take it back then.
B Yours is the best.
C I prefer it like that.

3 Is it OK to wear jeans to Sam's party?
A I'm not certain.
B Are you sure?
C He's OK, I think.

4 Can I borrow your leather jacket?
A Never mind!
B Well done!
C No problem!

5 Bring a warm sweater for later.
A Is it always warm?
B Do I really need one?
C How much are they?

Activity

Pass the hat

- For this game you need a dice and a hat per team of six.
- Give each person in the team a number from 1 to 6.
- Take turns to throw the dice. If your number is thrown, you must put on the hat and spell a clothes word.
- You get a point for every word you can spell correctly.
- You lose the hat after you have spelled three words correctly or if you spell a word wrongly. Then the dice is thrown again.
- The winner is the person with the most points.

Writing folder 2

Writing Part 7 Open cloze

In Part 7 of the Reading and Writing paper there is one text or two shorter texts with ten spaces (**41–50**). You must fill each space with one word.

There is an example at the beginning. The text is usually an email or a message left on the internet.

1   Here are some examples of the types of word that are tested in Part 7. Can you add other words to each set?

articles	*a*
pronouns	*it*
prepositions	*at*
quantifiers	*some*
auxiliary verbs	*did*
modal verbs	*can*

2   Decide what type of word should go in each space below, choosing from the list in exercise 1. Look at the words before and after the space to help you.

1 Are .... well? *pronoun*
2 How .... you know?
3 I went .... the cinema.
4 You .... eat more fruit.
5 Have you got .... stamps?
6 What .... pity!

3   Read these messages left on the internet by two friends and choose the correct words.

Hi Janusz!
We're having a lovely weekend (**1**) *in / at* Germany. We're staying near the centre of Berlin and there are (**2**) *any / some* great shops near the hotel. Yesterday we went shopping (**3**) *for / until* three hours! You really (**4**) *must / can* visit this amazing city soon. Give (**5**) *your / our* love to everyone.
Enrico and Paola

Hi Enrico and Paola
Thanks for your message (**6**) *from / by* Berlin. It sounds fantastic. How (**7**) *much / many* is your hotel? (**8**) *Will / Do* you think it is good? Please email me their website address (**9**) *so / because* I'd like to find out more about (**10**) *a / the* hotel.
Love, Janusz

Part 7	Do not write here
41	1 41 2
42	1 42 2
43	1 43 2
44	1 44 2
45	1 45 2
46	1 46 2
47	1 47 2
48	1 48 2
49	1 49 2
50	1 50 2

Part 7

Questions 41–50

Complete this email.

Write ONE word for each space.

For questions **41–50**, write the words on your answer sheet.

Example: | **0** | to |

Dear Maria,

I went (**0**) .... the town centre yesterday and I bought (**41**) .... new clothes. Let (**42**) .... tell you what I found. (**43**) .... was a sale in one shop and I got two pairs of jeans (**44**) .... the price of one! Then I decided to look in the market (**45**) .... they sell clothes and other things very cheaply. I saw a beautiful leather belt and (**46**) .... was only 10 euros.

You know I like T-shirts very (**47**) .... Well, I found a great one yesterday. The picture (**48**) .... the front is the Mona Lisa, but the colours (**49**) .... orange and green! This is now (**50**) .... favourite T-shirt.

What clothes have you bought?

Love,

Giulia

8.1 A great movie

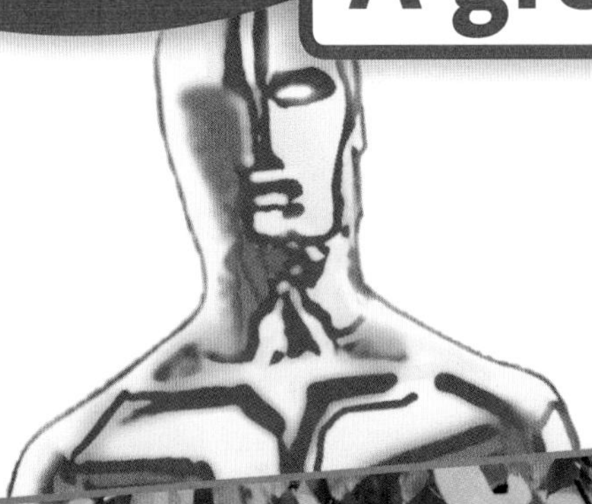

1 Can you name these films? Why are they popular? Choose from these phrases and add your own ideas.

Key speaking

well-known actors   amazing special effects
exciting story   awesome sound effects
excellent music   I love the part where …

2 Ask and answer these questions.

1 What's your favourite film?
2 Who are the main actors?
3 How long is the film?
4 What's the music like?
5 Which part of the film do you like most?

Grammar Modal verbs 1

3 Underline the modal verbs in these sentences.

1 I can understand most films in French.
2 Jenny may buy that DVD, but she's not sure.
3 You must book in advance for the 3D film.
4 I had to take my passport to the cinema to show my age.
5 When he was in New York, Roberto could see a different movie every night.
6 Cinema staff sometimes have to work very long hours.
7 My brother might have an extra ticket for tonight's film – I'll ask him.

4 Match a–e below with sentences 1–7 in exercise 3.

a talking about obligation in the present (two answers)
b talking about obligation in the past
c talking about possibility (two answers)
d talking about ability in the present
e talking about ability in the past

5 Complete the grammar notes and examples.

- We cannot use the word *must* in the past. Instead, we use ....
  EXAMPLE: *Last night, I* ....
  ....

- When we are talking about something we are unable to do, we use the word .... or the contracted form ....
  EXAMPLE: *I* .... , *but I'd like to be able to.*

- If we are talking about something we were unable to do in the past, we use .... or the contracted form ....
  EXAMPLE: *Before I was five, I* ....
  .... , *but now I can.*

G → page 141

6 Choose the correct word.

1 Elio's just phoned. He *can't / couldn't* come to the cinema with us tonight.
2 We *must / had to* sit at the side of the cinema last time because we booked so late.
3 We *couldn't / can't* see very well and the seats weren't very comfortable.
4 There was nothing we *must / could* do about it, but this time let's book earlier!
5 *May / Can* you buy the tickets for us at lunchtime?
6 We *may / must* all meet at the cinema no later than 7.15.
7 There *can / may* be time to have an ice cream after the film.
8 Perhaps, but I *could / have to* catch the 10 o'clock bus because that's the last one.

7 What might you do next weekend? Tick the table so that it is true for you. Then compare your information with other students, using *may* or *might*.

	Friday	Saturday	Sunday
see a film			
have a party			
buy some clothes			
go on Facebook			
play chess			
make pizza			
do some homework			
watch something new on TV			

Reading

8 Read the text about *Transformers 3*. Choose the best word (A, B or C) for each space.

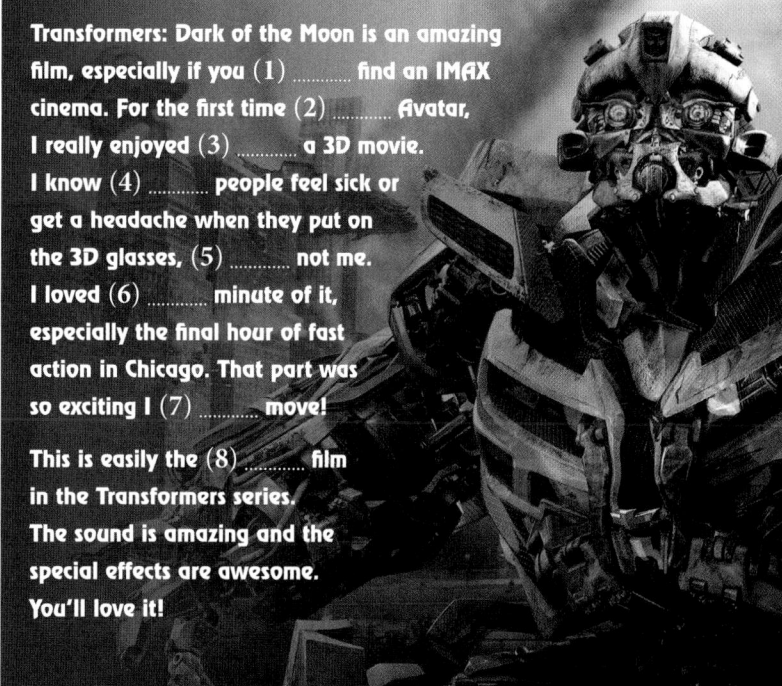

Transformers: Dark of the Moon is an amazing film, especially if you (1) .... find an IMAX cinema. For the first time (2) .... Avatar, I really enjoyed (3) .... a 3D movie. I know (4) .... people feel sick or get a headache when they put on the 3D glasses, (5) .... not me. I loved (6) .... minute of it, especially the final hour of fast action in Chicago. That part was so exciting I (7) .... move!

This is easily the (8) .... film in the Transformers series. The sound is amazing and the special effects are awesome. You'll love it!

1 **A** must   **B** can   **C** may
2 **A** from   **B** since   **C** for
3 **A** watch   **B** watched   **C** watching
4 **A** some   **B** much   **C** any
5 **A** and   **B** but   **C** so
6 **A** every   **B** all   **C** both
7 **A** can't   **B** mustn't   **C** couldn't
8 **A** good   **B** better   **C** best

8.2 Cool sounds

1 What kinds of music do you like? Write the names of your top five bands. Which is the most popular band in your class?

Vocabulary

2 Find eleven more music words in the word square (look → and ↓). The picture may help you. Then talk about the picture. Describe what you can see and say what each person in the band is doing.

s	l	q	f	b	s	p	l	a	y
i	d	w	e	a	t	i	t	e	t
n	d	w	s	t	d	a	n	c	e
g	u	i	t	a	r	n	j	o	x
e	l	n	i	o	u	o	w	n	e
r	i	t	v	k	m	v	s	c	i
p	g	x	a	e	s	u	a	e	b
b	h	a	l	b	u	m	r	r	a
o	t	a	m	p	d	a	t	t	n
l	s	p	e	a	k	e	r	s	d

Key words → page 150

Listening

3 🔊 1 26 You will hear five short conversations. For questions 1–5, put a tick under the right answer.

1 How much did Craig earn from the concert?

£50   £75   £150

A ☐   B ☐   C ☐

2 Which band did the girl see?

A ☐   B ☐   C ☐

3 Where is the next band from?

Australia   Brazil   Iceland

A ☐   B ☐   C ☐

4 What does Ben play?

A ☐   B ☐   C ☐

5 What must Kim bring to the party?

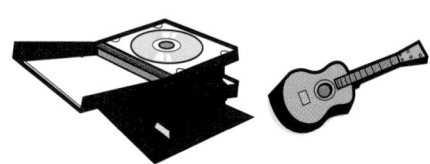

A ☐   B ☐   C ☐

Pronunciation

4 🔊 **1 27** Listen to Anna. How does she say the short questions below?

Boy   *Ray's ill.*

Anna   *Is he?*

Boy   *Here's your scarf. You left it at my house after the party.*

Anna   *Did I? Thanks.*

🔊 **1 28** Now listen to sentences 1–6. Choose the right short question from the list below. Write the sentence number on the square. There are some questions which you will not need to use. Then listen to check your answers.

EXAMPLE: You hear: **1** *Here's your scarf. You left it at my house after the party.*

Don't you?	☐	Isn't it?	☐
Have you?	☐	Must I?	☐
Can't you?	☐	Couldn't she?	☐
Did I?	1	Aren't they?	☐
Did they?	☐		

5 🔊 **1 29** Now listen again and choose a short phrase from the box to follow your question. Say the question and phrase aloud. More than one phrase may be possible.

EXAMPLE: You hear: **1** *Here's your scarf. You left it at my house after the party.*
You say: *Did I? Thanks a lot.*

Key speaking

That's a shame.	Thanks a lot.
That's too bad.	That's great!
What a pity.	Cool!
Never mind.	Fantastic!

6 Write conversations for the three questions you didn't use in exercise 4. Include one of the short phrases from exercise 5 after each question.

7 Here are some errors that candidates have made in the exam. Correct the sentences.

1 Yesterday I was at a beatiful rock concert.
2 It's my favrit cinema.
3 I'm selling my piano becouse I don't want it any more.
4 A lot of turists visit my town.
5 I went to a nightclub with my freends.
6 There are two musuems in the town.

Activity

Who is it?

- Look at the photo. Can you guess who's under the hat and sunglasses? Read the sentences below the picture to help you decide.

  This person sings hip hop and rap music. His album sales are more than 50 million worldwide. He is married to a famous singer.

- Make a poster for the classroom wall about a musician of your choice. Find a picture of him or her but make it difficult to see who it is. Include some sentences about your person below the picture, using some of the words from this unit.

Units 5–8 Revision

Speaking

1 Read these sentences with a partner. Say what you think about each one and give some extra information.

1 It's bad to keep animals in zoos.
2 Ten years ago, people in offices couldn't wear jeans.
3 The best thing about today's films is the special effects.
4 We must all look after the planet.
5 Children can get into museums and theme parks more cheaply than adults.

Grammar

2 In 1–4 only one sentence (A–C) is correct. Tick the correct sentence.

1 A I bought a green trousers yesterday.
   B I bought some green trouser yesterday.
   C I bought a pair of green trousers yesterday.
2 A We could to wait half an hour to go on our favourite ride.
   B We had to wait half an hour to go on our favourite ride.
   C We must to wait half an hour to go on our favourite ride.
3 A Enzo was playing the drums when he was dropping his drumstick.
   B Enzo played the drums when he dropped his drumstick.
   C Enzo was playing the drums when he dropped his drumstick.
4 A The band's new singer sings very well.
   B The band's new singer sings very best.
   C The band's new singer sings very good.

3 Read the text about a famous film. Choose the best word (A, B or C) for each space.

1 **A** by	**B** with	**C** from
2 **A** good	**B** better	**C** best
3 **A** but	**B** when	**C** if
4 **A** on	**B** into	**C** at
5 **A** takes	**B** taken	**C** took
6 **A** so	**B** and	**C** because
7 **A** much	**B** lots	**C** many
8 **A** also	**B** too	**C** both

The film 'Pirates of the Caribbean' had a wonderful story, (1) .... really great special effects. The (2) .... actor in the film was Johnny Depp, who played the pirate Jack Sparrow. Jack was a clever sailor (3) .... he lost his ship, the Black Pearl, to a very bad pirate called Captain Barbossa.

Barbossa sailed (4) .... the town of Port Royal and (5) .... a beautiful young girl called Elizabeth away as his prisoner. Jack Sparrow agreed to help find Elizabeth (6) .... he wanted to get his ship back.

Of course, there is (7) .... of adventure in this film. It is (8) .... very funny.

Vocabulary

4 Complete each sentence with an adjective from the box. Use each adjective once only.

> boring   dirty   fast   hot
> old   small   ~~tall~~   thin

1 Henry was so .... *tall* .... that he couldn't stand up straight in the room.
2 I'm going to change into a T-shirt – it's too .... to wear a sweater.
3 I had to clean my shoes as I had got them ....
4 This book is so .... – nothing interesting ever happens!
5 I've had these .... football boots for too long.
6 Eurostar trains go really .... so you can get to places quickly.
7 Because they diet a lot, most fashion models are very ....
8 Most dogs are not as .... as cats.

5 Put these words into four meaning groups.

~~album~~	~~bear~~	~~button~~
chess	climbing	concert
cycling	drums	elephant
fish	guitar	horse
jacket	jeans	lion
monkey	piano	pocket
shorts	skateboarding	socks
sweater	table tennis	trainers

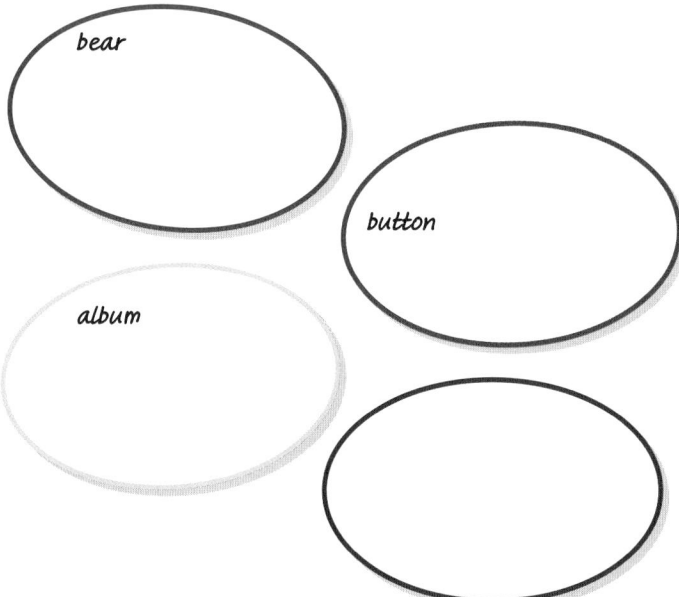

bear

button

album

Writing

6 Complete this letter about visiting a theme park in France. Write ONE word for each space.

Hi Steffi,

My parents took us **(1)** .... Parc Astérix, just north of Paris, yesterday. **(2)** .... was fantastic! In the morning, we **(3)** .... driving up the A1 motorway from Paris when my younger brother saw a big sign with a picture of Astérix on. He laughed and screamed – he was **(4)** .... excited than I was!

We spent eight hours **(5)** .... the park and enjoyed everything – the rides, the little plays outside and the wild boar sandwiches! The **(6)** .... thing for me was meeting Obélix **(7)** .... he is my favourite person in the stories. My brother asked him about **(8)** .... red hair and we got a photo of us all together.

We **(9)** .... go there again (my dad isn't sure). If we do, **(10)** .... don't you come too?

Love,

Amélie

9.1 Holiday plans

1 What's your idea of the perfect holiday? Tell your partner.

Listening

2 🔊1·30 Listen to four people talking about their plans for their next holiday. Match the people to the places and the type of holiday. The first one has been done for you.

1 Julia	Greece	sailing
2 Daniel	France	walking
3 Simon	Australia	camping
4 Natalie	Switzerland	beach

Then listen again and write down how they are going to travel.

5 Julia – by ....
6 Daniel – by ....
7 Simon – by ....
8 Natalie – by ....

Grammar The future with *going to*

- When we intend to do something in the future, we use *to be going to*.
  I'm going to do some walking in Switzerland.

  I decided to do it ———→ I'm going to do it ———→
  past   *now*   *future*

- With the verb *to go* we often don't repeat the *to go* and just say, for example, **I'm going to** the travel agent's tomorrow.

G→page 142

3 Look at the pictures below. Take turns to ask and answer questions.

EXAMPLE:
A: *Look at picture 1.*
   What's she going to do?
B: *She's going to catch a plane.*

4 Complete these sentences using *to be going to* + one of the verbs from the box.

> book   close   do   have   meet   ~~stay~~
> telephone   visit

1 I had a terrible holiday last year. Next year ....*I'm going to stay*.......... at home.
2 Peter .... the hotel and ask for a room with a view.
3 After lunch Alicia and Elena .... some shopping for souvenirs.
4 I .... my train ticket online tomorrow.
5 The cruise ship .... Athens, Naples and Nice.
6 The management .... the pool today because it needs cleaning.
7 We .... our friends later, in the café.
8 We .... a camping holiday again next year.

Pronunciation

5 Look at the words below. Underline the words which have the sound /h/.

hand   holiday   why   home   hill   when
honest   how   happy   hour   school   hotel

🎧 **1 31** Listen to check your answers.

6 Put the words in each sentence into the right order.

1 home hills has a he holiday in the
2 a hopes birthday Helena get horse for her she'll
3 homework him with his help
4 have holiday happy a
5 hire boat fun and have going I'm to a
6 helicopter me into the help

🎧 **1 32** Listen to check your answers and repeat the sentences.

7 🎧 **1 33** Listen and circle the word you hear.

1 eye / high   5 air / hair
2 old / hold   6 all / hall
3 it / hit   7 art / heart
4 and / hand

Reading

8 In Reading Part 3 you must complete a conversation.

Complete the conversation. What does Stella say to the travel agent? Choose from A–H below. There are two extra replies that you don't need to use.

EXAMPLE:

Travel agent	Good morning. Can I help you?
Stella	**0** _H_
Travel agent	Where would you like to go?
Stella	**1** ....
Travel agent	Florida is very popular.
Stella	**2** ....
Travel agent	It is all year, but there are lots of hotels.
Stella	**3** ....
Travel agent	Well, what about a holiday centre in Sardinia?
Stella	**4** ....
Travel agent	Yes, you can fly there easily and this year the price is only going to be 650 euros a week.
Stella	**5** ....
Travel agent	That's fine. Take some of these brochures so you can both look at them at home.

A Isn't it very busy in summer?
B Oh, that's more than I thought! I'm going to have to talk to my friend first.
C I'm not sure. I like places where I can do lots of things.
D Really? I thought the beach was good.
E That sounds more interesting. Is it easy to get to?
F No, I have a couple of weeks free.
G I'm not sure. What else do you have?
H Yes, please. I'd like to book a holiday.

Vocabulary

1 Match the words 1–10 with the explanations a–j. The first one has been done for you.

Key words

1	a hotel	a	when you travel from one place to another
2	a guidebook	b	all your bags when you travel
3	luggage	c	what you do when you put your clothes in your bag
4	a journey	d	a building where you eat and sleep
5	a passport	e	a picture which shows you where roads, towns etc. are
6	a suitcase	f	You put your clothes in this when you travel.
7	to go sightseeing	g	You go on one of these to see famous places.
8	to pack	h	You need this to leave and enter a country.
9	a map	i	to look at interesting places
10	a tour	j	a book which tells you about different places

2 What will holidays be like in the future? Tell your partner whether you agree with these sentences and say why / why not.

EXAMPLE: A: *We won't have holidays outside our country.*
B: *I think we will have holidays all over the world because everyone likes to see different places.*

1 We won't need a passport.
2 We will have hotels on the Moon.
3 We won't need suitcases.
4 We will travel by train underground from Europe to the USA.
5 We won't need guidebooks.
6 We won't travel by plane as there will be no oil.

Reading

3 Read the article about the future of travel and then write questions for 1–7.

1 Where / train / go? – Under the sea from London to New York.
   Where will the train go?
2 Where / have / holidays? – On the Moon.
3 How / travel? – In balloons instead of planes.
4 Where / mirrors? – In the bathroom.
5 What / mirrors / tell? – How healthy you are.
6 Why / curtains? – Because the windows will have special glass.
7 Where / food / come from? – The island's gardens.

TRAVEL IN THE FUTURE

Who knows what kind of holidays we will have in the future? People have lots of ideas. Some people think there will possibly be a railway under the sea between London and New York by 2025 and others believe that holidays on the Moon will certainly be possible by then too. Many people think that there will probably be hotels under the sea, and lots of people think that we will certainly travel in balloons instead of planes by 2025 and even that time travel will happen in the future.

Another report says that by 2030 there will be large islands which will be able to move from one place to another. There will be intelligent hotel rooms which tell you how much water you are using in the shower. They will also have special mirrors in the bathroom which tell you how healthy you are. The windows will have special glass so curtains won't be needed and all food will come from the island's gardens.

Grammar The future with *will*

- We use *will / 'll* + verb or *will not / won't* + verb to talk about the future.
  *There **will be** hotels under the sea.*
  *Curtains **won't be** needed.*
- We often use these words with *will*:
  certainly = 100%   probably = 70%   possibly = 40%
- When we are predicting something we also often use *think + will*.
  *Lots of people **think** that we **will travel** in balloons instead of planes.*

4 What will happen in the future? Write some sentences about each topic below. Use *will* or *won't*. Then, tell your partner about your ideas.

EXAMPLE   my holidays
I think that I will probably take my holidays in my own country in the future because it is easier. I don't think I will travel / I won't travel with my family because it is more fun to go with friends.

1 your holidays	**4** your favourite team
2 yourself	**5** your favourite band
3 your school	**6** your best friend

G → page 142

5 Read this email from Susie, who is on holiday on the moon. Which word best fits each space?

Moon Mail

To	Manuel Garcia
Subject	Holiday

Dear Manuel,
I'm having a lovely time on holiday at the Lunar Hotel. I arrived **(1)** .... Monday after **(2)** .... good flight on the space bus. I booked some trips today and tomorrow I'm **(3)** .... to take a trip to the Space Museum. My bedroom **(4)** .... under the ground **(5)** .... there's a restaurant on the surface with a great view of Earth from **(6)** .... large windows. I **(7)** .... even see Spain! The food is OK and **(8)** .... is a lot to do. Tonight, I'm going to the Space Club with **(9)** .... new friends. I'll see you next week when I get back. You **(10)** .... really like the photos!
Love,
Susie

1 (on)/ at	**4** is / has	**8** there / it
2 the / a	**5** or / but	**9** some / any
3 going / will	**6** their / its	**10** will / do
	7 must / can	

Spelling spot

Words ending in -y

- Usually when we add an ending to words ending in *-y*, the *-y* changes to *-i*.
  baby – babies, hurry – hurried, funny – funnier, carry – carries

- But *-y* does not change to *-i* if the word ends in *-ay*, *-ey*, *-oy* or *-uy*.
  boy – boys, stay – stayed

6 Complete each sentence with a word from the box in the correct form.

battery	buy	enjoy	family	happy
~~holiday~~	key	monkey	play	stay

1 We had many happy __holidays__ in Chile.
2 Shakespeare's .... are known all over the world.
3 Lucia is much .... now she has a new flat.
4 I've lost my .... and can't get into the house.
5 We like the .... best at the zoo.
6 I need new .... for my bicycle lights.
7 Dr Turner very much .... the film he saw last night.
8 Sheila always .... at the same hotel when she's in Rome.
9 I think big .... are much more fun than small ones.
10 She .... her clothes from a well-known designer.

Activity

Are you a World Traveller?

- Read the questionnaire on page 132 and ask and answer the questions with a partner.

- Look at the scores on page 134 to find out if your partner is a
  World Traveller
  Happy Tourist
  Stay-at-Home

Exam folder 5

Speaking Parts 1 and 2

There are two parts to the Speaking test. Part 1 lasts for 5–6 minutes and Part 2 lasts for 3–4 minutes. You do the Speaking test with another student.

There are two examiners – one who asks questions and one who listens.

EXAM ADVICE

- If you don't understand, ask the examiner: *Could you repeat the question, please?*
- Speak clearly.
- Don't worry if the other student knows more or less English than you do. It's what you say that is important.
- Practise giving information about yourself and what you like or dislike.
- Check you can talk about places and school subjects so you can answer questions about why you like something.
- Always say something, even if you are not sure you are right.
- Practise asking and answering questions using different question words such as *what, where,* etc. and different tenses.

Part 1

In Part 1 you are asked questions about yourself, your hobbies, your studies, etc. You will hear some examples of the type of questions on the recording.

1   **1 34** Listen to a student talking to an examiner. The first time, listen to get a general idea of what happens in Part 1.

Then listen again and complete this chart.

Surname:	
Town/country:	
Favourite subject:	
Countries visited:	
Free-time activities:	

2   **Ask and answer these questions.**

EXAMPLE:

What / name? *What's your name?*

How spell / surname?

Where / come from?

Where / study?

What subjects / study?

Which subject / like best?

Have / been to other countries?

What / do next weekend?

3   **Choose one of these things to talk about in pairs. Say to each other:**

Tell me something about …

… your favourite movie.

… your favourite music.

… your hobbies.

… your last holiday.

In Part 2 you will need to ask and answer questions. The examiner will give Candidate A a card with some information on it and Candidate B a card with some questions. Then Candidate B will get a card with some information on it and Candidate A will get a card with some questions.

4 Candidate A, here is some information about a holiday centre.
Candidate B, you don't know anything about the holiday centre, so ask A some questions about it. You will find the questions on page 131.

Holiday Centre

Westcliffe on Sea

★ Lots of fun for all the family!

★ Open March – November

★ Swimming pool and tennis courts

★ Excellent restaurant

Cost of a week in July: Adults £400 Children £250

---

5 Candidate B, here is some information about a cinema. Candidate A, you don't know anything about the cinema, so ask B some questions about it.

You will find the questions on page 133.

Burford Arts Cinema
68 Helman Street
Burford

This week only

The Return
of the
Martians

An adventure film starring Tom Schroder
Every day at 2.00 p.m.
Tickets: Adults £7.00 Children £3.50 Students £5.00

Eat at our Riverside Café – open all day and every evening.

Inside the home

Vocabulary

1 Match the words in the box with the pictures a–o.

Key words

1 bed	**6** curtains	**11** mirror
2 bookshelves	**7** desk	**12** pillow
3 carpet	**8** DVD player	**13** poster
4 chair	**9** lamp	**14** sofa
5 computer	**10** light	**15** wardrobe

2 Talk about your room. What's it like? You can use some of the ideas below.

> It's large.
> It's got a single bed.
> It's painted pink.
> There's a poster on the wall.
> It's very untidy.
> It's got a comfortable chair.
> It's on the first floor.

Spelling spot

Words ending in -f, -fe

- Nouns ending in -f or -fe usually change to -ves in the plural: *half – halves*
- Some nouns *don't* change: *roof – roofs, café – cafés*.

3 Make the underlined words plural.

1 There's a shelf in the kitchen.
   There are some shelves in the kitchen.
2 I have a bookshelf in my room.
3 The knife is on the table.
4 The roof is red.
5 His wife is in the kitchen.
6 I found a leaf on the floor.

Listening

4 Look at the objects 1–6, and the list of rooms. With a partner, decide which room or rooms the objects are usually found in.

EXAMPLE: *You usually find a desk in a teenager's bedroom.*

1 a desk	a bathroom
2 a sofa	a bedroom
3 a computer	a dining room
4 a TV	a hall
5 a mirror	a kitchen
6 a bookshelf	a living room

blue
black
brown
green
grey
orange
pink
red
white
yellow
purple

5 **1 35** Listen to a conversation between a girl called Lisa and her friend Tom about her family's new flat. She is telling him in which room (A–H) the family has put the objects 0–5.

For questions 1–5, write a letter A–H next to each object.

EXAMPLE:

0 the metal desk *E*

1 the leather sofa	**A**	the bathroom
2 the computer	**B**	the hall
3 the small TV	**C**	the living room
4 the large mirror	**D**	the dining room
5 the new bookshelves	**E**	the garage
	F	Lisa's bedroom
	G	the kitchen
	H	Lisa's parents' bedroom

Vocabulary

6 Ask and answer questions.

EXAMPLE: A: *What's the vase made of?*
B: *It's made of glass.*
B: *What are the curtains made of?*
A: *They're made of cotton.*

Key words

cotton	glass	gold	leather	metal
paper	plastic	silver	wood	wool

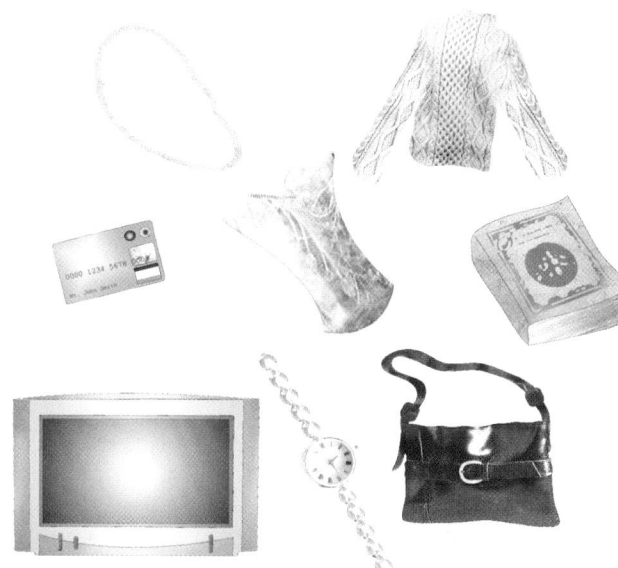

bag   book   bowl   credit card   curtains
necklace   sweater   TV   vase   watch   window

7 Match each adjective in box A with its opposite in Box B.

A | big   cold   double   expensive   high
large   long   narrow   new   noisy   soft

B | cheap   hard   hot   little   low   old
quiet   short   single   small   wide

8 Read the sentences about a flat. Choose the best word (A, B or C) for each space.

1 The bedroom is very .... and there isn't enough room for a double bed.
A short   **B** narrow   **C** single

2 The flat is .... at night because there's no traffic noise.
A soft   **B** low   **C** quiet

3 My new bed is very .... and hurts my back.
A hard   **B** long   **C** wide

4 Our flat is very .... so we have a good view of the park.
A high   **B** big   **C** new

5 I have a very .... computer in my bedroom.
A double   **B** expensive   **C** soft

Activity

In the classroom

Work with a partner. Talk about the objects in your classroom using the adjectives from exercises 6 and 7. Student A says a sentence which is wrong and B corrects it.

There is an old, metal desk.

No, the desk is new and made of wood.

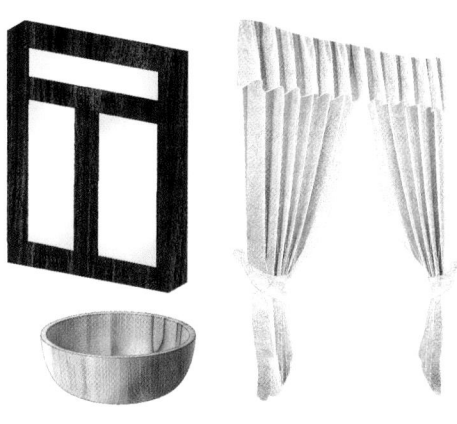

10.2 Famous buildings

1 Empire State Building

2 Opera House

3 Taj Mahal

4 Burj al Arab

5 Forbidden City

6 Great Pyramid

1 Look at the photos of famous buildings. Which building would you like to visit?

Match each building with the correct place and date. Who built or designed them? Don't worry if you don't know!

EXAMPLE: *The Taj Mahal was built in Agra, India in 1653.*

New York, USA	1999
Cairo, Egypt	1420
Beijing, China	1959–73
Agra, India	1931
Sydney, Australia	1653
Dubai, UAE	2500BC

Pronunciation

2 Write these dates as words.

EXAMPLE: *1173 – eleven seventy-three*

1 1292 3 1718 5 1963
2 1569 4 1890

▶ 36 Listen to check your answers.

3 ▶ 37 Listen and write down the dates you hear.

Grammar The passive

We can say:

*The government of the UAE **built** the Burj Al Arab in Dubai in 1999.*

This sentence is **active** and 'the government of the UAE' is the subject of the sentence.

Or we can say:

*The Burj Al Arab **was built** in Dubai by the government of the UAE in 1999.*

This sentence is **passive** and 'the Burj Al Arab' is now the subject of the sentence. This is an example of the **past simple passive**.

The passive is formed by using *to be* + the past participle of the verb. The past participle of a regular verb is the same as the past tense. If you are not sure what the past participle is of an irregular verb look at page 159.

An example of the **present simple passive** is: *My desk **is made** of wood.*

We use *by* to say who did the action if we know who it is/was and if we think that is important.

We often use the passive when we don't know or aren't interested in who exactly did something.

My bicycle was stolen today. TVs are made in China.

G → page 143

4 Complete these sentences with the verb in brackets in the present simple passive or past simple passive.

1 When Paul arrived at the White House he (take) _was taken_ to see the President.
2 My watch (make) .... by a factory in Switzerland.
3 A library is a place where books (borrow) ....
4 Kim's bedroom (paint) .... last month.
5 Their house (sell) .... for £450,000.
6 The Houses of Parliament (build) .... more than 150 years ago.
7 Children (teach) .... in schools.
8 The flat (buy) .... for her by her father.

5 Complete the article about the London Eye. For questions 1–6, you must decide which verb form to use. For questions 7–12, you will also need to decide how to form the verb.

The London Eye is one of the most popular attractions in London, and people (0) is visited / visit it from all over the UK and the world. It (1) designed / was designed by David Marks and Julia Barfield for a competition which (2) was organised / organised by a British newspaper in 1994. The newspaper (3) wanted / was wanted a new London building to celebrate the year 2000.

The Eye is 135 metres tall and it was the largest observation wheel in the world when it was built. Up to 800 people (4) are carried / carried on it at any one time. Marks and Barfield (5) were designed / designed the Eye and it (6) built / was built in less than 16 months. More than 1,700 people (7) .... (work) on the London Eye and much of it (8) .... (build) in other countries. The wheel (9) .... (develop) in the Netherlands. Experts in the Czech Republic and Italy (10) .... (make) some of the metal parts. The capsules which the people sit in (11) .... (make) in the French Alps and the glass (12) .... (produce) by an Italian company.

6 Complete the questions and find the answers in the article in exercise 5.

1 Who / design the London Eye?
Who designed the London Eye? It was designed by David Marks and Julia Barfield.
2 When / competition / organise?
3 How many / carry?
4 Where / wheel / develop?
5 Where / capsules / make?
6 Who / produce / glass?

Activity

What's the connection?

- Play in pairs.
- Your teacher will give you some cards. Place them in a pile between you.
- Each person takes a card in turn and has to say what the two things on the card have in common, using either the past simple passive or the present simple passive.

  EXAMPLE: *a helicopter and a plane*

  Possible answer:
  They are both flown by pilots.

- Only one answer is necessary and a correct answer gets a point.
- The winner is the person who gets the most points.

Exam folder 6

Reading Part 4 Right, Wrong, Doesn't say

In Part 4 of the Reading and Writing paper there is a text with an example and seven questions (**21–27**).

1   It is important in the exam that you don't answer the questions before reading the text, because the text may say something you don't expect. You *must* find the answer in the text to answer Right or Wrong. Try the following examples for practice. Sentences 1–3 all look like they could have the answer *Right*. However, read the text to see if this is true or not.

1   The castle is bigger than other houses in California.
2   Hearst Castle is one very large building.
3   Very famous American singers went to parties at Hearst Castle.

Part 4

21   A B C
22   A B C
23   A B C
24   A B C
25   A B C
26   A B C
27   A B C

EXAM ADVICE

- Read all the text carefully to get an idea of what it is about.
- For each question, find the part of the text that tells you the answer, then read it again carefully.
- The questions are in the order in which you will find the answers in the text.
- If the information isn't in the text, then the answer is *Doesn't say.*
- Don't worry if you don't understand every word.
- Practise filling in the answer on your answer sheets (see example).

Part 4

Questions 21–27

Read the article about a visit to Hearst Castle, a famous building in California.

Are the sentences **21–27** 'Right' (**A**) or 'Wrong' (**B**)?

If there is not enough information to answer 'Right' (**A**) or 'Wrong' (**B**), choose 'Doesn't say' (**C**).

Examples:

0   Hearst Castle was cheap to build.

0   A B C

*The answer is **B** (Wrong) because the text says the castle cost 'more than $30 million' to build.*

00   Theresa wanted to spend more time at Hearst Castle.

00   A B C

*The answer is **A** (Right) because the text says that Theresa 'spent all day looking around, but it wasn't enough'.*

000 Hearst Castle is on a mountain near the sea.

000   A B C

*The answer is **C** (Doesn't say) because there is no information in the text which tells you exactly where the castle is.*

A visit to Hearst Castle

by Theresa Martin

Last year, I had a great trip to Hearst Castle at San Simeon in California. Hearst Castle was built by William Randolph Hearst between 1922 and 1939, at a cost of more than $30 million – about $277 million today.

I spent all day looking around, but it wasn't enough. There was so much to see. Hearst Castle is really four houses. The main house, Casa Grande, is much bigger than the other three, which were used for guests. Many of these were Hollywood film stars, and they often came to Hearst's parties.

At Hearst Castle, there are 56 bedrooms, 61 bathrooms and 19 sitting rooms. There are also beautiful gardens, a garage for 25 large cars and two swimming pools, one inside and a larger one outside. I loved the one outside, the Neptune Pool – it was a pity we couldn't go swimming!

I found the tour very helpful. The guide told me that Hearst, at the age of ten, toured Europe with his mother, looking at paintings and castles. He never forgot this tour and decided that he wanted his house to look like a castle.

Hearst died in 1951, and Hearst Castle was given by his family to the people of California. It is now a museum.

21 Hearst's guests stayed in Casa Grande.

A Right   **B** Wrong   **C** Doesn't say

22 The swimming pools are the same size.

A Right   **B** Wrong   **C** Doesn't say

23 Theresa thought the tour was very useful.

A Right   **B** Wrong   **C** Doesn't say

24 Hearst enjoyed living at Hearst Castle.

A Right   **B** Wrong   **C** Doesn't say

25 Hearst remembered his trip to Europe all his life.

A Right   **B** Wrong   **C** Doesn't say

26 Hearst died in Hearst Castle.

A Right   **B** Wrong   **C** Doesn't say

27 The Hearst family still live at Hearst Castle.

A Right   **B** Wrong   **C** Doesn't say

11.1 Living for sport

1 surfing

2 tennis

3 baseball

4 basketball

5 snowboarding

6 volleyball

Vocabulary

1 Do you play/do any of the sports in the photos? Which sports do you enjoy watching? Why?

2 Say which words go with each sport in the photos. You can use some words more than once.

Key words

| ball | basket | bat | board | boots |
| court | glove(s) | net | racket | stadium |

3 **2 02** Listen to six teenagers talking about the sports in the photos. Say what each sport is. Do they *play/do* the sport or *watch* it?

	sport	play/do or watch?
Speaker 1		
Speaker 2		
Speaker 3		
Speaker 4		
Speaker 5		
Speaker 6		

Key words → page 151

Pronunciation

4 **2 03** Listen and repeat.

| basketball | bigger | boots | bought |
| vegetable | video | village | volleyball |

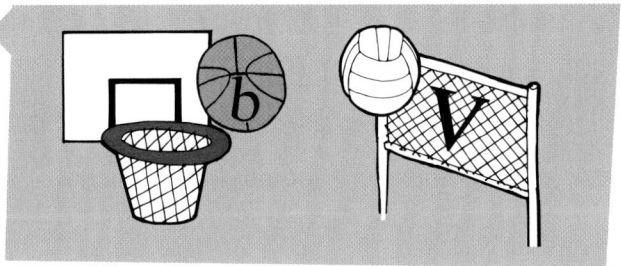

1 Bob plays basketball.
2 Bianca bought some new boots.
3 I live in a very small village.
4 There's a very good video on volleyball.
5 Bill eats bread and vegetables before he plays volleyball.

5 Write a sentence using as many words beginning with *b* and *v* as you can. It can be as funny as you like! Read your sentence to your classmates.

Reading

6 The England football player Eniola Aluko answered her fans' questions on a website. Decide which answer she gave to each question: A, B or C.

1 Meg
How old were you when you started playing football?

A I'm older now, but I still enjoy it as much as when I began.
B I kicked a ball around with my brother from the age of 6.
C I think it's amazing to play football when you are young.

2 Katie
Do you get to travel a lot?

A I think there are some good women's teams in Sweden.
B I learned a lot when we played Germany in the European final.
C When I'm in America, I visit a new city every other week for matches.

3 Eleanor
What is your best goal ever?

A It was against Finland. I went past five players and scored!
B I'd like to get the ball into the net more often this year.
C There's a competition on TV where you choose the best goal.

4 Liberty
Do you prefer playing in England or America?

A I play for my country and I belong to an American team.
B When you're my age it will be easier to earn money for playing in England.
C The US, I'm afraid. I get to wake up every morning and play football as a job there.

5 Amy
What exactly do you eat before a game?

A Sometimes I don't feel like it but I always have something to eat.
B Just enough to get my body ready – usually pasta or potato with chicken.
C At half-time I eat sweets to help me run faster during the rest of the match.

6 Rosie
I always put my left glove on first for good luck in goal! Do you do anything like this before every match?

A That's really cool! No, not really. Well done for playing in goal by the way, it's hard.
B Do you? I enjoy travelling back in the bus with the team after each match.
C No-one carries my boots for me. I have two hands so I can carry them myself!

7 What do you know about Eniola Aluko now? Write five short sentences about her, using some of the information in exercise 6.

EXAMPLE: *She plays for a team in the USA.*

Grammar extra

Word order in questions

Yes/No questions
Can you explain?
Does Eniola Aluko play for England?

Wh- questions
What happened?
(*What* is the subject of the sentence.)
Who scored the most goals?
(*Who* is the subject of the sentence.)
What do you know about Eniola Aluko?
(*What* is the object of the sentence.)

8 Put these words in the right order to make questions.

1 tennis / you / play / can
Can you play tennis?
2 team / Lionel Messi / which / does / play for
3 got / a snowboard / you / have
4 the next / World Cup / is / when
5 didn't / why / go / you / to the match
6 is / favourite / which / sport / your
7 does / the referee / where / come from
8 want to / in the competition / swim / you / do

9 Write five questions using the card below. Compare your questions with a partner. Then Student A ask the questions. Student B turn to page 133 and answer the questions.

SPORTS COMPETITION AT THIS COLLEGE

- when?
- sports?
- where?
- what / clothes?
- prizes?

11.2 Keeping fit

1 Do you do anything to keep fit or do you hate taking exercise?

2 Answer the questions in this chart and find out who you are like.

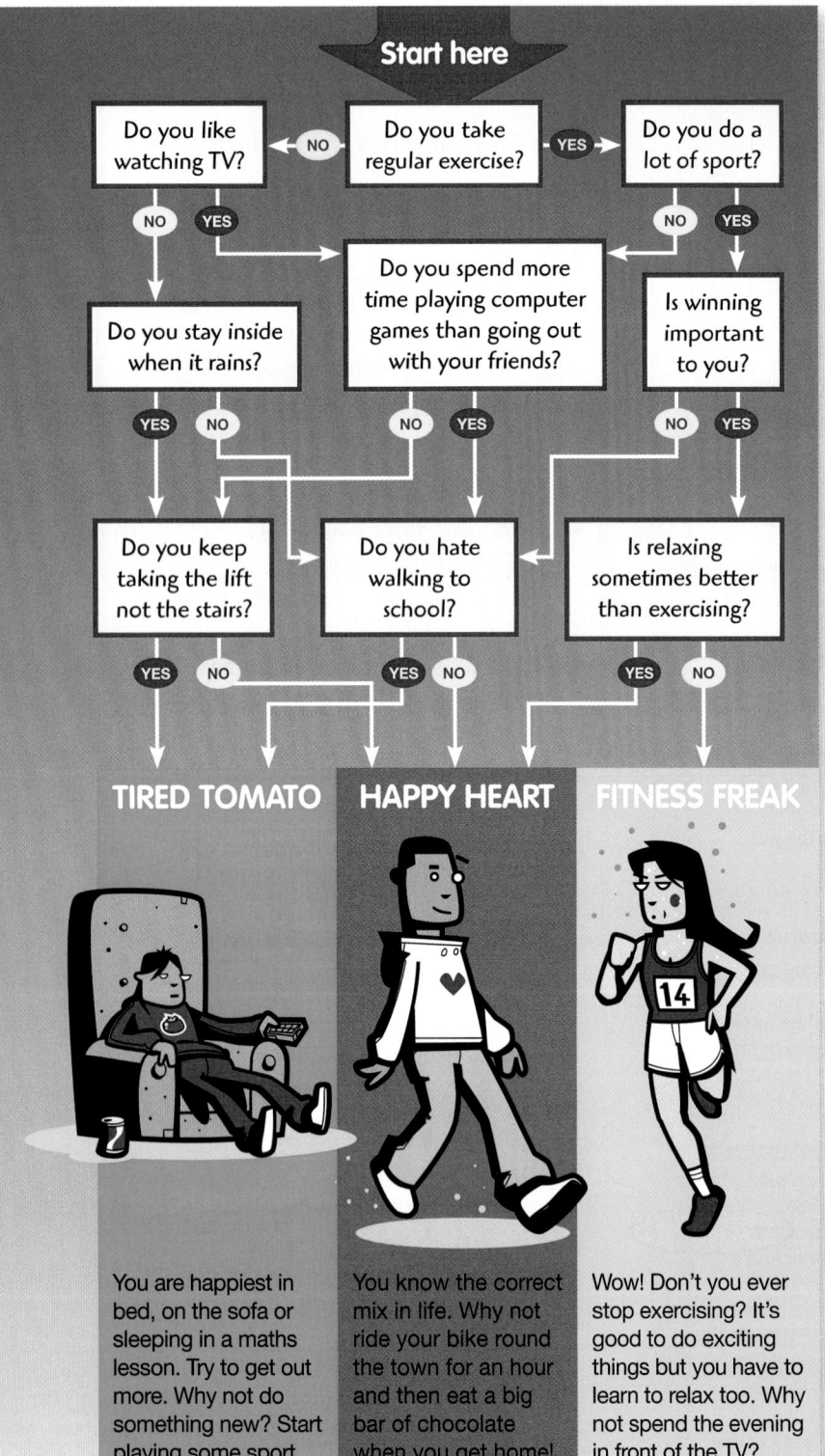

Start here

Do you like watching TV? — NO — Do you take regular exercise? — YES — Do you do a lot of sport?

Do you stay inside when it rains?

Do you spend more time playing computer games than going out with your friends?

Is winning important to you?

Do you keep taking the lift not the stairs?

Do you hate walking to school?

Is relaxing sometimes better than exercising?

TIRED TOMATO

You are happiest in bed, on the sofa or sleeping in a maths lesson. Try to get out more. Why not do something new? Start playing some sport.

HAPPY HEART

You know the correct mix in life. Why not ride your bike round the town for an hour and then eat a big bar of chocolate when you get home!

FITNESS FREAK

Wow! Don't you ever stop exercising? It's good to do exciting things but you have to learn to relax too. Why not spend the evening in front of the TV?

Grammar Verbs in the -ing form

3 There are several examples of verbs in the -ing form in the chart, for example, *Do you like <u>watching</u> TV?*

Find ten more examples in the chart and underline them.

4 The -ing is added to the infinitive of the verb: *watch + -ing = watching I enjoy watching TV.*

Sometimes there is a spelling change. Write the -ing forms of these verbs. Look back at the Spelling spot on page 45 if necessary.

1 sit	4 get	7 run
2 make	5 drive	8 throw
3 swim	6 play	9 carry

5 Complete these sentences with a verb from the box in the -ing form.

> go hit move play practise
> score ~~wait~~ walk win

1 Jess enjoys snowboarding but she hates ___*waiting*___ for the lifts up the mountain.
2 Please stop _____ the ball quite so hard – we'll lose it!
3 I feel like _____ for a run. Do you want to come?
4 Keep _____ your arms and legs or you'll get cold.
5 It'll take us about an hour to get there on foot, so let's start _____ now.
6 If the team keeps _____ all its matches, we'll soon be at the top!
7 I don't mind _____ in goal but I prefer _____ goals to saving them!
8 Mario doesn't spend enough time _____ his tennis.

6 Now say how you feel about the activities below, using verbs in the *-ing* form. You can add *really* to make the sentence stronger.

love   don't mind   hate
enjoy
like

EXAMPLE: *I really enjoy exercising at the gym!*

1 exercise at the gym
2 swim at the pool
3 run along the beach
4 walk to school
5 climb stairs
6 dance with my friends
7 play computer games
8 go for a bike ride

G → page 143

Listening

7 **2 04** You will hear some information about a sports centre. Listen and complete questions 1–5.

Solway Sports Centre

Opening hours: **(1)** 6.30 a.m. –
.... p.m.

For gym introduction, phone Jack Bergman: **(2)** 01453 ....

Swimming pool: **(3)** .... metres

To become a member, speak to:
(4) Mrs ....

Guided tours on: **(5)** ....
afternoon

Spelling spot

gu, qu

Remember you sometimes need to include the letter *u* after *g* if it is pronounced /g/, as in *guided tour*. The letter u always follows *q*, as in *queen*.

8 Spell the words that have these meanings.

1 fast (adverb)
  q _ _ _ _ _ _
2 one of four parts of something
  q _ _ _ _ _ _
3 a musical instrument
  g _ _ _ _ _
4 a person staying at a hotel
  g _ _ _ _
5 not saying anything (adjective)
  q _ _ _ _
6 if you don't know the answer, you have to do this
  g _ _ _ _

9 Read the descriptions of some sports. What is the word for each one? The first letter is already there.

1 You can get to the bottom of a mountain quite fast by doing this.
  s _ _ _ _ _
2 You need a bike to do this sport.
  c _ _ _ _ _ _
3 This sport lets you catch something to eat!
  f _ _ _ _ _ _
4 If you do this sport, practise on easy hills first.
  c _ _ _ _ _ _ _
5 Your boat needs some wind for this sport.
  s _ _ _ _ _ _

Activity

Find out who...

- Organise a class survey to find out who ...
  - takes the most exercise each week
  - plays the largest number of different sports
  - watches the most football matches
  - knows about an unusual sport.
- Write down the questions you need to ask to find out the information.
- Prepare a chart where you can write in the information you hear.

Writing folder 3

Writing Part 9 Short message

In Part 9 of the Reading and Writing paper (Question **56**), you must write something short, like a note, an email or a postcard to a friend. You must write about three different things. Either there will be instructions giving you the three things (see Writing folder 5 on page 122), or this information will be in a message from a friend, like the task on this page.

You must write between 25 and 35 words. If you write fewer than 25 words, you will get a lower mark. You will also get a lower mark if you forget to sign your note or postcard. It is possible to get up to five marks for Part 9.

Here is an example of the answer sheet for Part 9.

1 When you answer Part 9, you must write in sentences, using capital letters and full stops. Look at these exam answers and

- decide where the sentences should be
- correct the punctuation
- correct any other errors.

1

> I'll go to visit your town next friday I'd like to visit the sport club near your house, and I think it's very nice place, meet me at 7:00 o'clock p.m yours

2

> I think that the more interesting place near my town, a little lake because it is not noisy and there are a lot of animals. You can drive. Love

3

> Ok. we meet in the front of the football ground. At 17:00 o'clock. I want to buy a camera and a computer game. See you on Saturday.

4

> Hello: I have a basketball, a football, a computer and a television to sell. The basketball and football are very new I only played it once. The computer and television were used six month. But I want to sell them bye

2 What needs to be added to all four answers?

3 Read the exam task below and decide what *three* things you need to write about.
   Underline any important words.

Read this email from your English friend Alex.

Write Alex an email. Answer the questions.

Write **25–35** words.

Write the email on your answer sheet.

> Hi!
> I'm going to visit your town next month, so I have some questions for you. What's the swimming pool like? How do I get there from the town centre? When's the best time to go? Thanks for your help!
> Love,
> Alex

4 Which sample answer, A or B, is better? Think about these questions.

   1 How long is each answer?
   2 Does the writer answer all of Alex's questions?
   3 Is there enough information for Alex?

A
> Hi Alex
> There's a swimming pool near the motorway.
> Why not go at lunchtime or on Saturday?
> See you.
> Grazia

B
> Dear Alex
> It'll be nice to see you next month.
> The best pool is ten minutes by bus from the centre (bus number 34).
> The water's really warm! Swim in the morning, because it gets busy later.
> Love Juan

5 Write any extra information that is needed in the answer(s).

6 Which of Alex's questions (1–3) do sentences A–H answer? Write 1, 2 or 3 beside each sentence.

   1 What's the swimming pool like?
   2 How do I get there from the town centre?
   3 When's the best time to go to the swimming pool?

   A You can take a taxi from the main square.   *2*
   B It's 25 metres long and it's very wide.
   C I'd walk – it's only fifteen minutes away.
   D I think you should get there around five.
   E The building's made of glass and everything's very new.
   F You'll love going down the slides!
   G If you go in the afternoon, I can come with you.
   H Get a bike when you arrive, then you can cycle there in five minutes.

7 Now write your email. Remember to answer all Alex's questions and write between 25 and 35 words.

Family tree

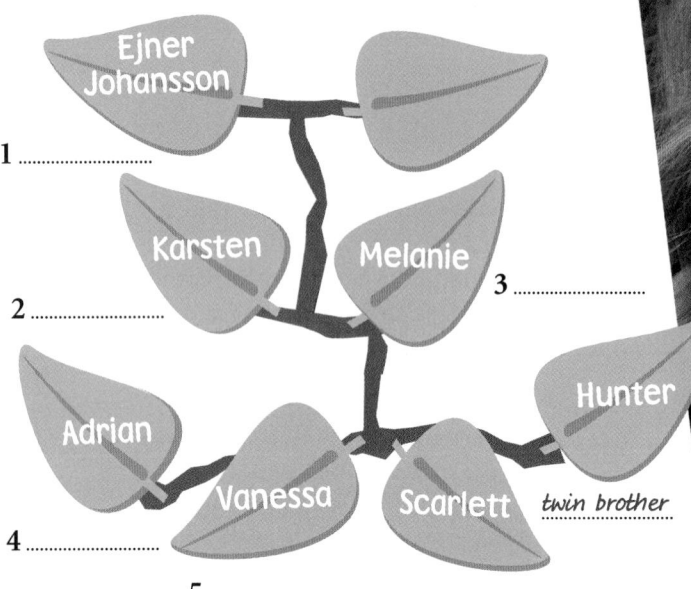

Vocabulary

1 Read the information about Scarlett Johansson and her family. Then complete the spaces in her family tree.

> Scarlett Johansson was born on November 22 1984. She and her twin brother Hunter are the youngest of four children. Their older brother is called Adrian and their sister's name is Vanessa. Mother, Melanie, lives in Los Angeles and their father, Karsten, is in New York. Karsten is half-Danish. (Scarlett's grandfather is the famous Danish writer Ejner Johansson.)

2 Write the words for other people in a family. Some letters are given to help you.

1 u _ _ _ _
2 a _ _ _
3 c _ _ _ _ _
4 g _ _ _ _ m _ _ _ _ _
5 g _ _ _ _ s _ _
6 g _ _ _ _ d _ _ _ _ _ _ _
7 g _ _ _ _ c _ _ _ _

3 Make your own family tree, which you will use later in this lesson.

Key words → page 151

Listening

4 **2 05** Listen to a girl called Helen asking Nick about their grandfather's party. For questions 1–5, tick A, B or C. Listen again to check your answers.

1 The party for their grandfather will be on
 A Friday.
 B Saturday.
 C Sunday.

2 Where will the party be?
 A at a restaurant
 B at a golf club
 C at Nick's house

3 The party will begin at
 A 2.45.
 B 3.30.
 C 4.00.

4 Who will Helen drive to the party?
 A Aunt Rose
 B Uncle Jack
 C Nick

5 Which present does Helen want to buy?
 A some DVDs
 B a mirror
 C a suitcase

Pronunciation

5 Write these words in group 1 or group 2 below.

all August draw house mouth now
or order out saw shout town

group 1 /aʊ/ *cow*	group 2 /ɔː/ *draw*

2 06 Listen to check your answers and repeat the words.

Spelling sp⦿t

Words ending in *-le*

6 The word *uncle* is often spelled wrongly as *uncel* by Key candidates. Sort the letters below to give other words with the same *-le* ending.

1 t a c l s e (a large old building)

— — — — — —

2 e c y b l c i (this has two wheels)

— — — — — — —

3 p a e l p (a good fruit to eat)

— — — — —

4 n i l g e s (not married)

— — — — — —

5 t i l l t e (small)

— — — — — —

6 p o l e p e (men, women and children)

— — — — — —

Possessive forms

Remember these forms:

adjective	pronoun
my	mine
your	yours
his	his
her	hers
our	ours
your	yours
their	theirs

- We use a possessive adjective before a noun:
  my car   your house   his party
- We use a possessive pronoun after a noun, to refer back to it:
  I can take you in my car.
  – Thanks, but I'll have mine. (= my car)
- We usually add *'s* to a noun or a name to show possession:
  granddad's party   Mario's restaurant

7 With a partner, look at the family trees you made in exercise 3. Compare the information. Use possessive forms.

EXAMPLES: *Your father is called …*
  Your brothers are older than mine.
  Their names are …

Report back to your classmates about what you found.

EXAMPLES: *Paul's father is called …*
  His brothers are older than mine.
  Our sisters are both older than us.

8 Get into pairs to play a guessing game. Choose nouns from the Vocabulary folder.

Student A look at Units 3 and 5.
Student B look at Units 7, 10 and 11.

EXAMPLES: Student A: *Mine is an animal. Its colour is grey and it's very big.*
  Student B: *An elephant!*
  Student A: *That's right. Tell me about yours.*
  Student B: *Well, mine is something you wear. Their colour is blue and everyone wears them.*

12.2 Large and small

1 What are the good and bad things about being part of a small family or a very large family?

2 Decide which of these things may not be possible in big families.

- being by yourself
- playing sport with others
- helping younger children
- living in a big house or flat
- keeping the place tidy
- having a low supermarket bill
- doing lots of washing
- travelling cheaply
- annoying your older brothers and sisters

Reading

3 Read what Sam Hayden says about his big family. Which brother is he close to? Which words tell you this?

> Hi, my name is Sam. I am nine and I live in a family of nine. I've got five brothers and their names are David aged sixteen, Michael aged fourteen, Joe aged twelve, Jacob aged seven and Isaac aged four. I've got a little sister Naomi aged two. My mother is called Pamela and my dad is called Bernie. I live in the county of Angus, which is in Scotland. I get on quite well with my brother Michael because he is kind and helps me. I don't get on so well with my brother Joe because he is a bit annoying. I like living in a big family and I wouldn't like to change anything.

4 Now read what Sam's brother Joe says. Who does he get on well with?

Hello, my name is Joe Hayden and I am twelve years old. My eldest brother David is sixteen and Michael is fourteen. I have three younger brothers. My little sister, who is called Naomi, is only two.

David, Michael and I are all into music, something we always enjoy. David plays the drums and Michael plays guitar, both quite loud but no one really minds. I get on well with David but not so much with my younger brothers Jacob and Sam. David, Michael and I are lucky because we all get to escape! We go to a school that is far, far away and we are only at home during the holidays.

It's good being in a big family. You can play games like football and cricket with everyone. In smaller families, this is not possible. Also, a big family means a big house, so you can always find somewhere to be by yourself. I like that sometimes.

The bad things are that you always get little kids bugging you. They can be so noisy! Everything around you is very busy and really messy, and there's lots of washing up and laundry to do. It also costs much more to go anywhere. But I prefer being in a big family.

5 Read what Joe says again. Are sentences 1–7 below 'Right' (A) or 'Wrong' (B)? If Joe doesn't tell you the answer, choose 'Doesn't say' (C).

1 Michael is older than Joe. *A*
2 When David and Michael play music, the others think they are too noisy.
3 Joe's school is very famous.
4 Joe comes home from school most weekends.
5 The Hayden children play more football than cricket.
6 Joe enjoys spending a bit of time alone.
7 Joe does all the washing up when he is at home.

Grammar Pronouns

6 All the underlined words are pronouns. Complete the table.

He is kind and helps <u>me.</u>
<u>You</u> can be by <u>yourself</u>.

subject pronouns	object pronouns	reflexive pronouns
I	me	
you		yourself
.... , ... , it	.... , ... , it	.... , ... , itself
		ourselves

7 Finish the second sentences so that they mean the same. Use some of the pronouns from exercise 6.

1 My brother and I took some sweets from the dish.
My brother and I helped *ourselves* to some sweets from the dish.
2 I made Mum's birthday cake without any help.
I made Mum's birthday cake by ....
3 Let's visit grandma and grandpa soon – they're nice.
Grandma and grandpa are nice – let's visit .... soon.
4 Dad made a big bowl of pasta and ate it all!
Dad made a big bowl of pasta for ....

5 My cousin broke my favourite model car.
My favourite model car is broken.
.... was broken by my cousin.
6 Jenny wanted to be alone for an hour.
Jenny wanted to be by .... for an hour.
7 Did your brothers have fun on their skiing trip?
Did your brothers enjoy .... on their skiing trip?

8 The underlined words below are also pronouns. Complete the table.

I wouldn't like to change <u>anything</u>.
You can play games like football and cricket with <u>everyone.</u>

things	people
	/ someone
	anybody /
everything	/
	/ no one

9 Complete the sentences with the correct pronoun from the table in exercise 8.

1 I'm really bored – there's ..... *nothing* ..... to do.
2 .... is on the phone for you, Mum.
3 Why doesn't Granddad remember .... about his schooldays?
4 Have you got a minute? I want to ask you ....
5 There was .... at tennis practice yesterday – only me!
6 Are you sure you've got .... you need?
7 This is important for .... else in the class, so listen carefully.
8 There wasn't .... in the playground because it was raining.

G → page 144

Activity

Family fun

Tomorrow, you and your teenage cousin are going to look after a family of five children between two and eleven years old. Decide what activities you would all enjoy and plan how to spend your day together.

Units 9–12 Revision

Speaking

1 Match questions 1–8 with sentences A–H. Then answer the questions with a partner.

EXAMPLE: *1 G*
I think a lot of people will drive electric cars.

1 What kind of cars will people drive in ten years' time?
2 Will people go on holiday into space in the next ten years?
3 What's your bedroom like?
4 Are you going to play any sport next weekend?
5 Where was your jacket made?
6 When was your school built?
7 Can you tell me something about your last holiday?
8 Does anyone in your family make you laugh?

A My sister is very funny sometimes.
B We spent two weeks at the beach and I played volleyball every day.
C In Italy, I think.
D I'm not sure, but it's very old.
E Almost certainly, but I won't be one of them.
F Yes, the school basketball team has a match on Saturday.
G I'm not sure. Perhaps they'll have hydrogen, not petrol.
H It's painted purple and I've got some great posters on the walls.

Grammar

2 Correct the mistakes that exam candidates have made in these sentences.

1 I enjoyed to see your family.
2 I will at the station wait for you.
3 This is the best book for to learn English.
4 I think it's will cost £30.
5 You don't need to ask nobody.
6 I don't mind to get the bus to your place.
7 We can ride horses and we can fishing in the lake.
8 If anybody are interested, call this number.
9 You can coming to London by train.
10 The village is famous because it has built from three Roman emperors.

3 Complete each second sentence using the passive.

1 We sent James a letter about the skiing trip.
A letter _____ *was sent* _____ to James about the skiing trip.
2 A taxi took me to the airport.
I _____ to the airport by taxi.
3 Alex showed me round the city.
I _____ round the city by Alex.
4 Someone famous wore this silver necklace.
This silver necklace _____ by someone famous.
5 A Greek actor wrote this song.
This song _____ by a Greek actor.
6 Everybody in the village knows the story about the castle.
The story about the castle _____ by everybody in the village.
7 My parents gave me snowboarding lessons for my birthday.
I _____ snowboarding lessons for my birthday.
8 My uncle built the biggest house in the town.
The biggest house in the town _____ by my uncle.

Vocabulary

4 Read the descriptions of some things you use in different sports. What is the word for each one? The first letter is already there.

1 You hit a tennis ball with this.

r _ _ _ _ _

2 The two teams stand on opposite sides of this in volleyball.

n _ _

3 In football, you must wear these on your hands if you are in goal.

g _ _ _ _ _

4 This is made of wood and you use it in baseball or table tennis.

b _ _

5 Wear special boots to stand on this and go down the mountain.

s _ _ _ _ _ _ _ _

5 Decide which word is the odd one out.

1 aunt	mother	cousin	granddaughter
2 mirror	poster	desk	bookshelf
3 sofa	bed	curtains	wardrobe
4 grey	pink	red	orange
5 sailing	golf	surfing	swimming
6 wood	metal	silver	glass

6 Read the sentences about a holiday. Choose the best word (A, B or C) for each space.

1 Some friends of mine .... to visit Ireland for a week.

A would   **B** enjoy   **C** want

2 I'm .... during that week and I'm going to go with them.

A empty   **B** free   **C** ready

3 We're going to take our bikes so we can go ....

A walking   **B** cycling   **C** driving

4 We won't take much .... with us, but we'll need to carry a tent.

A luggage   **B** suitcase   **C** bags

5 We'll .... a campsite by a lake and go swimming if the weather's good.

A look   **B** find   **C** arrive

Writing

7 Add the punctuation in these emails. Then say which email answers each question below. One question does not match any of the emails.

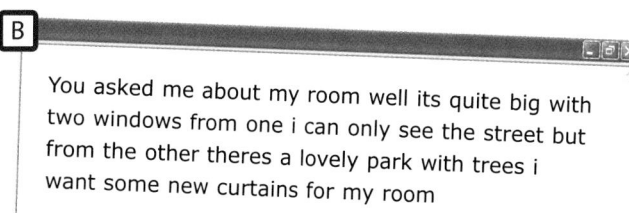

A

Id love to come sailing with you and your family andrea I go sailing about ten times a year so ive got something to wear can I borrow a life jacket

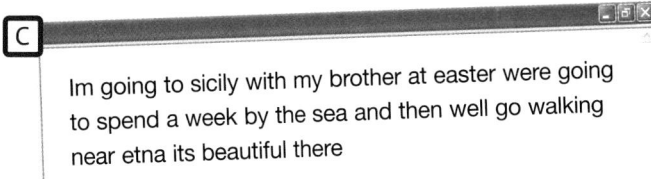

B

You asked me about my room well its quite big with two windows from one i can only see the street but from the other theres a lovely park with trees i want some new curtains for my room

C

Im going to sicily with my brother at easter were going to spend a week by the sea and then well go walking near etna its beautiful there

1 How big is your bedroom? *B*
2 Where do you think you'll go?
3 Are you good at sailing?
4 Why will you be late?
5 When are you going to have a holiday?
6 Is there anything you'd like for your room?
7 What will you do there?
8 Would you like to come on our boat next weekend?
9 What can you see from your window?
10 Will you need any special clothes?

13.1 Sun, rain or snow?

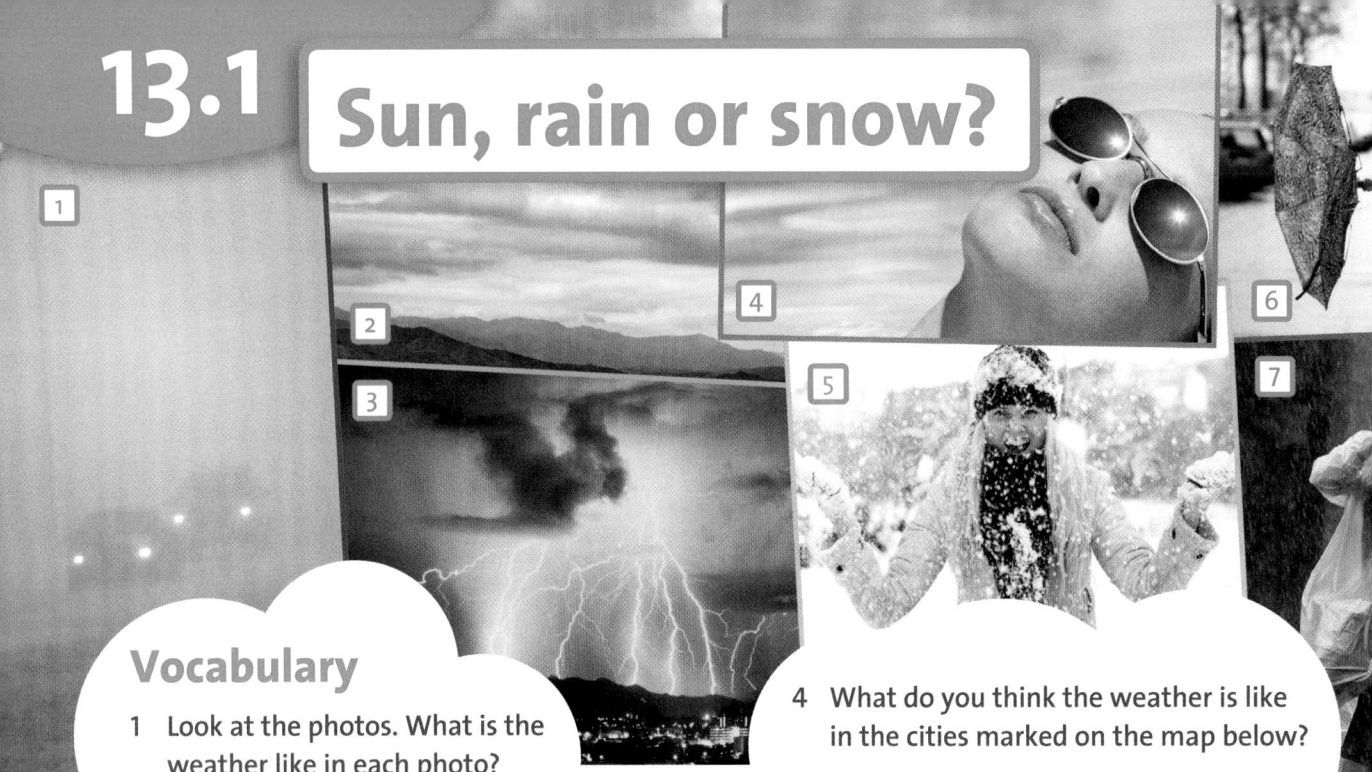

Vocabulary

1 Look at the photos. What is the weather like in each photo?

2 Find nine weather words in the word square (→ ↓ and ↑) and complete the sentences below. The first one has been done for you.

Key words → page 151

d	u	r	w	e	t	y
r	p	a	s	y	o	s
y	w	i	n	d	y	t
g	y	n	o	u	n	o
g	e	i	w	o	n	r
o	o	n	m	l	u	m
f	r	g	y	c	s	s

1 It's very w _ _ _y today – let's fly our kites.
2 It's r _ _ _ _ _g in Bogotá at the moment.
3 It's a lovely s _ _ _y day for a bike ride.
4 It's c _ _ _ _y so we can't see the sun.
5 It's w _t in my country in November.
6 It's very f _ _ _y outside – I can't see far.
7 There are many s _ _ _ _s in the summer, sometimes with thunder and lightning.
8 It's d _y at the moment, so let's go for a walk.
9 There was s _ _w when I went to Beijing in January.

3 What's the weather like where you live ... today? ... in December? ... in July?

Which is the hottest / coldest / wettest / driest place in your country?

4 What do you think the weather is like in the cities marked on the map below?

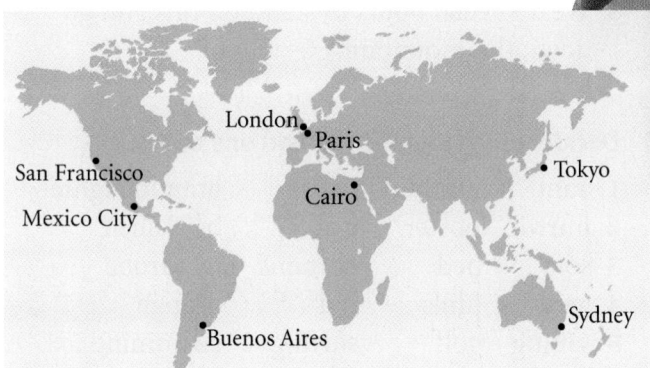

EXAMPLE: *I think that Cairo is very hot in summer and dry in winter.*

Listening

5 **2 07** Listen to Dan talking about his round-the-world trip with a friend.

What was the weather like in each place? Match the places (1–5) with the weather (A–H).

EXAMPLE:
0 London *D*

1 Paris	**A** cloud
2 Cairo	**B** fog
3 Sydney	**C** ice
4 Tokyo	**D** rain
5 San Francisco	**E** snow
	F storms
	G sun
	H wind

(not) as ... as

- On the recording Dan said:

  *It **wasn't as hot as** in summer.*

  Does this mean that

  a Cairo is colder in the summer?

  b Cairo is the same temperature in winter and summer?

  c Cairo is hotter in summer?

  *It **wasn't as expensive as** Tokyo.*

  Does this mean that

  a Tokyo was more expensive than Sydney?

  b things in Tokyo cost the same as in Sydney?

  c Tokyo was less expensive than Sydney?

- When we compare things that are the same, we can use:

  the same as *The weather today is **the same as** yesterday.*

  as ... as *It's **as cold today as** it was yesterday.*

6 With a partner, talk about the weather report below. Use *(not) as ... as*, *the same as ...* or a comparative adjective + *than*.

  EXAMPLES:

  The weather in Athens yesterday was not as hot as in Delhi.

  The weather in Rio de Janeiro was wet, the same as in Tokyo.

  Madrid was colder than Mexico City.

Around the world yesterday		
Athens	15°	
Beijing	7°	
Delhi	34°	
Madrid	15°	
Mexico City	23°	
Moscow	–1°	
Rio de Janeiro	29°	
Rome	13°	
Sydney	22°	
Tokyo	10°	
Vancouver	6°	

= rain   = cloudy   = sunny   = snow

Pronunciation

7 What words are missing from these sentences?

  1 You went .... Paris.

  2 Paris was .... bit cloudy.

  3 We had .... great time.

  4 I'd love .... go there.

  5 We stayed in .... hotel.

  6 We did .... shopping there.

  7 There was no rain .... all.

  8 It was warmer .... some of the other places.

  2·08 Listen to check your answers. What do the missing words have in common?

8 Read these sentences about a camping trip. Underline the unstressed words which have the sound /ə/. Some sentences have more than one /ə/ sound.

  1 Bob went camping with <u>a</u> friend.

  2 Both of them like camping.

  3 They got to the campsite late.

  4 They slept for ten hours.

  5 There was a good view from their tent.

  6 They had hot chocolate to drink.

  7 Bob took some great photos.

  2·09 Listen to check your answers.

1 Look at 1–4. Are they true or false?

Crazy weather round the world!

1
In Libya, in 1922, the temperature reached 57.8 degrees centigrade. It was <u>hot enough</u> to fry an egg on the road!

2
It's <u>too dangerous</u> to go outside if there is a tornado. People in parts of the USA have a special 'safe' room to go to, usually under the ground.

3
It's very dry in the Atacama Desert in Chile. It only gets 15 mm of rain a year. It's <u>too dry</u> to grow anything.

4
The UK gets tornadoes but they are usually <u>not big enough</u> to worry about.

Grammar *enough* and *too*

- Look at the underlined phrases in exercise 1:
  adjective + *enough* – *hot enough*
  too + adjective   – *too dangerous*

- We can also use *to* + infinitive after these:
  adjective + *enough* – *hot enough* **to fry** an egg
  too + adjective   – *too dangerous* **to go** outside

G → page 144

2 Look at the pictures. What is each person saying?

1 *It's too cold to go swimming.*
2
3
4
5
6

3 Complete these sentences using *too* or *enough*, plus one of the adjectives and one of the verbs.

adjectives windy cold cloudy ~~wet~~ icy foggy hot
verbs   to see to switch on ~~to go out~~ to walk
        to wear to lie to see

1 It was ....*too wet to go out*........ without an umbrella.
2 It wasn't .... on the beach, so we went to the cinema.
3 It was .... the road in front of the car.
4 It's .... any stars in the sky tonight.
5 It isn't .... the heating in the evenings.
6 It's .... a hat – it will blow away.
7 My grandmother thought it was .... to the shops. She could easily fall.

Reading

4 Read this article about a man called Warren Faidley, who has an unusual job. Choose the best word (A, B or C) for each space.

The man who loves tornadoes

Warren Faidley has **(0)** .... unusual job – he likes bad weather so much that he follows storms, really bad storms like tornadoes. He **(1)** .... born in the middle of the USA. This part of the world has **(2)** .... tornadoes than the rest of the country. Warren travels all over North America to find tornadoes and other storms. **(3)** .... he finds one he makes a film **(4)** .... it and uses his computer to give him extra information. He says he enjoys **(5)** .... photos of bad weather. He believes it is **(6)** .... important for people to know about bad weather. He works for the government and also for Hollywood. He helped on the film *Twister*, which was about tornadoes. He says his job **(7)** .... be very frightening but he does **(8)** .... he needs to do to keep himself safe.

0 (A) an	**B** a	**C** the
1 A is	**B** was	**C** were
2 A most	**B** more	**C** lots
3 A When	**B** Where	**C** Because
4 A by	**B** of	**C** at
5 A took	**B** take	**C** taking
6 A too	**B** very	**C** enough
7 A can	**B** must	**C** have
8 A something	**B** nothing	**C** everything

Spelling spot

to, too and two

Be careful with the spelling of *to*, *too* and *two*.

5 Complete the sentences with the correct word.

1 I went .... Tokyo last year for .... weeks.
2 My cousin went ....
3 We took taxis .... places because it was .... difficult for us .... use the subway.
4 When I got home I tried .... cook some Japanese food.
5 I made some sushi and invited .... friends for a meal.
6 They wanted .... know how .... make it so they could cook it ....

6 Correct the mistakes that exam candidates have made in these sentences.

1 The weather are very sunny.
2 This year the weather colder than last year.
3 What does the weather like in Australia?
4 The weather in Caracas is hotter as in Santiago.
5 It was not enough hot to go swimming.
6 I like sunny weather too much.

Activity

Seasons

- Get into four teams, one for each season: spring, summer, autumn and winter.
- Take it in turns to say a sentence about your season, for example:

  In winter I like being inside where it is warm and cosy.

- The team scores a point for each correct sentence.
- The team with the most points is the winner.
- Write a paragraph about your favourite season and also say why you don't like other seasons as much.

Exam folder 7

Listening Part 2 Multiple matching

In Part 2 of the Listening paper there are five questions (**6–10**) and a choice of eight answers (**A–H**). There are always two speakers (usually two friends). You must choose from **A–H** the correct letter to answer questions **6–10**. There is an example first to help you.

6–10 can be names, days of the week, months, etc. and **A–H** can be words from topic sets such as sports, presents, etc.

1 Give a title to each of the following topic sets and add as many words as you can.

   1 Monday, Tuesday ... *Days of the week – Wednesday, Thursday ...*
   2 January, February ...
   3 football, swimming ...
   4 blue, red ...
   5 dress, jacket ...
   6 aunt, sister ...
   7 apples, soup ...

2 Look at the exam task on the opposite page. Here is the first part of the recording script. It is possible to divide it into sections.

Introduction
Girl Hi, Nick.
Boy Hi, Penny. How was your holiday in Switzerland?

The example – Nick
Girl It was great – hot and sunny every day and some nice shops! Look, Nick, I bought you a mug. See, it's got 'Switzerland' written on it.

First question – James
Boy Oh, thanks! Did you get James a pen? He's always taking mine.
Girl I got him an album of a local band – he likes anything to do with music.

In the example you usually hear just one object mentioned, but for the questions you may hear one or two. You must listen carefully to make sure you choose the correct answer. In question 6, both 'pen' and 'album' are mentioned. 'Album' is the correct answer. Sometimes on the recording you don't hear the word from the question, but you hear a different word that has the same meaning.

Before you listen

- Read the questions and answers very carefully.
- The questions, 6–10, will be in the order in which you hear them. **A–H** are in alphabetical order.

First listening

- If two things are mentioned (objects, places, days, etc.), think about which is the correct answer. Write down both words or letters next to the number if you aren't sure.

Second listening

- Check your choice of answer is correct. You can only choose one answer for each question.
- At the end of the Listening test, copy your answers onto your answer sheet. Opposite is an example of the answer sheet for Part 2.

Part 2								
6	A	B	C	D	E	F	G	H
7	A	B	C	D	E	F	G	H
8	A	B	C	D	E	F	G	H
9	A	B	C	D	E	F	G	H
10	A	B	C	D	E	F	G	H

2 10

Part 2

Questions 6–10

Listen to Penny talking to her cousin about the presents she bought on holiday for her friends.

Which friend got each present?

For questions **6–10**, write a letter (**A–H**) next to each friend.

You will hear the conversation twice.

Example:

0 Nick [D]

Friends		**Presents**	
6 James ☐		**A** album
7 Becky ☐		**B** book
8 Alice ☐		**C** comb
9 Tom ☐		**D** mug
10 Lucy ☐		**E** pen
		F picture
		G soap
		H watch

Speaking

1 Do this questionnaire with a partner.

Who reads the most in the class?

Which type of book is the most popular in your class?

1 How many books do you read each year?
A fewer than 5
B 6–20
C more than 20

2 Where do you read?
A at the beach
B in my bedroom
C in the bath

3 What kind of books do you like?
A picture books / comics
B love stories
C adventure stories
D books that make you laugh
E detective stories
F science fiction books

Reading

2 Three people were asked what they read, and this is what they said. Read the texts and answer questions 1–7. Don't worry about the underlined phrases at the moment. For each question, choose the answer A, B or C.
A = Luis
B = Joanna
C = Sam

Luis
I like to read in bed before I turn my light off. I don't like science fiction or comics. I'm really lucky because my parents buy me a lot of books. My friends enjoy borrowing them. One book I enjoyed is called *The Lake* by Tom Davis. It's about a girl who lived a hundred years ago and worked at a hotel. One day a guest is found in the deep, blue lake. Lena thinks she knows who killed her.

Joanna
I never buy books, I always go to my local library. I like stories about modern life where boy meets girl, not about what happened years ago. A book I enjoyed is called *The Dream* by Dorrie Williams. Lois has left school and is now a famous pop singer. Lois meets Mike – a good-looking Australian guitar player in a band. Her friends don't like him but she does. Does she take her friends' advice or does she go out with Mike? Read it and find out!

Sam
I don't often buy books, I prefer to get comics – often ones that make me laugh, not stupid love stories which send me to sleep. Anyway, I read a good book called *Will* by Gary Hahn. It's about a boy who wakes up in someone else's bedroom and has a different face and body. He remembers playing great, new computer games with his friend Jack and then going home but he doesn't remember getting home … This is an awesome story because it's really different.

0 Who buys more comics than books? *C*
1 Who enjoys reading funny stories?
2 Who prefers love stories?
3 Who reads before going to sleep?
4 Who read a book about something terrible happening?
5 Who enjoyed a book because it was unusual?
6 Who read a book about the past?
7 Who always borrows books?

3 What do you think about the books Luis, Joanna and Sam have read? Which of these books would you like to read?

Grammar Position of adjectives

- If there is more than one adjective before a noun, they are put in a special order.
  For example, opinion (e.g. *nice*) is before fact (e.g. *old*).
  We say *nice old house* NOT *nice and old house*.

4 Complete this chart with the words underlined in the reading texts.

1 What's it like? opinion	2 How big? size	3 How old? age	4 What colour?	5 Where's it from? nationality	6 What kind?	NOUN
						lake
						player
						games

5 Put these words in the right order.

1 a   book   boring   old
2 a   magazine   colourful   new
3 a   computer   modern   Japanese
4 the   library   new   school   excellent
5 the   book   long   adventure
6 the   bag   expensive   leather   little
7 a   dress   beautiful   white
8 a   writer   young   clever

G → page 145

6 With a partner, describe the following:

1 your favourite book
2 your favourite item of clothing
3 your best friend
4 a film
5 a pop star

EXAMPLE:

My favourite book is about a friendly, Italian girl who travels to a dangerous foreign country to try to find her young sister.

Pronunciation

7 All these words from the reading texts have a silent consonant. Draw a circle round the silent letter(s) in each of them.

1 light   4 what
2 knows   5 who
3 guitar   6 often

2 11 Listen to check.

8 All the silent letters are missing in the words below. Match the silent letter with the right word so the spelling is correct.

t   n   h   s   b   k   d   l

1 i _s_ land   5 autum _
2 cas _ le   6 _ nife
3 ha _ f   7 We _ nesday
4 clim _   8 _ our

2 12 With a partner, say the words and then listen to check.

Spelling spot

Words which are often confused

bed – bad
buy – by – Bye
than – then
things – thinks
want – won't

9 Complete these sentences with the correct word.

1 .... Suzy ran into the sea, but it was colder .... it looked.
2 The weather was really .... when I was on holiday.
3 You don't .... to stay in .... all day, do you?
4 She said '.....................' and went out to .... a book.
5 We are going to get some .... from town.
6 I .... be home late tonight.

Learn something new!

Vocabulary

1 Put these school subjects in order. Tell your partner why.

1 = You like this subject best.
8 = You like this subject least.

Try to use some of the words below.

EXAMPLE: *For me, maths is awesome.*

Key speaking

- 😊 I think it's awesome, brilliant, cool, great.
- 😊 It's horrible, terrible, boring.
- 😊 It's crazy, strange.
- 😞 It isn't very exciting, interesting.
- 😐 It's OK / all right. It isn't boring.

maths	
history	
languages	
sport	
art	
geography	
music	
science	

2 Is there any subject you would like to do but can't do at your school?

Tell your partner.

Listening

3 **2 13** Sylvia is 14 and wants to be an actor. You will hear her asking for information about Saturday morning classes at a theatre school in London.

Listen and write the missing information.

> **Theatre School**
> 0 Day: Saturday
> 1 Date of new classes: 3rd ....
> 2 Send cheque for: £..................
> 3 Time classes begin: ....
> 4 Address: .... High Street
> 5 Best bus to get: ....

Reading

4 Match sentences 1–4 from Sylvia's conversation with responses A–D.

1 Can I help you?
2 Could I visit the school to see what it's like?
3 When can I come and visit?
4 Thank you very much.

A You're welcome.
B Any time.
C Yes, please.
D Of course.

2 13 Listen again to check your answers.

5 Now do the same with 1–10 and A–J.

1 I can't come on the school trip.
2 What are you doing?
3 I've got an exam tomorrow.
4 I've passed all my exams.
5 Would you mind opening the classroom window?
6 Where's the library?
7 Hi! How are you?
8 Is that your teacher?
9 Can I sit here?
10 Let's study together tonight.

A Fine, thanks.
B Sorry, I can't – I'm going swimming.
C I'm afraid it's taken.
D No, it's not.
E Chemistry homework.
F Sure, I can do that.
G What a pity.
H Congratulations!
I Good luck!
J On the first floor.

2 14 Listen to check your answers.

Vocabulary

6 Complete the crossword.

Across

3 French is an example of this.
4 You can get books from this place.
6 The teacher writes on this.
7 You must do this when the teacher is talking.
9 The person who teaches you.
11 You study this to know about the past.
13 You do this after school.

Down

1 You write with this.
2 What you do at school.
5 You put books on this.
8 You sit at this in class.
10 A place to keep things in.
12 Past simple of *see*.

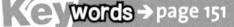 Key words → page 151

Key words → page 151

Grammar extra

I prefer / I'd like

Sylvia says: *Can I get a bus? I prefer buses to the underground.*

I prefer
I prefer Maths to History.
I prefer watching an adventure story on TV to reading one.
Do you prefer art or music?

I'd like
I'd like to go to a bigger school.
Would you like to start school earlier?

7 Complete the questions with *prefer* or *would like* and the correct from of the verb in brackets. Then give true answers to a partner.

1 <u>*Do you prefer reading*</u> (read) or
<u>*listening*</u> (listen) to music?
2 .... (marry) someone famous or someone who isn't famous?
3 .... (eat) in restaurants or
.... (go) on a picnic?
4 .... (meet) Angelina Jolie and Brad Pitt?
5 On your next holiday,
.... (go) to New York or Malibu Beach?
6 .... (get up) early or
.... (stay) in bed?
7 Where .... (live)?

Activity

- In groups, talk about your school. First of all, talk about what the school is like now. Talk about the building, the subjects you study, the classrooms, etc.

- Now talk about the changes you want to make. You can change the length of the school day, the types of lessons you have – anything!

- When you have finished, give a talk to the rest of the class.

I think we need a new modern building with a swimming pool.

I'd like to have more school trips so we can see different places.

Exam folder 8

Reading Part 3 Multiple choice

Part 3 of the Reading and Writing paper tests the type of English you use every day in conversation. Part 3 is divided into two parts:

Questions **11–15** have an example and five multiple-choice questions.

Questions **16–20** are based on a conversation and contain an example and a conversation with five spaces. You must match each space with one of eight possible answers, **A–H**.

It's important not to choose an answer just because it uses the same words as the question. Do this example for practice.

Hi! Is that Sally speaking? **A** Yes, Sally is here.
                                          B No, it's Lisa.
                                          C It's her.
                                          Answer: ....

EXAM ADVICE

- For questions **11–15**, think about where or when you can say each question or statement.
- For questions **16–20**, read through the instructions and the example, as they will tell you what the conversation is about.
- Make sure you read the whole conversation before you choose your answers.
- Cross out the example letter so that you don't choose it again by accident.
- Check your answers carefully when you transfer them to your answer sheet. An example of the answer sheet for Part 3 is on the page opposite.

Part 3

Questions 11–15

Complete the five conversations.

For questions **11–15**, mark **A**, **B** or **C** on your answer sheet.

Example:

0  What do you do?

          A I'm studying.

          B I'm a doctor.

          C I'll see you tomorrow.

Answer: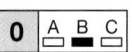

---

11 Can I help you?   **A** No problem.
                                B You're welcome.
                                C Yes, can I pay for this here?

12 Are you ready?   **A** I agree.
                                B Not yet!
                                C Here it is!

13 Where's the bus stop?   **A**   It's over there.
                                            B   Nowhere.
                                            C   I don't mind.

14 It's hot in here.   **A**   That's fine.
                                            B   Yes, isn't it?
                                            C   Let's open it.

15 That'll be £3.98, please.   **A**   Here you are.
                                            B   I'm afraid I can't.
                                            C   That's nice.

Part 3		
11 A B C	**16** A B C D E F G H
12 A B C	**17** A B C D E F G H
13 A B C	**18** A B C D E F G H
14 A B C	**19** A B C D E F G H
15 A B C	**20** A B C D E F G H

Questions 16–20

Complete the conversation between two friends.

What does Jenny say to Marco?

For questions **16–20**, mark the correct letter **A–H** on your answer sheet.

Example:

Marco: Who's your favourite writer, Jenny?

Jenny: **0** ....   *Answer:* **0**   A B C D E F ■ H

Marco: Oh, yes. I love all his Alex Rider books.

Jenny: **16** ....

Marco: You'll have to wait, I think.

Jenny: **17** ....

Marco: Have you seen the film *Stormbreaker*?

Jenny: **18** ....

Marco: My brother's got the computer game.

Jenny: **19** ....

Marco: That's a good idea. When are you free?

Jenny: **20** ....

Marco: That's great. See you then.

A   I know. I read somewhere that he hasn't started writing it yet.

B   It's a book I'm reading at the moment.

C   What about playing it together?

D   Me too! I can't wait to read the next one.

E   I got it last Saturday.

F   Friday is best because I don't have any homework.

G   I think it must be Anthony Horowitz.

H   No, I missed it.

Working hours

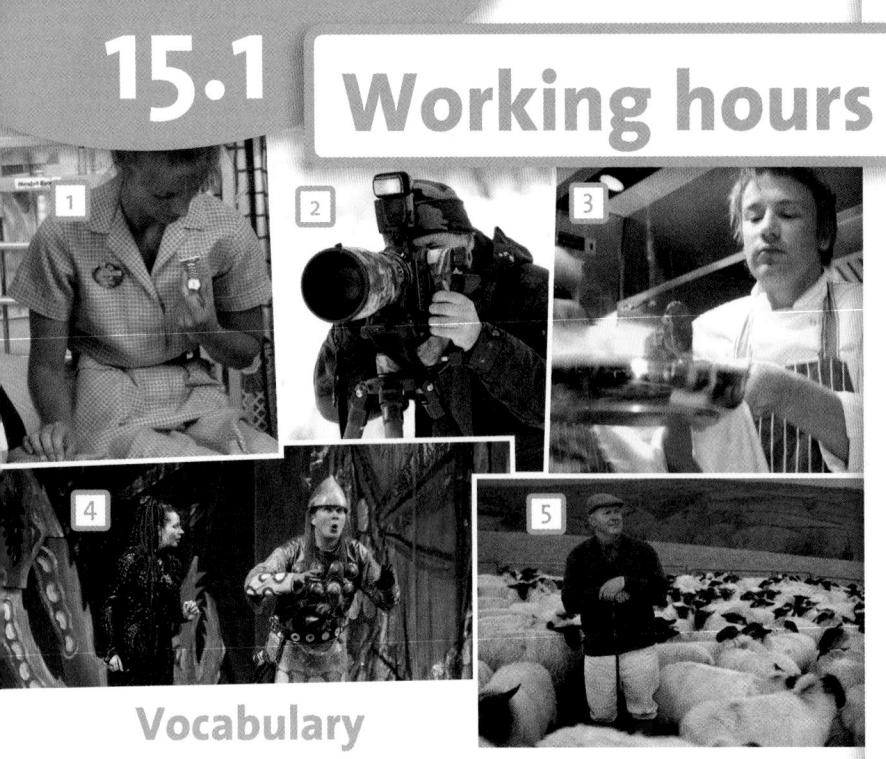

FAMOUS FOR
FIFTEEN

Jamie Oliver is Britain's most famous chef. He made his first TV cooking programmes when he was only 23, got married at 25 and was given a special award by the Queen at 28. A top supermarket used him in their advertisements for many years, his books on cooking sell better than any other food writer's, and journalists are always writing articles about him.

A few years ago, Jamie opened the restaurant *Fifteen* in London. The name doesn't describe where the restaurant is – it's because he chose this number of young people to become cooks there. Not one of them knew how to cook so Jamie sent them to college in the year before he opened the restaurant. They also visited other restaurants to learn more.

Fifteen started because of a conversation Jamie had with his wife's friend. She worked with difficult children and found that they always enjoyed cooking, so Jamie decided to start a restaurant business to help young people with problems.

The number of people working at *Fifteen* has grown. The restaurant in London is always full and Jamie has several receptionists answering phone calls. There is another *Fifteen* in Amsterdam. Like the London restaurant, it trains several young people every year. Its chefs also give cooking lessons in Dutch schools. The children have fun learning to cook and afterwards, they can enter a national competition called Junior Chefs. Those with the best cooking ideas are invited to a party at *Fifteen*, where the winner is decided.

Vocabulary

1 Match five of these jobs to photos 1–5.

Key words

actor	chef	dentist	engineer
farmer	journalist	nurse	photographer
receptionist	tour guide		

2 Now match the other five jobs to their descriptions.

1 looks after people's teeth
2 helps people when they arrive at a hotel or office
3 shows visitors a place or area
4 designs and builds roads and bridges
5 writes articles for newspapers and magazines

3 What job would you like to do in the future? Why?

Reading

4 Read the article and answer the questions. The colours show you the right part of the text.

1 At the age of 23, Jamie Oliver
A got married.
B went on television.
C met the Queen.

2 Now, Jamie Oliver
A is the top-selling writer on cooking in Britain.
B writes articles for several newspapers.
C does some work for a supermarket.

3 Jamie's restaurant is called *Fifteen* because of
A the first staff there.
B the opening hours.
C the street number.

4 The cooks who joined *Fifteen*
A came from other restaurants.
B had no training in cooking.
C were already at a college.

5 The idea for *Fifteen* came from
A Jamie.
B Jamie's wife.
C a friend of Jamie's wife.

6 How is the London *Fifteen* different now?
A It has more staff than it did.
B It no longer trains any students.
C It is less busy than it was.

7 The winner of the Junior Chefs competition
A must live in Amsterdam.
B is chosen before the day of the party.
C has had a lesson with a chef from *Fifteen*.

Grammar Present perfect

5 Question 6 could say: *How <u>has</u> the London Fifteen <u>changed</u>?*

The possible answers could be:
The number of staff **has grown**.
Only trained cooks **have found** *jobs there.*
The restaurant **hasn't been** *so busy recently.*

These are all examples of the present perfect. How is it formed?

6 When is the present perfect used? Choose A or B for sentences 1–4.

A something that started in the past and is still true in the present

B something that happened recently (we aren't told when)

1 Jamie Oliver has written a new book.
2 Jamie Oliver has always enjoyed cooking.
3 *Fifteen* has been full every night.
4 I've booked a table at *Fifteen* for your birthday.

Be careful! You cannot say: *~~I've booked~~ a table two hours ago.* Which tense should you use here? Why?

Which sentence (5–7) is not correct? Why? Choose A or B for the other two sentences.

5 *Fifteen* has been open for ten years.
6 *Fifteen* has opened in 2003.
7 *Fifteen* has been open since 2003.

G → page 145

7 Correct any mistakes with verbs in these sentences. Some sentences are correct.

1 Jamie Oliver has made a new TV programme.
2 His books have sold well for several years.
3 The supermarket has advertised for more staff last week.
4 I haven't been to this restaurant since August.
5 Marion has become a doctor in 2011.
6 Have you always worked from home?
7 Lee has arrived for his meeting an hour ago.
8 The company has opened offices in different parts of Spain.

8 Put the verbs in brackets into the present perfect or the past simple.

> Tom Stone works in south-east England as an engineer. Two years ago, he (**1**) .....*bought*..... (buy) a house in France and (**2**) .... (move) there with his family. Both his children like their French schools and they (**3**) .... (make) lots of new friends. For two years, Tom (**4**) .... (travel) to work every day on Le Shuttle, a train that takes cars to England. When he (**5**) .... (begin) doing this journey, he (**6**) .... (decide) to catch the train at 5 a.m. This (**7**) .... (mean) leaving his house at 3.30! Tom (**8**) .... (be + not) sure about doing this every day, but says he soon (**9**) .... (find) it easy to get up early. He (**10**) .... (take) the same train ever since, because then he can be home again by 6 p.m.

9 Have you ever …

… met a chef?   … seen a famous person?
… been to hospital?   … wanted to be rich?

Now ask and answer the questions above, and add one of the questions below.

Why? / Why not?   What did you do?
When was that?   Who did you meet/see?

Spelling sp⊙t

-er/-or

Many words for jobs end in -er, e.g. *teacher*, but a few end in -or, e.g. *inventor*.

10 Read the descriptions of some jobs. What is the word for each one? The first letter is already there. What is the job in the yellow box?

1 This person uses a camera.
2 Ask this person to change the colour of your walls.
3 This person works for a newspaper or on TV.
4 You will find this person in a theatre.
5 See this person if you are feeling ill.

1 p _ _ _ _ _ _ _ _ _ _ _ _
2   p _ _ _ _ _
3   j _ _ _ _ _ _ _ _ _
4   a _ _ _ _
5   d _ _ _ _ _

Part-time jobs

1 Have you ever wanted to get a job in the evenings or at weekends? Why? / Why not?

2 Answer these questions about the job advertisements by choosing A, B or C.

 1 Which job is only for one day a week?
 2 Which job can you do if you are only 13?
 3 Which job pays nothing?

A

Paper boys/girls wanted

Hours 6–8 a.m. and 5–6 p.m.

Must have own bike and be 13 or older
£16.50 per day, more at weekends

B

Extra help needed on Saturdays ...

... in our busy music shop (open 10–6)

Suitable for student 16+

Earn some money **and** get a discount on DVDs!

C

Do you care about old people?

**Then help our staff at Sunnydale Care Home.
We can't pay you but you'll find your visits good fun!**

Play games, read stories, or just talk to someone – it's your choice.

If you are over 14 and have a few hours a week free after school or at weekends, phone us now on 0124 426638.

---

3 What do you feel about working for no money? Would you ever do that? Why? / Why not?

Grammar extra

just and yet

These words are often used with the present perfect.

• *Just* means that something has happened very recently.
 I've just got a new job.
 Have you just arrived?

• *Yet* means that something hasn't happened but will probably happen soon.
 Carmen hasn't taken her driving test yet.
 Haven't you done your homework yet?

4 Write out the sentences and complete them with *just* or *yet* and the present perfect of the verb in brackets. Remember to make the verb negative with *yet*.

EXAMPLES:
Isabel (finish) her nursing course. ✓
Isabel has just finished her nursing course.
Isabel (finish) her nursing course. ✗
Isabel hasn't finished her nursing course yet.

 1 The receptionist at the sports centre (leave) a message for you. ✓
 2 Tom (meet) his new boss. ✗
 3 They (send) me any information about the job. ✗
 4 Nick's dad (stop) working at the hospital. ✓
 5 My uncle (give) me a job in his café. ✓
 6 Charlotte and Andy (find) a photographer for their wedding. ✗
 7 I (choose) a computer course to go on. ✓
 8 The supermarket manager (pay) Mike for his extra hours. ✗

Listening

5 Before you listen, spend 20 seconds reading the questions below.

🔊 **2 15** Listen to Sam phoning Kate Richards about a Saturday job at her music shop. For questions 1–5, tick A, B or C.

1 The hours for the Saturday job are
   A 8 a.m. – 8 p.m.
   B 9 a.m. – 7 p.m.
   C 10 a.m. – 6 p.m.

2 The job will be mainly
   A adding up money.
   B cleaning the shop.
   C serving customers.

3 How much can Sam earn when he starts?
   A £5.25 an hour
   B £6.30 an hour
   C £7.00 an hour

4 Where is the music shop?
   A near the university
   B in the centre of town
   C across the river from Sam's home

5 Which day will Sam visit the shop?
   A Wednesday
   B Thursday
   C Friday

Pronunciation

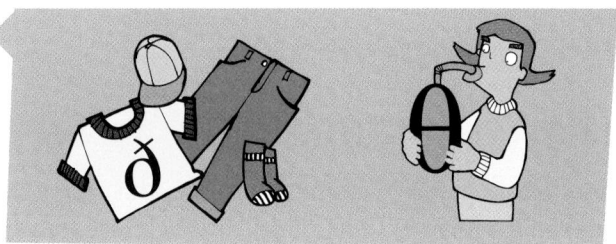

6 🔊 **2 16** You will hear these sentences from the recording in exercise 5 again. Listen carefully to the underlined and circled sounds because they are different.

<u>Th</u>at's true. Well, any o<u>th</u>er questions?
How about ⓉⒽursday or Friday?
Say the words aloud.

🔊 **2 17** Then listen to and repeat some more words and write them in group 1 or group 2.

group 1 /ð/ *that, other*	group 2 /θ/ *Thursday*

7 🔊 **2 18** Now listen to sentences 1–6 twice. The first time you listen underline any /ð/ sounds you hear. The second time circle any /θ/ sounds.

1 I've worked for the last two months in my father's shop.
2 Let's look at all these job adverts together.
3 I thought you were working at the museum. Have you finished there?
4 Jenny, thanks for looking through my article.
5 That footballer earns a hundred and thirty thousand pounds a month!
6 My brother's just got a job in the north of Sweden.

Activity

101 jobs

- Get into groups of three or four.
- Your teacher will write the names of some places on the board. Write down as many different jobs as you can for each place.

EXAMPLE:
school: secretary, teacher, receptionist, gardener, cook, cleaner

Writing folder 4

Writing Part 8 Information transfer

In Part 8 of the Reading and Writing paper you must copy information from two texts onto a form or a set of notes. There are five spaces (**51–55**) to complete. The information will come from both texts.

1   Look at these texts and say what each one is.

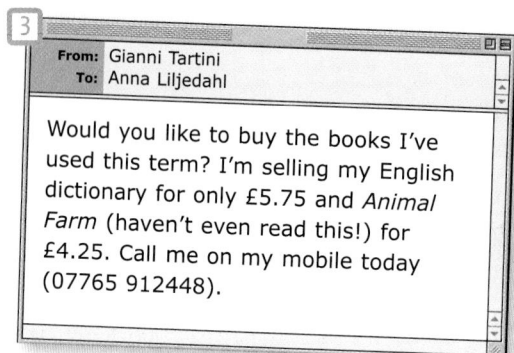

2   Find the following information in the texts. Be careful to copy everything correctly.

1 Phone number ....

2 Name of book ....

3 Last date to see play ....

4 Name of guitar player ....

5 Student ticket price ....

6 Time of concert ....

7 Where to see play ....

8 Price of dictionary ....

EXAM ADVICE

- Read both texts quickly to find out the topic.
- Look at the notes or form (questions **51–55**).
- Decide if each space needs a number or word(s).
- Read the texts again carefully to find the answers.
- Write all your answers on the question paper first.
- Don't write more than you need to.
- Write any numbers in figures, not words.
- Check your copying of numbers carefully.
- Check spelling and use of capital letters in names, days of the week, months, etc.
- Write your answers on your answer sheet. Opposite is an example of the answer sheet for Part 8.

Part 8		Do not write here
51		1 41 2
52		1 42 2
53		1 43 2
54		1 44 2
55		1 45 2

Part 8

Questions 51–55

Read all the information about holiday jobs in Britain.

Fill in Laura's form.

For questions **51–55**, write the information on your answer sheet.

AU PAIR JOBS IN BRITAIN

Welcoming families in Derby (close to beautiful hills) and Eastbourne (by the sea).

Start dates 16/23/30 June

If you are 18 or over, complete our form today – you only pay £60 (£40 if you worked last summer).

From: Hana Stankova hanastan@scworld.com
To: Laura Tournier lauratou@free.fr

Thanks for the job advert. We're both just old enough! I can begin on June 23 too. Choose the town near the beach like me! Good luck.

FORM FOR AU PAIR, ENGLAND

Name:	Laura Tournier
Email address:	**51**
Age:	**52**
Date can start work:	**53**
Town chosen:	**54**
Payment:	**55** £

16.1 Journeys

1 Decide if these sentences about transport are true or false.

> London Heathrow is the largest airport in the world.

> A man in Canada put wheels on his wife's bed and cycled her to work as she slept.

> If you put all the railways in the USA end to end, they would go round the world six times.

> In 1783 in France, the first hot-air balloon passengers were a sheep, a duck and a snake.

Vocabulary

2 Put the letters in the right order to spell different kinds of transport.

1 a i t n r
2 h c a o c
3 y c c b l i e
4 t a b o
5 e l a p n
6 o r m k e t i b o
7 c t e i h p e r o l
8 s r h e o

3 Match each picture to a word from exercise 2. Can you add any more transport words?

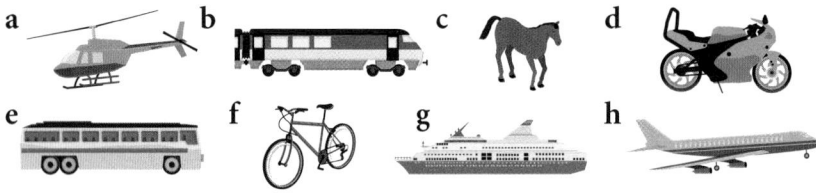

Key words → page 152

4 Now match these verbs to each kind of transport in exercise 2. Most verbs go with more than one type of transport.

Key words

> board   catch   drive   fly   get   get off
> get on   park   ride   sail   take off

EXAMPLE: *board – a coach, train, plane, helicopter, boat*

Grammar   Modal verbs 2

5 What is the difference between these two examples? Which girl can choose what she does?

1

> You should take the train because it's quicker than the bus.

2

> You must go to Gate 43 by six o'clock.

What is the difference in meaning between the two sentences below?

3 You mustn't go to Gate 43 later than six o'clock.

4 You don't have to go to Gate 43 before six o'clock.

6 Complete the text using *should, must, mustn't* and *don't have to*. Use each verb once only.

7 Now look at these examples. Which modal verbs in exercise 6 are closest in meaning to the underlined verbs?

1 You <u>need to</u> stay with your luggage at all times.
2 You <u>needn't</u> show your passport again until you board the plane.

G → page 146

Passengers on **Jetaway flights**
(**1**) .... leave themselves at least 10 minutes to get to Gates 44–54. If you are travelling with only one piece of hand luggage, you (**2**) .... check it in. However, your hand luggage (**3**) .... be no larger than 55 x 40 x 20 cm and (**4**) .... weigh over 10 kg.

8 Read the notices and choose the correct modal verb in the sentences below.

> **Please have enough change ready for the bus driver**

1 You *needn't / need to* give the driver the correct money.

2 If you aren't driving, you *should / needn't* get on the boat now.

> **Why not visit our duty-free shop before your flight leaves?**

3 You *need to / should* look inside the shop.

> Coach to city centre 15 euros
> Tickets on sale only inside airport

4 You *need to / don't have to* pay before you get on the coach.

> **Passengers only beyond this point – please show boarding pass**

5 If you aren't travelling, you *don't need to / mustn't* go through here.

9 Look at the first diagram and read the example, which describes how to get from Melbourne to Heron Island. Then look at the second diagram and describe how to get from London to Vizzavona in the same way. Then describe a journey of your choice, using as many different means of transport as possible!

EXAMPLE **Melbourne to Heron Island (Australia)**

You should fly from Melbourne to Brisbane. You need to change there and take another plane to Gladstone. From Gladstone you needn't take a boat, because there's a helicopter to Heron Island.

London to Vizzavona (Corsica)

16.2 A day out

Vocabulary

1 What do you enjoy doing on a day out with family or friends? Say what things you could do when:

- visiting a big city
- hiking in the countryside
- spending a day at the beach

2 Join these verbs and nouns to make free-time activities.

Key words

build	a picnic
climb	a football
fly	a Frisbee
have	a sand castle
kick	a kite
throw	a hill
visit	a museum

Speaking

3 Are these sentences about Speaking Part 2 right or wrong? Say why.

1 You must ask another student five questions in this part.
2 You needn't include the information on the card in your answers.
3 You mustn't talk to the examiner during this part.
4 You should only use the words that are on the card.
5 You need to relax!

4 Student A turn to page 133 and ask Student B questions about a trip to the beach. Student B turn to page 134 and answer A's questions.

5 Now Student B turn to page 134 and ask Student A about a hiking trip. Student A turn to page 135 and answer B's questions.

Listening

6 **2 19** You will hear five short conversations. You will hear each conversation twice. For questions 1–5, put a tick under the right answer.

1 Which train is leaving first?

A ☐   B ☐   C ☐

2 How will the girl get to the cinema?

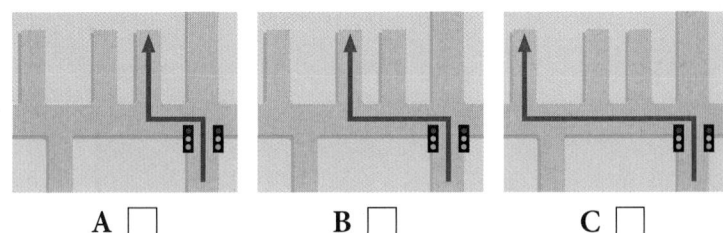

A ☐   B ☐   C ☐

3 Where is Kate's boat now?

A ☐   B ☐   C ☐

4 How will the woman get to work today?

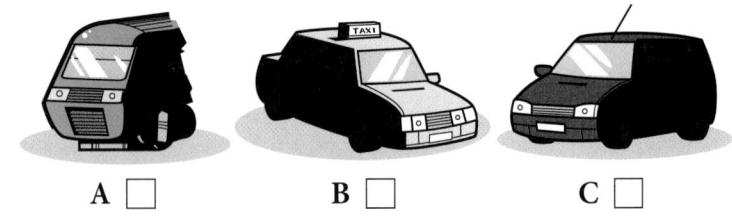

A ☐   B ☐   C ☐

5 Where is the nearest petrol station?

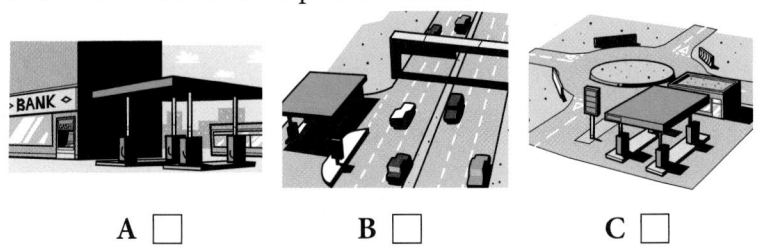

A ☐   B ☐   C ☐

Pronunciation

7 ♪2 [20] Some words have a 'weak' and a 'strong' form. We usually say the weak form of the word *of*. Listen again to these examples from the recording.

a quarter of an hour ago
because of last night's winds

♪2 [21] Now listen to these sentences. Does the underlined word sound weak or strong? Write W or S beside each one.

1 We've got <u>some</u> heavy luggage. *W*
2 Why did you go to Greenland, <u>of</u> all places?
3 <u>Some</u> people travel a lot for work.
4 Can I ask you a couple <u>of</u> questions?
5 The journey's by train <u>and</u> coach.
6 Kate's emailed us <u>some</u> directions to the house.
7 My hotel room's very dark, there are no towels, <u>and</u> the TV doesn't work!
8 On the left <u>of</u> the square there's a bank.

Practise saying these sentences to improve your pronunciation.

Spelling sp●t

i or *e*?

Exam candidates often confuse the letters *i* and *e*, and make spelling mistakes such as *expirience* (for *experience*).

8 Here are some spelling mistakes that candidates have made in the exam. Correct the sentences. One sentence is correct.

1 Cross the bridge, turn right and the musium is on your left.
2 When you leave the aeroport by car, take the third turning off the roundabout and drive for 5 km.
3 To get to the hospetal, go up Silver Street and turn left at the lights.
4 Go straight past the cinema and turn right at the petrol station.
5 You need to walk along the river, cross the univirsity footbridge and then take the second turning on the right.

Activity

How to get there

- Choose a place on the map. Don't tell your partner.
- Give your partner directions to the place. Your partner must say which place it is.

EXAMPLE:
A: *Go over the bridge. Turn right. Take the first turning on the left. This place is on your right. What is it?*
B: *It's the hotel.*

1 Petrol station
2 School
3 Library
4 Theatre
5 Supermarket
6 Police station
7 Hotel
8 Bus station
9 Museum

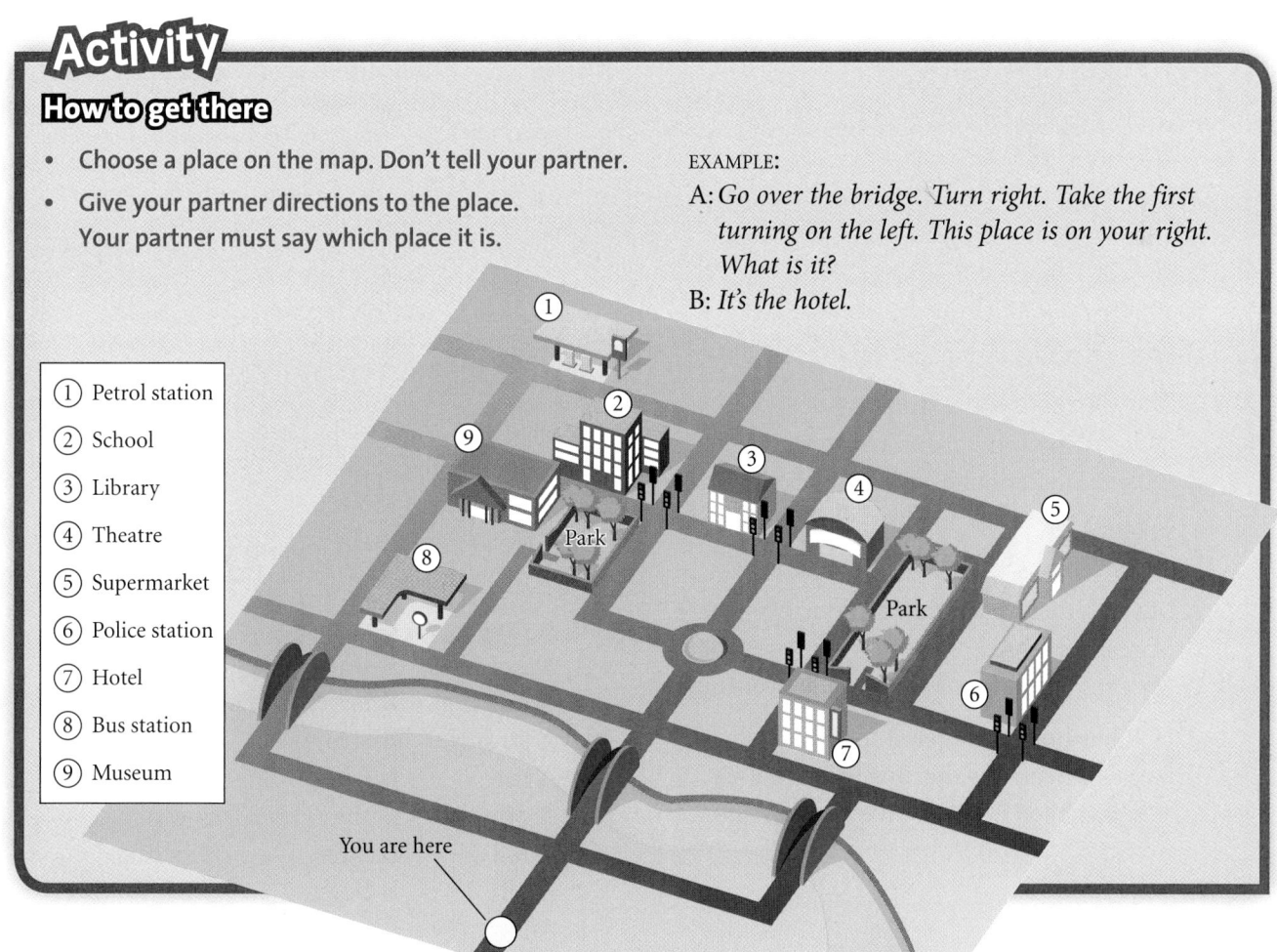

You are here

Units 13–16 Revision

Speaking

1 Write questions for these answers. Then ask your partner the questions. Try to give answers as long as number 8, or longer.

EXAMPLE: *(1) What job would you like to do after you leave school?*

1 I'm not sure, but I'd like to work for an advertising company.
2 It isn't really hot enough today.
3 Sorry, I mustn't be late home this evening.
4 My favourite is an old Italian leather one with deep pockets.
5 I think it's going to rain on Saturday.
6 You don't have to pay anything.
7 I've been to Buenos Aires.
8 The best one I've read this year is a detective story by George Pelecanos.

Grammar

2 In 1–4 only one sentence is correct. Tick the correct sentence (A–C).

1 **A** Foot passengers need to board the ship until 4.45.
   B Foot passengers don't have to board the ship before 4.45.
   C Foot passengers mustn't board the ship since 4.45.

2 **A** It's snowing too hard to cycle into town.
   B It's snowing enough hard to cycle into town.
   C It's snowing very hard to cycle into town.

3 **A** My car's the French new red one over there.
   B My car's the red French new one over there.
   C My car's the new red French one over there.

4 **A** Jack has been a waiter since five months.
   B Jack has been a waiter for five months.
   C Jack has been a waiter five months ago.

3 Read this text about the weather. Choose the best word (A, B or C) for each space.

World weather

In (**0**) .... parts of the world, the weather (**1**) .... change from one minute to the next. The sun (**2**) .... covered by dark clouds, the wind gets (**3**) .... than before and it starts to rain. Usually, it doesn't take (**4**) .... long for the sunny weather to return.

In the Tropics, which are near the Equator, the weather doesn't change for months at (**5**) .... time. It is very hot and heavy rain (**6**) .... every day.

At the North and South Poles, it is always cold and there is ice (**7**) .... year. No plants grow at the Poles. However, in summer there are some plants in the Arctic. These plants grow close to the ground because of the wind and complete (**8**) .... life cycle in a few weeks.

0	**A** much	**B** many	**C** lots
1	**A** need	**B** must	**C** can
2	**A** has	**B** is	**C** was
3	**A** strong	**B** stronger	**C** strongest
4	**A** too	**B** more	**C** enough
5	**A** one	**B** the	**C** a
6	**A** fall	**B** falls	**C** falling
7	**A** all	**B** both	**C** some
8	**A** its	**B** your	**C** their

Vocabulary

4 Put the words below into the correct circle. Put the nouns on the left and the verbs on the right. If a word is a noun and a verb, write it in both places.

EXAMPLE:

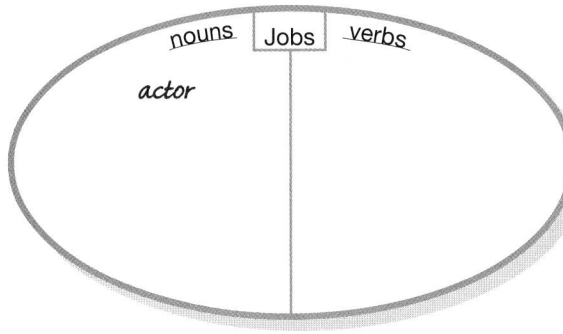

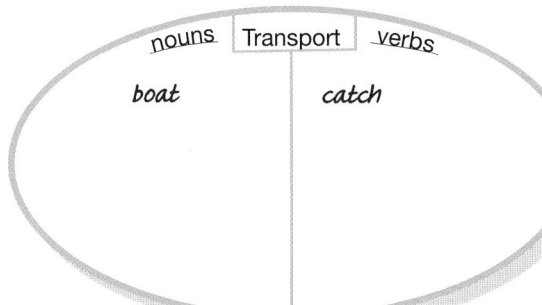

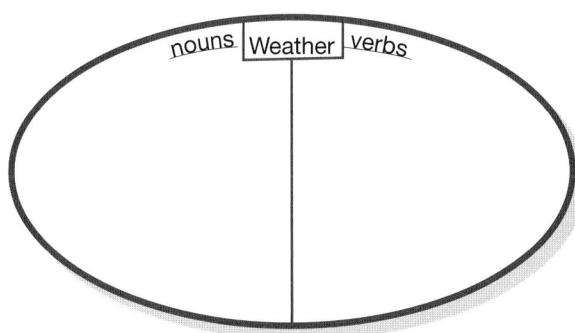

actor	boat	build
car	catch	cloud
chef	dentist	drive
farmer	fly	fog
get off	grow	helicopter
journalist	motorbike	park
phone	photographer	plane
rain	receptionist	sail
snow	storm	take off
tour guide	wind	write

5 Choose the correct answer, A, B or C.

1 Which subject needs a lot of maps?
A art　　　**B** music　　　**C** geography

2 Who looks after people in a hospital?
A a pilot　　　**B** a nurse　　　**C** a tour guide

3 Who doesn't work outside?
A a farmer　　**B** a chef　　**C** a tennis player

4 How can you sail to Mallorca?
A by ship　　　**B** by taxi　　　**C** by plane

5 What will the roads be like if it's –10°C?
A icy　　　**B** cloudy　　　**C** foggy

6 Where do science fiction stories usually happen?
A at the beach　**B** in space　　**C** under the sea

7 What does a dentist check?
A your hair　　**B** your teeth　　**C** your feet

8 Which subject teaches you how to add numbers?
A history　　　**B** science　　　**C** maths

Writing

6 Complete this email about a new magazine for teenagers. Write ONE word for each space.

> To: David
> From: Dimitri
> Subject: Magazines
>
> Hi David
>
> How are you? Have you read (**1**) .... good magazines recently? I've just bought a new (**2**) .... called *Coolclub*, which only started a week (**3**) .... Inside, there are really great photos and (**4**) .... of articles about all our favourite singers and bands.
>
> There's going to be a competition (**5**) .... month, with excellent prizes.
>
> The magazine also has a letters page and they pay £25 for the (**6**) .... interesting letter or email. I think I'll try to write (**7**) .... funny, to win £25. Perhaps I'll describe our journey (**8**) .... boat round the island. Do you remember? You (**9**) .... taking a photo of me and I suddenly fell in the sea! I've (**10**) .... laughed so much!
>
> Write and tell me about the magazines you enjoy reading.
>
> With love from Dimitri

17.1 Totally Techno

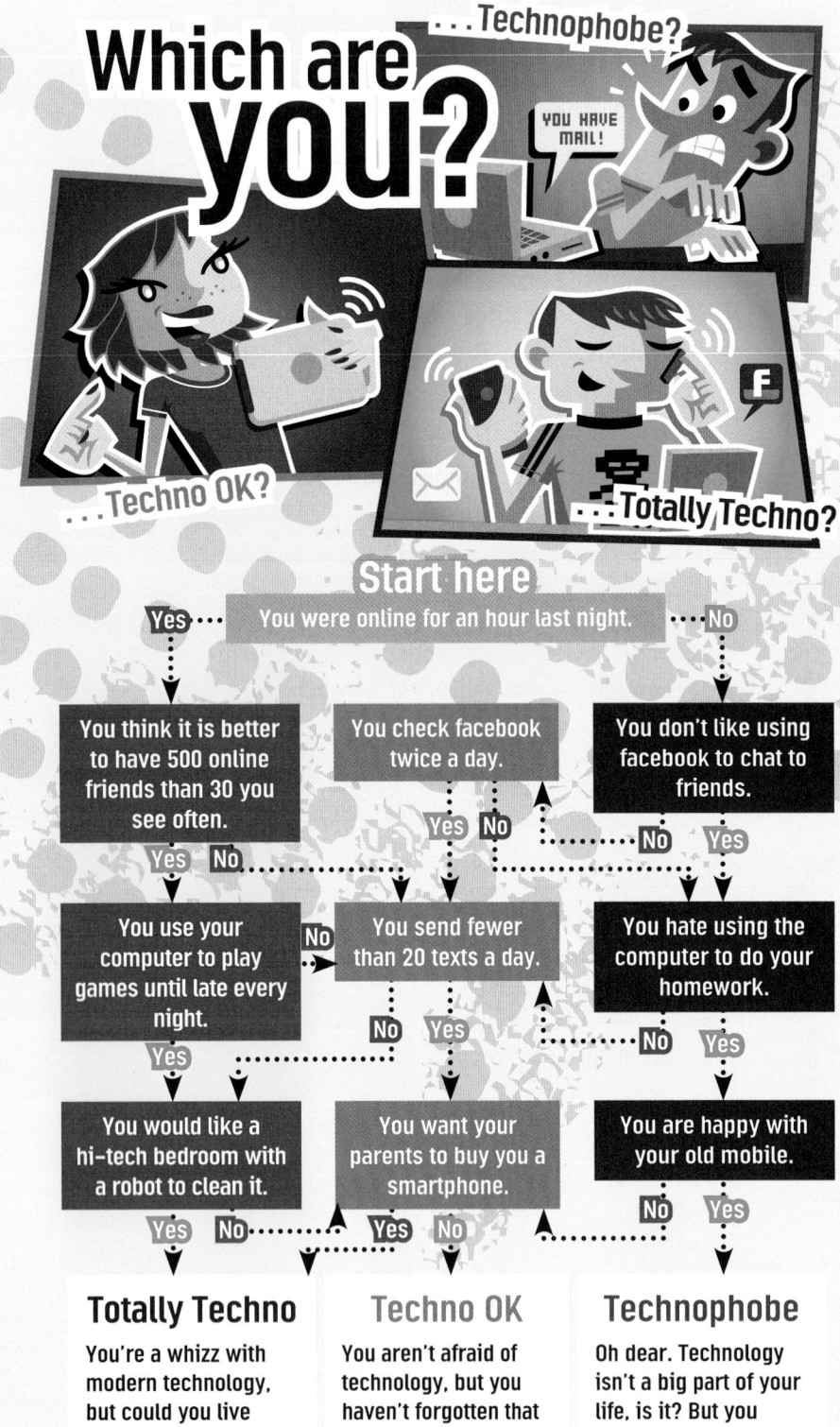

Which are you?

...Technophobe?

YOU HAVE MAIL!

...Techno OK?

...Totally Techno?

Start here

Yes .... You were online for an hour last night. .... No

You think it is better to have 500 online friends than 30 you see often.

You check facebook twice a day.

You don't like using facebook to chat to friends.

Yes No

You use your computer to play games until late every night.

No

You send fewer than 20 texts a day.

You hate using the computer to do your homework.

No Yes

You would like a hi-tech bedroom with a robot to clean it.

You want your parents to buy you a smartphone.

You are happy with your old mobile.

No Yes

Totally Techno

You're a whizz with modern technology, but could you live without it? Do you have time to meet your friends?

Techno OK

You aren't afraid of technology, but you haven't forgotten that people are important too. Remember to send your friends a card on their birthday!

Technophobe

Oh dear. Technology isn't a big part of your life, is it? But you could use it to help your social life and your schoolwork. Why don't you give it a try?

Reading

1 Are you a Technophobe, a Techno OK or are you Totally Techno? Find out by answering the questions in the chart opposite.

Grammar

Infinitive of purpose

2 We often use the infinitive (*to* + verb) to say *why* we do things. Find four examples in the quiz and underline them.

G → page 146

3 Complete each sentence with the infinitive form of a verb from the box.

buy   call   download   ~~help~~
keep   listen   study   turn on

1 You can find a robot _to help_ you with the housework.

2 We click on a web page .... a program.

3 You use this switch .... the laptop.

4 Emily needs a mobile phone .... her friends.

5 A fridge is useful .... food cool.

6 Paula has a smartphone .... to her favourite music on the bus to school.

7 Carlos went to university .... computer science.

8 My brother is saving all his money .... the latest computer game.

4 Talk about why people do these things.

EXAMPLE: *I think people go to university …*
… to learn more about a subject.
… to get a good job when they leave.

1 go to university
2 use Google
3 buy electric cars
4 go to other countries
5 play computer games
6 use a laptop computer
7 read magazines
8 play team sports
9 learn English
10 buy the latest technology

5 Think about life with no electricity. Would you be happy? Why? / Why not?

Did you know?

The word 'robot' was first used in 1921 by a man called Karel Capek. 'Robot' means 'a slave worker' in the Czech language!

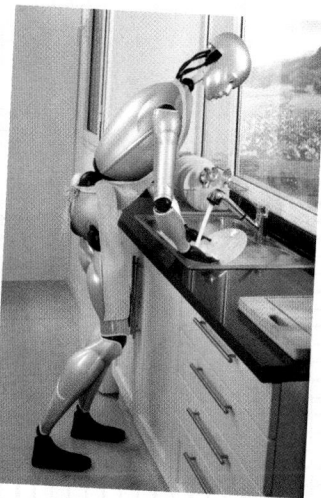

Did you know?

An Englishman called Charles Babbage built the first 'computer' in 1834.
The machine was as big as a bus!

Can you say?

anna@yahoo.co.uk   www.cambridge.org

6 Read the article about teenagers and social networking sites. Choose the best word (A, B or C) for each space.

Ruby, 14, (**0**) .... a Terrible Time. 'My family went (**1**) .... holiday to a house with no TV, no wifi, (**2**) .... I couldn't use my phone. It was so hard – I couldn't talk to my friends for two weeks!'

We can't live (**3**) .... technology in our modern world. A new study says that 55% of (**4**) .... North American teenagers use social networking sites (**5**) .... Facebook. (**6**) .... teenagers go to their computer immediately when they come home from school to chat to their friends. Ruby has 732 online friends and says she knows 'most' of them. 'I'm very popular,' she says. (**7**) .... does she use the site for? 'To share photos and videos, make plans for parties and to chat to people. Being online (**8**) .... good fun.'

0	**A** remembers	**B** remembering	**C** remember
1	**A** on	**B** at	**C** for
2	**A** because	**B** if	**C** and
3	**A** without	**B** except	**C** from
4	**A** every	**B** all	**C** both
5	**A** among	**B** like	**C** as
6	**A** Many	**B** Much	**C** Lot
7	**A** Who	**B** When	**C** What
8	**A** are	**B** is	**C** have

17.2 New ideas

a solar robot toy

an underwater mask with a built-in camera

a backpack with a solar cell

an iTeddy – a multi-media player with a small screen and speakers

1 What do you think of these gadgets? Which gadget would you like to own and why?

Listening

2 **2 22** Listen to Vanessa telling her friend Edward about a visit to see a special gadget show in London.

For questions 1–6, tick A, B or C.

0 Vanessa's ticket cost   A £5.95.
                        B £9.50. ✓
                        C £15.00.

1 Vanessa went to the show   A on foot.
                        B on the underground.
                        C on the bus.

2 Vanessa really liked seeing the   A Games Hall.
                        B Test Space.
                        C 3D Theatre.

3 The show opens at   A 9.00 a.m.
                        B 10.00 a.m.
                        C 11.30 a.m.

4 For lunch Vanessa decided to   A take a picnic.
                        B have a hot meal.
                        C get a snack.

5 The show will finish on   A 23rd April.
                        B 24th April.
                        C 27th April.

Pronunciation

3 **2 23** Listen again to these sentences from the recording, then repeat them.

You <u>can't</u> go in until ten.
We <u>didn't</u> get there until eleven thirty.
There <u>wasn't</u> enough time to see everything.
<u>I'd</u> really like to go.
<u>I'm</u> free next Saturday – <u>that's</u> 23rd April.
<u>I'll</u> go on the 24th.

Write the full version of the underlined contractions.

4 With a partner, underline the words you can contract in the following sentences and then say them aloud. There are two sentences where you can't contract the words.

1 I am going to buy a new calculator.
2 Are you not coming to my house tonight?
3 Who is playing with my PlayStation?
4 I would like a new phone for my birthday.
5 Who is it?
6 Dan has borrowed my laptop again.
7 They cannot get any batteries because the shop is closed.
8 Has she been shopping yet? Yes, she has.

2 24 Listen to check your answers.

Vocabulary

5 In the recording, Vanessa <u>got the bus</u> to the gadget show and she <u>had fun</u> there.

There are many words in English that go together. Match the verbs below with the nouns. Sometimes there is more than one answer.

Key words

get	a party	
give	a bus	a job
have	a film	a noise
make	friends	someone a call
see	a good time	TV
watch		

6 Choose the correct word in these questions and then ask your partner the questions.

1 How often do you *make / have* a noise when you are with your friends?
2 What job do you think you will *get / give* when you leave college?
3 Do you find it easy to *get / make* friends?
4 What do you usually *watch / see* on TV?
5 When do you usually *see / watch* your friends?
6 Have you *given / got* any good parties this year?
7 How often do you *give / make* your friends a call?

Spelling spot

Correcting mistakes

7 Read this email from Carl to his friends. Correct the spelling mistakes and add commas, capital letters and full stops.

○ ○ ○

From Carl
To Josh, Danny, Miriam, Ravi, Gurgei, Oli

Hi everyone

i want to sell my phone becose my girlfriend bougth me a new won last weakend it is too monts old the prize was about $100 and im seling it for $50 does enyone want to by it?

Carl

Grammar extra

The infinitive – with and without *to*

- A number of verbs are followed by *to* + infinitive:

decide	*They decided **to buy** their son a solar bicycle.*
go	*She went **to see** the new gadget show.*
hope	
learn	
need	
want	
would like	

- These modal verbs are followed by the infinitive **without** *to*:

can / could	*We couldn't **find** the right house.*
must	*You must **tell** someone.*
may / might	
shall / should	
will / would	

8 Correct the mistakes that candidates have made with infinitives.

1 I'd like for see you next weekend.
2 I must to arrive home at 10.00.
3 I would like sell my books.
4 I want buy it.
5 You can to go to a museum there.
6 I have decided study chemistry.
7 She should to visiting London.
8 I hope see you soon.
9 We need doing our homework tonight.
10 We went to London see the London Eye.

Activity

Guess the object

Write a short description of something you use every day. Read it aloud and let everyone guess what it is.

EXAMPLE:
It is made of metal and plastic and is quite small. I use it every day. It has numbers on it. I use it to make appointments or find out information.

Exam folder 9

Listening Part 3 Multiple choice

In Part 3 of the Listening paper you must listen to a conversation. There are always two speakers, usually one male and one female. There are five questions (**11–15**), each with a choice of three answers (**A**, **B** or **C**). These choices can be numbers or words.

You must choose the correct answer. There is also an example at the beginning.

EXAM ADVICE

Before you listen
- Read through the questions carefully. You have 20 seconds to do this.

First listening
- You hear the conversation twice, so don't worry if you don't hear all the answers the first time you listen.
- The first time you listen, tick your answers on the question paper. You have time at the end of the test to transfer your answers to your answer sheet.

Second listening
- The second time you listen, check to make sure your answers are correct.
- This is an example of the answer sheet for Part 3.

Here are some example questions. Read the question and recording script. All three choices are mentioned in the recording script, but only one choice answers the question.

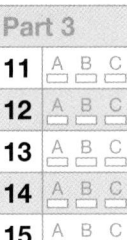

Part 3			
11	A	B	C
12	A	B	C
13	A	B	C
14	A	B	C
15	A	B	C

1 Sam bought the DVD for **A** £15.00.
                                   B £16.00.
                                   C £19.50.

Judy   The DVD that you wanted costs £16.00 in the supermarket.
Sam   I know, but I was really lucky and got it for £15.00 from a local shop. Last week they were selling it for £19.50, so I'm really pleased.

The answer is A.

2 Joe goes to an extra science class every **A** Monday.
                                            B Tuesday.
                                            C Thursday.

Sue   There's an extra science class on Tuesdays, isn't there?
Joe   That one's for the under 14s. I'm in an older class – that's on Thursdays, and there's one on Mondays as well, but I play football then.

What is the answer?

Part 3

Questions 11–15

Listen to Ellie talking to Chris about Lynne, his sister.

For questions **11–15**, tick (✓) **A**, **B** or **C**.

You will hear the conversation twice.

Example:

0	Lynne arrived home on	**A**	Monday.	☐
		B	Wednesday.	✓
		C	Saturday.	☐

11	At the moment Lynne is working in	**A**	Hong Kong.	☐
		B	New York.	☐
		C	London.	☐

12	Lynne learnt how to use a computer	**A**	at home.	☐
		B	at school.	☐
		C	at university.	☐

13	Next year Lynne will get	**A**	four weeks' holiday.	☐
		B	five weeks' holiday.	☐
		C	six weeks' holiday.	☐

14	Lynne is free	**A**	in the morning.	☐
		B	at lunchtime.	☐
		C	in the afternoon.	☐

15	Chris has bought Lynne	**A**	a computer game.	☐
		B	a camera.	☐
		C	a watch.	☐

Keeping well!

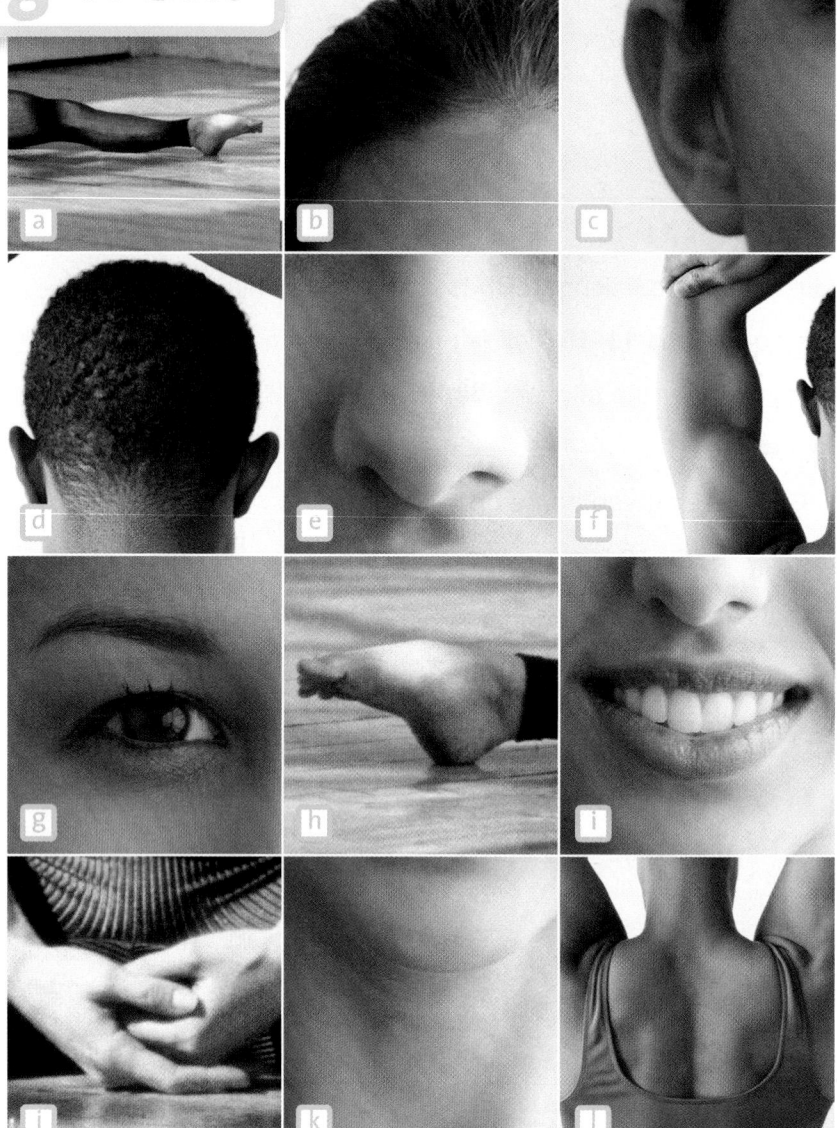

Vocabulary

1 Put the letters in the right order to spell the name of a part of the body or face.

Then match the words with the photos.

EXAMPLE: *head – d*

The body	*The face*
1 e a d h	**9** r a e
2 a i r h	**10** h t m o u
3 n e k c	**11** s e o n
4 m r a	**12** y e e
5 n a h d s	
6 c k b a	
7 e g l	
8 f o t o	

2 Read the descriptions of words to do with health.

What is the word for each one? The first letter is already there.

1 A doctor helps people who are like this.

s _ _ _

2 This person helps people who are ill in hospital.

n _ _ _ _

3 People telephone to ask this to take them to hospital.

a _ _ _ _ _ _ _ _

4 It's important to take this if you want to get better.

m _ _ _ _ _ _ _

5 If this is high, you feel ill.

t _ _ _ _ _ _ _ _ _ _

6 This shop sells things to make people feel better.

c _ _ _ _ _ _

3 Match the problems 1–10 with the advice A–J. (Sometimes there is more than one answer.)

EXAMPLE: *1 H*

1 I'm very tired.	**A** You probably need an X-ray.
2 I've got a terrible headache.	**B** Why don't you go on a diet?
3 I've got a cold.	**C** Terrible. I think I'll stay in bed.
4 I'm too fat.	**D** Go and lie down.
5 How do you feel today?	**E** You need a hot lemon drink.
6 My foot hurts.	**F** Don't go running today.
7 I've cut my hand.	**G** Try not to talk.
8 I've broken my arm.	**H** Try going to bed earlier.
9 I've got a sore throat.	**I** You need a plaster.
10 I've got stomach ache.	**J** You should take an aspirin.

Key**words** → page 152

4 Look at the pictures below. Tell your partner what the problem is. Your partner will give you some advice.

Begin: *I've …*
Answer: *You should … / You need to … / Why don't you …?*

Listening

5 **2 26** You will hear some information about which chemists are open in the local area.

Listen and complete questions 1–5.

Information

Date: 15th–21st December

<u>Bridges</u> in Sandford
Opening hours (Mon–Fri):
(**1**) 8.45 a.m. – ....

<u>Nearest chemist when Bridges is closed</u>
Name of shop: (**2**) ....
Address: (**3**) .... The High Street, Dursley.
Opposite: (**4**) ....
Telephone no: (**5**) ....

Grammar eXtra

Word order of time phrases

- In the recording in exercise 5 the speaker said:
  Ring this number if you need to talk to the chemist at night.
- The time phrase (*at night*) is used after the object (*the chemist*).
- We usually use a time phrase either at the beginning of a sentence/clause or at the end.
  *We went running after school **last Saturday**.*
  ***Last Saturday** we went running after school.*

6 Here are some errors that exam candidates have made. Correct the sentences.

1 I was last night at a big party.
2 I'll come on Saturday shopping.
3 We have been every day to the beach.
4 I went after work to the chemist.
5 They at night usually sleep well.
6 I bought today some new trainers.

Pronunciation

When we speak we link together the consonant sound at the end of a word and the vowel sound at the beginning of the next word.

7 **2 27** Listen and mark the linking in these sentences.

EXAMPLES: *He's got‿a broken‿arm.*
We're here to make‿an‿appointment.

1 Can you call an ambulance?
2 Fruit and vegetables are very good for you.
3 You should do some exercise every day.
4 Watching TV all weekend is not good for you.
5 Make sure you get enough sleep at night.

A long and happy life

Speaking

1 Some people say that if you sleep about six to seven hours a night, you will have a long and happy life. Ask three people about their sleeping habits and write their answers on the chart on page 135. Then report back to the class.

1 How many hours a night do you sleep?
2 How many hours did you sleep last night?
3 Do you sleep on your back, your side or your front?
4 Do you remember your dreams?
5 Have you ever had a bad dream?
6 What do you do if you wake up in the night?
7 What do you do if you have problems getting to sleep?

Reading

2 Read the article quickly to find out who is the oldest person mentioned.

Now read it again more slowly. Are sentences 1–8 'Right' (A) or 'Wrong' (B)? If there is not enough information to answer 'Right' (A) or 'Wrong' (B), choose 'Doesn't say' (C).

1 Doctors now think that Shirali Muslimov was probably younger than he thought he was.
   A Right   B Wrong   C Doesn't say
2 Yone Minagawa lived a long life because she only ate vegetables.
   A Right   B Wrong   C Doesn't say
3 Joan Riudavets Moll slept more when he was old than he did when he was younger.
   A Right   B Wrong   C Doesn't say
4 Joan's first job was working in a hospital.
   A Right   B Wrong   C Doesn't say
5 Joan was married three times.
   A Right   B Wrong   C Doesn't say
6 Joan spent most of his time in his house.
   A Right   B Wrong   C Doesn't say
7 Joan remembered life without electricity.
   A Right   B Wrong   C Doesn't say
8 Joan hated sport.
   A Right   B Wrong   C Doesn't say

Some of the oldest people in the world are said to live in Azerbaijan. The most famous of all was Shirali Muslimov, who died on 2 September 1973 at the age of 168. Today, doctors do not think this is possible, but he was a very old man – probably nearer 120 than 160!

Another person who was once the oldest person in the world was Yone Minagawa who died in 2007 aged 114 years and 221 days. She had five children and worked selling flowers and vegetables for many years. She enjoyed eating sweets and thought eating well and getting a good night's sleep was the reason why she lived so long.

Joan Riudavets Moll was born on 15 December 1889, on the Balearic Island of Menorca. He lived there until he died aged 114 years and 81 days. In the last years of his life he was spending up to 14 hours a day asleep. Riudavets really wanted to be a doctor but he became a shoemaker, working at home in the family business. He had three daughters in all, with five grandsons and six great-grandchildren. He rarely left his home. He thought planes and electricity were the most important changes he had seen in his life. During his life he played a lot of football – his favourite game – and still enjoyed singing and playing the guitar when he was very old. Joan Riudavets Moll said, 'If you eat a little but often, you will live a long life.'

Grammar First conditional

- Find the sentence in the text which begins with *If* ...
  If _____ .
- Which tenses are used?
  If + _____ .
- We use this structure to express a possible condition.

3 Match the sentence beginnings 1–6 with their endings A–F.

1 If I get up 7 o'clock,	**A** I'll get a good job.
2 If I go swimming every day,	**B** I'll travel round the world.
	C I'll sleep better at night.
3 If I work hard at school,	**D** I'll get fit.
4 If I save my money,	**E** I won't be late for school.
5 If I win the lottery,	**F** I'll buy a TV for my
6 If I drink less coffee,	bedroom.

- When the sentence begins with *if*, we often use a comma. We can also use *if* in the middle of a sentence without a comma.

G → page 147

4 We all need enough sleep at night. What other things will make you healthier? Talk to your partner about the things below and add two more ideas of your own.

1 eating burgers	4 too much stress
2 riding a motorbike	5 having a holiday
3 working long hours	6 watching TV all day

EXAMPLE: *If you eat fewer burgers and more vegetables you will feel better.*

5 You are going on a camping holiday in the mountains with a friend. Talk about what you will do if you have problems.

EXAMPLE: *A: What will you do if you have an accident?*
  B: I'll use my mobile phone to ring someone.

6 Complete the sentences.

If I work harder, I will ...
If I don't ...
If I get up ...
If ...

7 Write a note to a friend about what you are going to do to become healthier. Say:
- why you want to get fit
- what you are going to do
- when or how often you are going to do it.

Write 25–35 words.

Spelling spot

Words which don't double their last letter

The last letter isn't doubled if a word ends in
- two consonants:
  help helped helping
- two vowels and a consonant:
  need needed needing

8 Are these words correct? Put a tick or a cross beside each one.

1 cheaper
2 fastter
3 getting
4 stoping
5 waiting
6 running
7 thiner
8 swiming

Activity

An interview

For homework interview the oldest person you know – maybe a grandparent or a neighbour or even your parents! Prepare a chart where you can write in the information. Report back to the class what you found out.

Use these words to make questions:
1 when / you / born
2 how / you / keep / healthy
3 what / you / eat
4 what / changes / you / see
5 what / you / think of / internet/

Exam folder 10

Reading Part 4 Multiple choice

In Part 4 of the Reading and Writing paper, there can be different types of task. You will only have to answer one of these in the exam. See Exam folder 6 on page 66 for information about the 'Right, Wrong, Doesn't Say' task.

For the multiple-choice task, you will have to read one long article or three short articles. There are seven questions (**21–27**) and an example at the beginning. Each question has a choice of three answers (**A**, **B** or **C**). You must choose the correct answer.

Part 4			
21	A	B	C
22	A	B	C
23	A	B	C
24	A	B	C
25	A	B	C
26	A	B	C
27	A	B	C

One long article

1 Read the instructions and the article about John Flynn quickly.
   What is it about?

   A An Australian sheep farmer.
   B A British doctor living in Australia.
   C An Australian who had a new idea.

2 Now do the exam task, following the advice.

EXAM ADVICE

- Read the instructions to find out what the article is about.
- Read the whole article quickly before you answer any of the questions.
- Don't worry if there is a word you don't understand.
- Read each question very carefully. The questions are in the order in which you will find the answers in the article.
- Underline the place in the article where you find each answer.
- Decide on the correct answer (A, B or C).
- Look at the article to check that the other choices are wrong.
- Mark your answers on your answer sheet. There is an example of the answer sheet for Part 4 above.

Part 4

Questions 21–27

Read the article about a famous Australian man, called John Flynn.

For questions **21–27**, mark **A**, **B** or **C** on your answer sheet.

> # *The Flying Doctor*
>
> John Flynn was born in Australia in 1880. His father was a schoolteacher. John studied hard and in 1911 he left the city of Melbourne and went to work in South Australia for a church. The church wanted to help the sheep farmers who lived in the outback – the countryside area many kilometres from towns and cities. They built a number of small hospitals and found nurses to work in them. But at that time there were only two doctors in all of South Australia.
>
> One story Flynn often told was of Jimmy Darcy. One day Jimmy had an accident on his farm so friends took him to see F.W. Tuckett, who worked at the post office at Halls Creek. It was a journey of 22 km. Tuckett was the only person in the area who knew anything about medicine. He wanted to help but Jimmy was too ill. Tuckett finally talked by radio to a doctor in Perth, a city 1500 km away. The doctor took ten days to arrive. He travelled by car, by horse and on foot and when he arrived, he found that Jimmy was already dead.
>
> Flynn saw that planes could really help people in the outback. He wrote about his idea for a 'Flying Doctor' in 1917 but it wasn't until 1928 that one actually took off. By the 1930s there was a Flying Doctor plane in every part of Australia.

Example:

0 John Flynn's job was   **A** teaching at a school.
                            B helping with sheep farming.
                            C working for the church.   *Answer:* **0** A B C

---

21 Flynn worked in

     A a city.
     B the countryside.
     C a small town.

22 What was the problem in South Australia?

     A The nurses weren't very good.
     B There were no hospitals.
     C There weren't enough doctors.

23 What does Flynn tell us about Jimmy?

     A He lived at Halls Creek.
     B He was a farmer.
     C He was often ill.

24 Why did Jimmy and his friends go to see F.W. Tuckett?

     A He helped sick people.
     B He worked at a post office.
     C He was a doctor.

25 What did F.W. Tuckett decide to do?

     A to give Jimmy some medicine
     B to go with Jimmy to the city
     C to use a radio to get help for Jimmy

26 What do we know about the doctor from Perth?

     A He travelled too slowly to save Jimmy.
     B He had problems with his car.
     C He didn't know the way to Halls Creek.

27 The first Flying Doctor plane flew in

     A 1917.
     B 1928.
     C 1930.

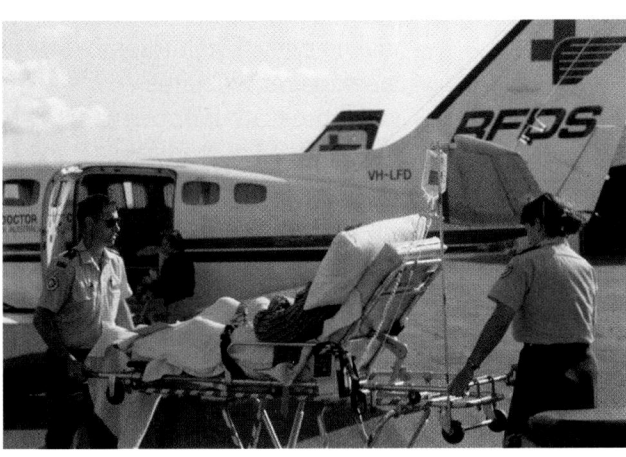

Turn over.

There is another Part 4 exam task on the next page.

Reading Part 4 Multiple choice

EXAM ADVICE

- Read the instructions to find out what the articles are about.
- Read all three articles quickly before you answer any of the questions.
- Don't worry if you don't understand every word.
- Read each question carefully and underline the important words.
- Find the information in the articles that matches these words.
- Decide which article gives the correct answer (A, B or C).
- Underline the part of the article where you found the answer.
- Remember that there will be some 'distraction' in the other articles – for example, another article will use some of the words from the question.
- Check your answers by reading the parts you underlined in the articles.
- Mark your answers on your answer sheet.

Part 4

Questions 21–27

Read the articles about three teenagers and their smartphones and then answer the questions.

For questions **21–27**, mark **A**, **B** or **C** on your answer sheet.

LEE	KIM	ALEX
My cousin gave me this phone last year when she got a new one. It can take great pictures but I don't use it for that. I've downloaded lots of free fun things to play, like chess and different puzzles. I've only ever bought one app, to help me plan my homework and tennis practice. My phone's so useful! I can get facts I need for history and geography before my next class.	I lost my last phone when I was sailing – it fell in the sea! This one is only three weeks old and I haven't put any games on it yet. I don't buy many apps and there's only one that I use often. I've got friends all over the world and we email each other cool photos while we're at parties and concerts. It's really important to talk to them too, so I use free websites for that.	My phone was a present from my parents when I became a teenager. It was the latest model then, but that was two years ago! To begin with I used it just to text and speak to my school friends. Now I go online every day to know what's happening at big football matches and find out about my favourite movie stars. I visit foreign newspaper websites sometimes, to improve the languages I'm studying.

Example:

0 Who has the newest phone?

 A Lee   **B** Kim   **C** Alex   *Answer:*   0 | A B C |

---

21 Who was given the phone as a birthday gift?

 A Lee   **B** Kim   **C** Alex

22 Who has put several games on their phone?

 A Lee   **B** Kim   **C** Alex

23 Who had an accident with an earlier phone?

 A Lee   **B** Kim   **C** Alex

24 Who uses their phone to find out information about school subjects quickly?

 A Lee   **B** Kim   **C** Alex

25 Who takes pictures on their phone and sends them to friends immediately?

 A Lee   **B** Kim   **C** Alex

26 Who uses their phone to check on the latest sports information?

 A Lee   **B** Kim   **C** Alex

27 Who chats to friends in other countries without having to pay anything?

 A Lee   **B** Kim   **C** Alex

19.1 Let's communicate!

Vocabulary

1 Find fifteen words to do with communicating in the word square (look → and ↓). Use the pictures to help you. One has been done for you.

c	a	l	l	r	o	m	a	y	i
w	e	n	v	e	l	o	p	e	n
i	t	f	a	c	e	b	o	o	k
n	s	u	f	e	a	i	s	r	n
t	e	x	t	i	l	l	t	i	o
e	n	e	e	v	l	e	c	n	t
r	d	b	m	e	s	s	a	g	e
n	c	k	a	t	o	m	r	i	t
e	w	r	i	t	e	n	d	a	l
t	t	e	l	e	p	h	o	n	e

Key words → page 152

2 Which ways of communicating are best in these situations? Decide on your answers. Then talk to another student about them, using words from the word square.

1 Your friend in Australia has a birthday in a couple of days, so it's too late to post anything.
2 You've heard that your cousin in another town is getting married.
3 You can't meet your friends tonight and want to say sorry.
4 You want to tell your family where you'll be this evening but no one is at home.
5 You're on holiday and want to show your brother what the place is like.
6 A friend who lives near you has just had some bad news.

Listening

3 **2 28** Listen to Paul telling a friend how he has communicated some good news. Which way of communicating has he used for each person?

For questions 1–5, write a letter (A–H) next to each person.

EXAMPLE: **0**   *Ruth*   B

People
1 Mario ☐
2 Anna ☐
3 Jack ☐
4 Tessa ☐
5 Paul's professor ☐

Ways of communicating
A email
B Facebook
C letter
D mobile phone call
E note
F phone message
G postcard
H text message

Pronunciation

4 ♪2|29 **Listen again to the parts of the recording below. On the words which are broken into syllables, put a star above the stressed syllable.**

1 Con|gra|tu|la*|tions on get*|ting the job!
2 Mario's tra|vel|ling up to Scot|land to|day.
3 I spoke to him on his mo|bile in|stead.
4 I left a mess|age on her phone.
5 Yes, in Ar|gen|ti|na.
6 Re|mem|ber to phone your pro|fess|or and tell him.
7 The num|ber at the u|ni|ver|si|ty has changed.
8 I bought one of that Mo|rocc|an car|pet we saw at the mu|se|um.

Now practise saying the sentences.

Grammar Prepositions of place

In the recording, you heard several phrases with prepositions, for example *at the museum*.

5 **Complete each phrase with a preposition from the box and add another similar phrase of your own.**

| at | in | on |

1 __at__ home   __at work__
2 .... the floor
3 .... Argentina
4 .... New Street
5 .... 25 Broad Street
6 .... Madrid
7 .... the bus stop

6 **Correct the mistakes that exam candidates made with prepositions. One sentence is correct.**

1 You can call me at my cell phone: 22 59 67 81.
2 I'll meet you on the supermarket in West Street.
3 I'm in holiday now in Istanbul.
4 You can stay on my house.
5 The hotel is at the centre of the town.
6 We live on a new house in Magka.
7 On the walls there are some posters.
8 If you are interested in joining the club, find me at room 12.

G→**page 147**

7 **Complete this letter. Write ONE word for each space.**

Dear Margareta

How are you? I don't write too (**1**) .... letters, but I'm sending you this one (**2**) .... I know you like to receive them. I've bought (**3**) .... beautiful stamps to put (**4**) .... the envelope, too. (**5**) .... my country, the post office often sells stamps showing different birds, like (**6**) .... ones. I think they're great! (**7**) .... one is your favourite?

If you get a smartphone for your birthday, (**8**) .... it have a new number? Please let (**9**) .... know about that. My mum and dad and (**10**) .... else in the family send you their best wishes.

Love,

Agnes

Spelling spot

Spelling the sound /iː/

- The sound /iː/ is spelled in different ways in English.

beginning	middle	end
email	been	see
easy	mean	tea
	these	we
	police	
	believe	
	ceiling	

8 **Fill in the missing vowels.**

1 Have you rec_ _ved an email from Jan yet?
2 Here's a fr_ _ pen for you. They cost six euros _ _ch in the shops!
3 Can I sp_ _k to Mrs Lee?
4 What animals are in that f_ _ld over there?
5 I'm going to be away all next w_ _k.
6 I'd like a k_lo of apples.

1 How many languages do you speak? Do you speak a different language or dialect at home? Do your grandparents?

2 Answer this quiz about world languages by saying Right or Wrong. Then discuss your ideas with another student.

1 Spanish is spoken by more people than any other language.
2 Japanese is one of the six official languages of the United Nations.
3 More than 700 languages are spoken in Indonesia.
4 At least one in three people in Italy speak a dialect as well as Italian.
5 Cornish and Irish belong to the same language group.

Reading

3 Read this article about the Cornish language. Choose the best word for each space, A, B or C.

	A	B	C
0	(A ago)	B before	C since
1	A This	B Them	C These
2	A on	B in	C at
3	A another	B others	C other
4	A to	B until	C for
5	A more	B much	C many
6	A is	B has	C was
7	A its	B their	C her
8	A bring	B bringing	C brought

The history of Cornish

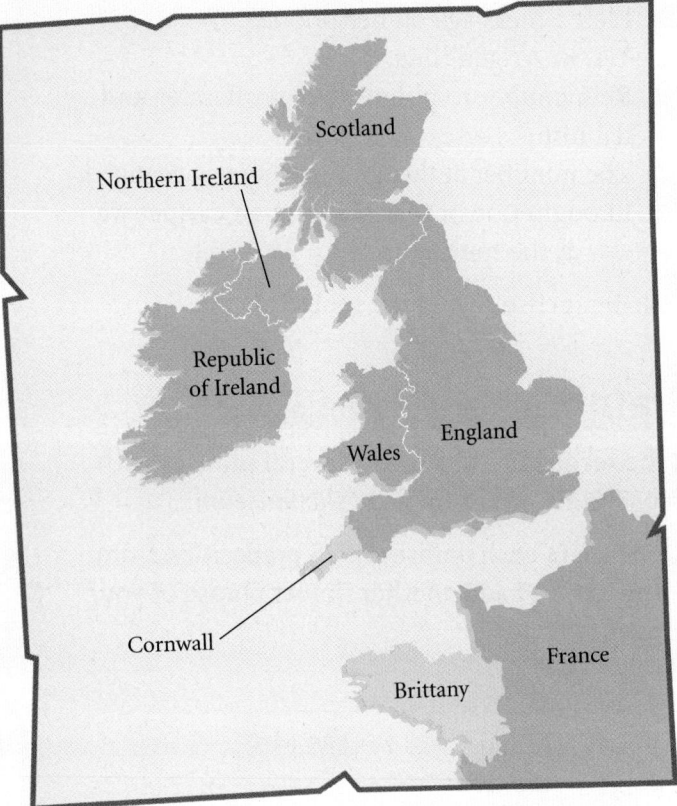

Around 4000 years (0) .... , the group of languages now called the Celtic languages started to develop. (1) .... languages then became two different groups. Cornish, Welsh and Breton – the language spoken (2) .... north-west France – are one group, and Irish and Scots Gaelic are part of the (3) ....

Cornish grew like a modern European language (4) .... the 17th century, when English became (5) .... important in Cornwall than earlier. English (6) .... used to buy and sell things and because of that, Cornish people began to think badly of (7) .... language and saw Cornish only as the language of poor people.

By the end of the 19th century, Cornish was no longer spoken. But a man called Henry Jenner studied the language and (8) .... it back to life. Now, you can even learn Cornish on the internet!

Grammar Prepositions of time

4 What do you know about prepositions? Fill in the missing prepositions of time: *at, in, on.*

- We use .... with:

  years 1953
  centuries .... the 20th century
  seasons .... (the) summer
  months .... November
  parts of the day .... the afternoon

- We use .... with:

  days of the week .... Saturday
  special days .... New Year's Day
  dates .... 1 March 2013

- We use .... with:

  times .... ten o'clock / 10.00
  meals .... breakfast
  festivals .... Easter
  periods of time .... the weekend

G → page 148

5 Lara studies German and Russian. Ask and answer questions to complete her timetable, using prepositions of time. Student B should turn to page 135 now.

Student A's questions

- Which day … German/Russian Conversation?
- What time?
- When … free?

Do the same for these classes in each language:

Conversation   Grammar
Reading   Writing
Listening

EXAMPLE:
A: *Which day does she have German conversation?*
B: *On Monday.*
A: *What time?*
B: *At three o'clock.*

Vocabulary

6 How many languages do you know the names of? Remember that sometimes the word used for the language is the same word as the nationality. Complete the table.

country	nationality	language(s) spoken
Argentina	Argentinian	
Brazil	Brazilian	
Chile	Chilean	
France	French	
Greece	Greek	
Italy	Italian	
Mexico	Mexican	
Morocco	Moroccan	
Switzerland	Swiss	

Key words → page 152

Activity

What do they speak in …?

- Get into two teams. (And close your books!) Your teacher will give each of you a number.
- When your number is called, say the name of a country. The person with the same number on the opposite team must tell you any one language which is spoken in that country.

  EXAMPLE: Team A person: *Poland*
  Team B person: *Polish*

- Score one point for your team for every language you name correctly.

	Monday	Tuesday	Wednesday	Thursday	Friday
9.00					
10.00					
11.00					
12.00					
1.00	LUNCH				
2.00					
3.00	*German Conversation*				

Writing folder 5

Writing Part 9 Short message

In Part 9 (Question **56**) of the Reading and Writing paper, you must write about three different things, using between 25 and 35 words. Sometimes, as in Writing folder 3 (see page 72), you will have to reply to a message from a friend. Sometimes there will just be instructions about what you have to write.

1 Look at these exam answers and decide what three things the candidates were asked to write about. Choose from A–E in the box below.

1

Dear Pat
I'll be free at 10 a.m. We can meet us to Paul's caffe. I'd like to buy a skirt. See you on Saturday.
Love Anya

2

Dear Pat
I will go for two hours. I will meet with John and I will want buy a red bicycle. Your friend

3

Dear Pat I think it is a great idea to go shopping together. We could meet in the bus stop at 12 o'clock in the morning. I'd like to buy some pens. See you soon. Claudia

4

Yes, I coming with you to shopping on Saturday. I'll probably be free at the lunch. We'll meet us to the shopping centre in town. I want to buy me two trousers and a top. Perhaps, I want to buy also a robe. And you, what do you want to buy?
From your best friend
Sylvie

> **A** when you can meet your friend Pat on Saturday
> **B** who you will invite to go shopping with you on Saturday
> **C** where you suggest meeting your friend Pat on Saturday
> **D** what you would like to buy on Saturday
> **E** how you will get to the shopping centre on Saturday

2 Decide which answer is the best and which is the worst. Explain why.

3 Correct any wrong prepositions in the answers and underline other errors.

4 Rewrite answer 4, correcting the errors. Write between 25 and 35 words.

Part 9 (Question 56): Write your answer below.

Part 9

Question 56

You are going to meet your friend Jan at the cinema tomorrow. Write an email to Jan.

Say:

- **when** you will meet at the cinema
- **which film** you want to see
- **why** Jan would enjoy this film.

Write **25–35** words.

Write your email on the answer sheet.

Famous people

1 Who are these people? Why are they famous? Will they still be famous in five years' time? Why? / Why not?

2 Are you interested in famous people?

Who are you a fan of? How do you find out about them?

3 With a partner, guess the answers to the questions below by choosing A, B or C.

A Emma Watson
B Cesc Fabregas
C Shakira

1 Who was born in 1987?
2 Who met President Obama in 2010?
3 Who has a French grandmother?
4 Who recorded an album at the age of 13?
5 Who went to a football match as a baby?

Grammar   Review of tenses

4 Choose the correct tense.

1 Shakira *has sold / sold* almost 60 million albums since her first one.
2 In 2010, Emma Watson *has become / became* Hollywood's highest paid female star.
3 I think Cesc Fabregas *won't play / doesn't play* again for Arsenal.
4 Shakira loved listening to 'merengue' dance music when she *was growing up / grew up* in Colombia.
5 Emma Watson *talks / is talking* to her co-star Daniel Radcliffe quite often.

G → page 148

5 Who are the most famous man and woman in your country today? Write sentences about them, saying:

– when and where they were born
– what has happened in their lives
– how they became famous
– what they are doing at the moment
– what their lives will be like in five years' time.

6 Tick any tenses you have used in your sentences in exercise 5.

present simple	past continuous
present continuous	present perfect
past simple	future with *will*

Reading

7 Read the article about Emma Watson. Then answer the questions by choosing A, B or C.

EMMA WATSON

Even as a child, Emma Watson wanted to be an actor. From the age of six, she was learning how to dance and sing after school, and was in many school plays. Her first paid acting job was as Hermione in the *Harry Potter* films. She didn't know then how big this project would be!

She often missed school because of *Harry Potter* but she and her co-stars had lessons each day at the places they were filming. She got excellent marks in her exams, which meant she could go to university anywhere. She chose the USA because she could study various subjects together, instead of just one in Britain.

Her student years have been fun and being famous hasn't given her many problems. She's had to speak to journalists since she was nine, so answering students' questions is OK – but she doesn't want her friends to see her as different, which most of them have understood.

Emma earned more than ten million pounds from her *Harry Potter* work and will never need to work for money again. However, she still enjoys acting, as well as working in fashion, which she feels she understands because of her art studies at school.

Daniel Radcliffe (Harry) is special to Emma. During the filming of *Harry Potter* he always understood his job as an actor, but what mattered to her was that he kept everyone else interested in the whole project. Daniel says they are 'very much like brother and sister'.

Emma Watson and Daniel Radcliffe at the opening of a *Harry Potter* film

1 When she was 6, Emma
   A was already able to dance well.
   B took extra lessons outside school.
   C started singing in a school band.

2 Before she played Hermione in *Harry Potter*, Emma
   A earned money from other acting.
   B knew exactly how much work it was.
   C was only in school plays.

3 While she was filming *Harry Potter*, Emma
   A was usually able to get to her school.
   B spent part of her day in a special class.
   C had to study everything by herself.

4 Why did Emma choose to study in the USA?
   A She preferred the courses in American universities.
   B Her marks weren't good enough to study in Britain.
   C The one subject she wanted to study was only available there.

5 During her time at university, Emma
   A has spent a lot of time with journalists.
   B has hated being such a well-known actor.
   C has been able to enjoy a normal life.

6 Why is Emma happy to work in fashion?
   A She has become a bit bored with acting.
   B She needs to earn more money as an adult.
   C She knows something about it after studying art.

7 The article says that Daniel Radcliffe is important to Emma
   A because of what he has done for the *Harry Potter* project.
   B because she thinks of him more as a brother than a friend.
   C because he helped her to understand how to be a better actor.

8 Find examples in the article of five of the tenses listed in exercise 6. Which one isn't included?

1 Do you believe that some people have better luck than others? Why? / Why not?

2 Sports stars often do strange things, like asking for the same tennis ball, putting drinks bottles down in a certain way, or wearing the same shirt. Why do they do this? Can you think of other examples?

3 Answer the questions in this chart.

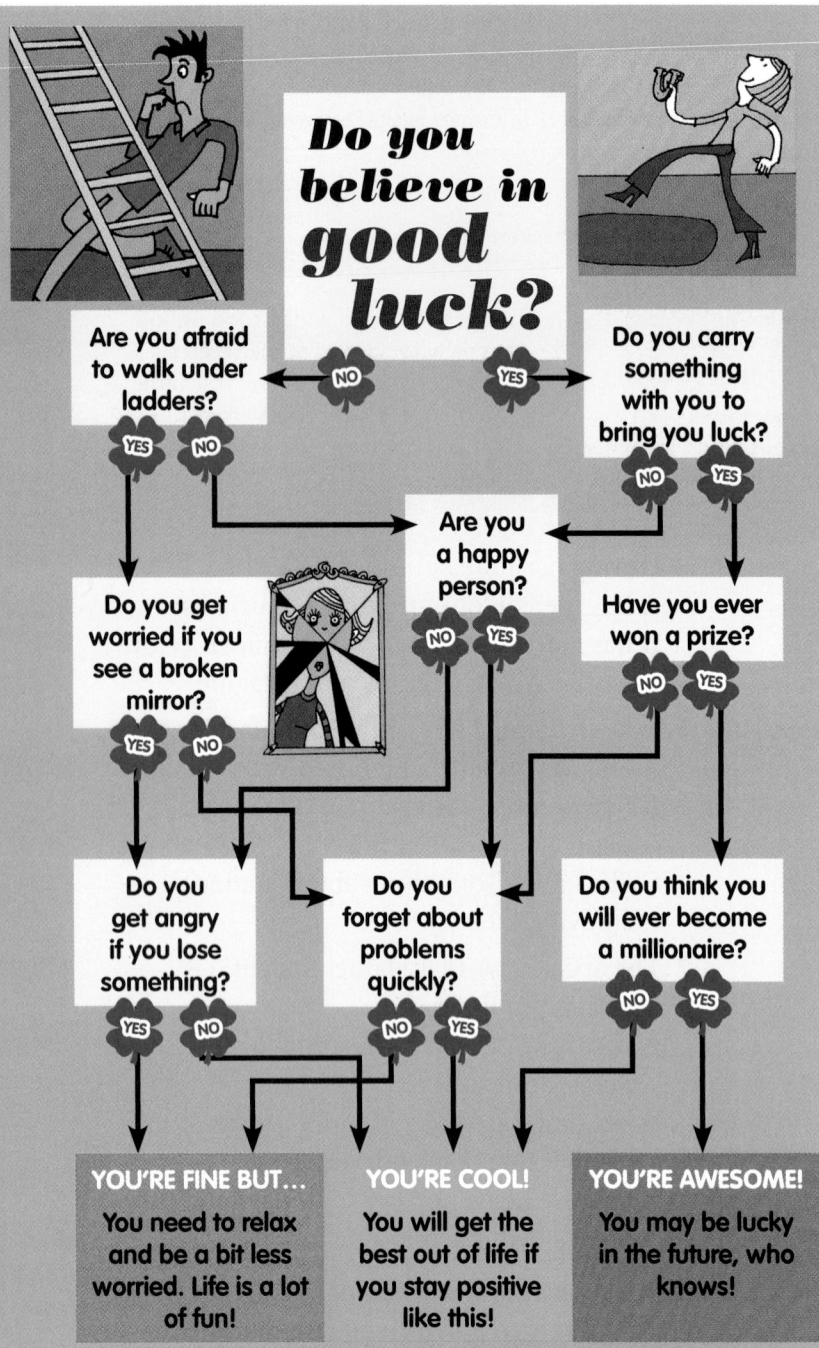

Do you believe in good luck?

Are you afraid to walk under ladders?

Do you carry something with you to bring you luck?

Are you a happy person?

Do you get worried if you see a broken mirror?

Have you ever won a prize?

Do you get angry if you lose something?

Do you forget about problems quickly?

Do you think you will ever become a millionaire?

YOU'RE FINE BUT...
You need to relax and be a bit less worried. Life is a lot of fun!

YOU'RE COOL!
You will get the best out of life if you stay positive like this!

YOU'RE AWESOME!
You may be lucky in the future, who knows!

4 You have had some good luck and have won a competition. Your prize is to visit the city of your choice with one other person. Where will you go? Why? Who will you take?

Listening

5 🔊 **2 30** You will hear a girl called Ruth phoning a radio station about a prize she has won. Listen and complete questions 1–5.

STAR RADIO
COMPETITION

Prize: trip to (**0**) *Venice*

Type of transport: (**1**) ....

Latest date to travel: (**2**) .... *April*

Radio station's address:
(**3**) *47* .... *Road*

Day to visit the office: (**4**) ....

Time to arrive: (**5**) ....

Pronunciation

6 🔊 **2 31** Listen again to how Ruth asks these questions. Underline the word she stresses most in each one.

1 What have I won?
2 When do we have to use them by?
3 Will you send me the tickets?
4 Where are you?
5 When shall I come?
6 What time?

Speaking

7 Now it's your turn to ask questions.

Student A should turn to page 133.
Student B should turn to page 135.

Vocabulary

8 Read the descriptions of some adjectives about people. What is the word for each one? What is the adjective in the yellow box? Explain what it means.

1 Your best friend is this, because they are more important to you than other people. s _ _ _ _ _ _

2 Those who help other people are said to be this. k _ _ _

3 This word describes someone who is not married. s _ _ _ _ _

4 Anyone who gets excellent marks at school is this. c _ _ _ _ _

5 If you are laughing, this is how you feel. h _ _ _ _

Reading

9 Read the sentences about a teenage millionaire. Choose the best word (A, B or C) for each space.

1 Jason Richards has always .... to play computer games.
   A enjoyed
   B loved
   C invited

2 When he was 15, he had a good .... for a new game.
   A example
   B study
   C idea

3 Jason went to several computer .... to talk about his game.
   A stations
   B companies
   C houses

4 Nobody was .... in selling Jason's game.
   A interested
   B ready
   C pleased

5 Jason .... to sell his game himself on the internet.
   A thought
   B agreed
   C decided

6 In less than a year, Jason .... over £1,000,000 in sales.
   A earned
   B paid
   C spent

Spelling spot

ck or k?

- If the vowel before the /k/ sound is short, the spelling is 'ck': *back* *luck*
- With a short double vowel before the /k/ sound, there is no 'c': *look*
- If the vowel sound is long, there is no 'c': *break* *like*
- If a vowel is followed by a consonant, there is no 'c': *milk* *bank*

10 Sort the letters in these words and use them in the sentences below.

o o b
g k n i

k j
a c
t e

c i k
n e
h c

k o
l
c c

l
u y
k c

c t i
s k
t e

1 There's something good on TV at nine o'............................ .
2 Can I borrow your .... to wear to the theatre?
3 Let's phone the .... office now and get some .... for the festival.
4 How .... are you! You've won first prize again!
5 This .... and rice dish is wonderful. Is there any more?

Activity

Millionaire quiz

Answer your teacher's questions and win money for your team!

Units 17–20 Revision

Speaking

1 Ask and answer these questions with a partner.

1 Why do people go on diets?
2 What will you do if you pass *Cambridge English Key*?
3 Where is the city of Salamanca?
4 Which film actors or directors have won an Oscar?
5 Who do you think you will see next weekend?
6 How much fruit do you eat in a week?
7 When is your birthday?
8 What time will today's lesson finish?

Grammar

2 Match a phrase from A with a phrase from B and make conditional sentences.

EXAMPLE: *If I buy a new phone, I'll be able to send photos.*

A	B
1 buy a new phone	invite all my friends
2 get a Saturday job	visit some new websites
3 become famous	go out with my friends
4 eat more healthily	be able to send photos
5 have a party	earn some money
6 do all my homework	get a cup of coffee
7 go on the internet	feel better
8 take a break soon	build a house with a pool

3 Correct any wrong prepositions in this text about the island of Martinique.

Martinique is the largest island on the area of the eastern Caribbean. Over 300,000 people live at the island – many on the capital city, Fort-de-France. People speak French and it is taught on schools.

The mountains on Martinique are old volcanoes. The highest one is Mount Pelée, which is 1,397 metres high. At 1902, Mount Pelée erupted and about 30,000 people were killed.

The weather at Martinique is warm and quite wet – perfect for the farmers to grow bananas in their land. Bananas from Martinique are sent all over the world, so look at the bananas on your fruit bowl. If they are from Martinique, they will have a blue sticker in them.

Vocabulary

4 Decide which word is the odd one out.

1 laptop	internet	robot	website
2 ear	mouth	eye	back
3 email	letter	postcard	envelope
4 German	Japanese	Italian	Spanish
5 prize	exam	test	competition
6 lucky	happy	special	ready

5 Read the sentences about recording a TV programme. Choose the best word (A, B or C) for each space.

1 I wanted to .... a football match on the TV.

   A take   **B** look   **C** watch

2 My sister was .... with me because there was a programme about lions on at the same time.

   A upset   **B** sorry   **C** difficult

3 She .... me to record the programme for her.

   A invited **B** asked   **C** decided

4 By mistake, I chose the .... TV channel.

   A bad   **B** wrong   **C** open

5 My sister was mad when she .... there was a history programme instead of the one about lions.

   A found   **B** turned   **C** kept

Writing

6 Read questions A and B and decide which sentences (1–6 below) go with each question. Then put each set of sentences in order, adding a few more words to make a 35-word email that answers each question.

A

> You saw someone famous when you were in your capital city last week.
> Write an email to your friend, saying:
> - which famous person you saw
> - where you were at the time
> - how you felt.

B

> You would like to invite your friend to a party.
> Write an email to your friend, saying:
> - when you are going to have the party
> - who else you have invited
> - what you would like your friend to bring.

1 Heidi and Lorna can come as well.

2 It was amazing and I couldn't believe it!

3 Could I borrow some of your party albums?

4 It'll be on Saturday 15th November, starting at 8.30 p.m.

5 Tom Cruise walked by just in front of me.

6 I was looking at a painting in an art gallery.

Extra material

1.2 Activity

Questionnaire

Name	
Age	
Address	
Favourite music	
Favourite place(s)	
What makes you laugh?	

3.1 Activity

Question	Student 1	Student 2	Student 3
What time do you get up?	At	At	At
What do you have for breakfast?			
What time do you have lunch?	At	At	At
What do you prefer for lunch?			
What time do you have dinner?	At	At	At
What do you like best for dinner?			

6.2 Activity

Group A

How often do you watch TV?

every night   only at weekends   not often

What is your favourite free-time activity at home?

playing music   reading books

playing chess   seeing friends

playing computer games   something else

....

What is your least favourite free-time activity at home?

....

Add some more questions here:

....

....

....

....

....

Group B

What is your favourite free-time physical activity?

football   swimming

tennis   skateboarding

running   something else

....

How often do you do a physical activity?

every day   three times a week

once a week   less than once a week

What is your least favourite free-time physical activity?

....

Add some more questions here:

....

....

....

....

Exam folder 5
Candidate B questions

Holiday Centre

★ where?

★ what / do?

★ price / adult?

★ open / all year?

★ place / eat?

ARE YOU A WORLD TRAVELLER?

1 How often do you go on holiday?

  A hardly ever
  B once a year
  C twice a year or more

2 How many countries have you visited?

  A two
  B none
  C six or more

3 You win the lottery – where will you go?

  A to Disney World for a month
  B to an expensive hotel in my country
  C on a trip round the world

4 What type of holiday do you like?

  A staying at home doing nothing
  B activity holidays such as sailing
  C lying on a sandy beach and dancing
    at night

5 Your hotel room isn't very nice. Do you

  A complain to the manager?
  B not worry about it?
  C not notice?

6 What do you buy on holiday?

  A presents for all your friends
  B one or two souvenirs
  C some sweets for yourself

7 Do you send postcards?

  A no – never
  B yes – to everyone I know
  C yes – to a few friends

8 Who do you like to go on holiday with?

  A no one – I prefer to be alone
  B my best friend
  C my family

Now turn to page 134 to find your score.

11.1 Exercise 9

College Sports Day

College Sports Field
Saturday 12 June (10.00–3.30)

Football, volleyball and running for everyone.

Win one of 50 T-shirts!

Don't forget your shorts and trainers!

Exam folder 5

Candidate A questions

Cinema

- what / see?
- film / start?
- eat?
- what / address?
- student ticket / £?

16.2 Exercise 4

Student A questions

DAY TRIP FOR STUDENTS

- where?
- when?
- cost?
- transport?
- things to do?

20.2 Exercise 7

Student A questions

Ask Student B about his/her favourite holiday place.

What … favourite holiday place?
Where …?
How … get there?
What … like best about it?

9.2 Activity

ARE YOU A WORLD TRAVELLER?

World Traveller 21–24 points
You really like holidays and enjoy everything about them: buying presents, seeing friends and having fun. But remember, you can have fun at home too!

Key

1	A 1	B 2	C 3
2	A 2	B 1	C 3
3	A 2	B 1	C 3
4	A 1	B 2	C 3
5	A 3	B 2	C 1
6	A 3	B 2	C 1
7	A 1	B 3	C 2
8	A 3	B 2	C 1

Happy Tourist 12–20 points
You like to go to new places. You enjoy quiet holidays with a few friends and you prefer not to spend too much money.

Stay-at-Home 8–11 points
You quite like going away, but you prefer to be with people you know. You are also happy at home. You believe holidays should be relaxing.

16.2 Exercise 4

Student B answers

HAVE FUN ON OUR SCHOOL TRIP TO BRIGHTON

Only £12.50 for students at this school!

Price includes lunch and return coach journey

Free time for shopping or visiting the beach

Saturday 7 April (book by Wednesday 4 April)

16.2 Exercise 5

Student B's questions

Hiking trip
- date?
- price?
- how far?
- what clothes?
- things to take?

Question	Name	Name	Name ....
1 How many hours a night do you sleep?			
2 How many hours did you sleep last night?			
3 Do you sleep on your back, your side or your front?			
4 Do you remember your dreams?			
5 Have you ever had a bad dream?			
6 What do you do if you wake up in the night?			
7 What do you do if you have problems getting to sleep?			

16.2 Exercise 5

Student A's answers

TAKE SOME EXERCISE ON OUR FULL-DAY HIKING TRIP!

20-kilometre path in the beautiful Hassett Hills

Bring a water bottle and picnic food
Dress for rain and wind!

Saturday April 14, bus leaves 7.15 (back 21.00)

£13.75 including transport

20.2 Exercise 7

Student B questions

Ask Student A about his/her luckiest moment.

What … was your luckiest moment?
When … happen?
Why … happen?
How … feel?
What … do afterwards?

19.2 Exercise 5

	Monday	Tuesday	Wednesday	Thursday	Friday
9.00	German Grammar		Russian Reading		Russian Grammar
10.00		German Writing			Russian Writing
11.00			Russian Conversation		
12.00	Russian Listening			German Reading	
1.00	LUNCH				
2.00			German Listening		
3.00	German Conversation				

Grammar folder

Unit 1

Yes/No questions in the present

- With **have got**, *have* comes first and *got* comes after the subject.
  Have *you* **got** *any money with you?*

- With **be**, the verb comes first.
  Is *Giulio one of your friends?*

- With **can**, this verb comes first and the main verb comes after the subject.
  Can *I borrow your music magazine?*

- With **other verbs**, we start the question with *Do* or *Does* and the main verb comes after the subject.
  Do *you* **want** *a cup of coffee?*
  Does *Sandro* **help** *you with your homework?*

1A Change the word order to make Yes/No questions.

1 got / my phone / you / have
   Have you got my phone?
2 tomorrow / your sister / come / can
3 Carmen and Maria / are / Brazil / from
4 like / dogs / you / do
5 it / time / to go / is
6 Arturo / catch / does / the same bus

Wh- questions in the present

- With **be**, **have got** and **can**, the verb comes after the question word.
  What's the time?
  Who **have** *you* **got** *in your maths class?*
  How **can** *I get to your house?*

- With **other verbs**, *do* or *does* comes after the question word. The subject comes next and the main verb comes after the subject.
  Why **do you want** *my phone number?*
  When **does Jana get** *home?*

1B Make Wh- questions. Add the subject you if you need it.

1 When / meet me / can
   When can you meet me?
2 How / get to school / do
3 Where / your house / is
4 What / in your bag / have got
5 Why / angry / are
6 Who / know / Ingrid / does

Suggestions

- We use **Why don't/doesn't ...** to make suggestions.
  Why don't *we meet at school?*
  Why doesn't *Ruth come with us?*

- We also use **How about ...** to make suggestions. (Use the *-ing* verb after *How about*.)
  How about *seeing a film tonight?*

Unit 2

Some/any

- We use **_some_** with uncountable nouns in affirmative sentences.
  I've got **some** chocolate.

- We use **_some_** with countable nouns in affirmative sentences.
  That shop has got **some** new computer games.

- We use **_some_** for a request.
  Can I look at **some** trainers?

- We always use **_any_** in negative sentences.
  We don't sell **any** magazines here.

- We usually use **_any_** in questions.
  Have you got **any** city maps?

2 Complete the sentences with _some_ or _any_.

  1 I'd like _some_ tennis balls, please.
  2 There aren't .... cheap DVDs here.
  3 Have you got .... shops near your flat?
  4 Can I buy .... apples?
  5 I want .... lemon shampoo.
  6 Is there .... juice left?
  7 We've got .... cameras in the sale.
  8 Do you get .... emails about online shopping?

Unit 3

Present simple

We use the present simple to talk about:

- what we do every day
  I **have breakfast** at 7.30 a.m.

- facts
  Bookshops often **sell** birthday cards.
  Cats **eat** fish.

affirmative
I/You/We/They **drink** coffee. He/She/It **drinks** water.

question
What **do** I/you/we/they **eat**? What **does** he/she/it **drink**?

negative
I/You/We/They **don't eat (do not eat)** potatoes. He/She/It **doesn't drink (does not drink)** water.

3A Complete the sentences using the verb in brackets.

  1 I _prefer_ (prefer) coffee to tea.
  2 .... Pete really .... (hate) carrots?
  3 Both Katie and Jack .... (love) chocolate.
  4 My brother .... (not eat) fish.
  5 Rafael .... (go) to restaurants three times a week.
  6 .... you usually .... (go) to a party at New Year?
  7 Supermarkets .... (not sell) computers.

Telling the time

Asking the time	Saying what the time is
What time is it? What's the time? Could you tell me the time, please?	It's ... 7.05 seven (oh) five *or* five past seven 7.10 seven ten *or* ten past seven 7.15 seven fifteen *or* (a) quarter past seven 7.25 seven twenty-five *or* twenty-five past seven 7.30 seven thirty *or* half past seven 7.35 seven thirty-five *or* twenty-five to eight 7.45 seven forty-five *or* (a) quarter to eight 7.50 seven fifty *or* ten to eight 8.00 eight o'clock

For other times, for example 7.03, 7.17, 7.43, we say <u>minutes</u> to/past seven/eight:
three minutes past seven
twenty-seven minutes to eight

3B Match the times with the clocks.

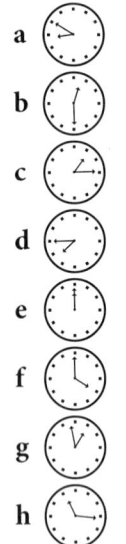

a
b
c
d
e
f
g
h

1 one fifteen   *c*
2 two minutes to one
3 quarter to eight
4 ten to nine
5 midday
6 sixteen minutes past eleven
7 half past twelve
8 four o'clock

Unit 4

Past simple

We use the past simple to talk about:

- things that happened in the past
  Men **travelled** from all over the world.

- past states
  He **liked** gold.

The verb *be*

affirmative
I/He/She/It **was** right. You/We/They **were** right.

question
Was I/he/she/it right? **Were** you/we/they right? Yes, I/he/she/it **was**. Yes, you/we/they **were**. No, I/he/she/it **wasn't (was not)**. No, you/we/they **weren't (were not)**.

negative
I/He/She/It **wasn't (was not)** right. You/We/They **weren't (were not)** right.

Regular verbs, e.g. *arrive*

affirmative
I/You/He/She/It/We/They **arrived** home.

question
Did I/you/he/she/it/we/they **arrive** home? Yes, I/you/he/she/it/we/they **did**. No, I/you/he/she/it/we/they **didn't (did not)**.

Irregular verbs, e.g. *see*

Many verbs are irregular in the past tense, for example *see – saw*. See the list on page 159.

affirmative

I/You/He/She/It/We/They **saw** Skookum Jim.

question

Did I/you/he/she/it/we/they **see** Skookum Jim?
Yes, I/you/he/she/it/we/they **did**.
No, I/you/he/she/it/we/they **didn't (did not)**.

negative

I/You/He/She/It/We/They **didn't see** Skookum Jim.

4 Complete the sentences using the verb in brackets in the past simple.

1 How long *did you stay* (you stay) in London?
2 .... (you enjoy) the boat trip?
3 The coach .... (not arrive) back at school on time.
4 My mother .... (make) me some sandwiches for the trip.
5 We .... (travel) to Rome by plane.
6 What .... (Lyn see) in India?
7 When .... (Pete go) to Peru?
8 He .... (not speak) Spanish on his holiday.
9 How much .... (she spend) on holiday?
10 Where .... (she buy) that present?

Unit 5
Conjunctions

and   but   or   because

We use conjunctions to join two clauses or sentences to make one longer sentence.

Sentence A   *Polar bears weigh from 350 to 650 kg.*   **AND**
Sentence B   *Polar bears are two and a half to three metres long.*

Polar bears weigh from 350 to 650 kg and are two and a half to three metres long.

- We use **and** when we want to *add* one fact or idea to another.
  *I saw a polar bear **and** there were two cubs with her.*

- We use **but** when there is a *contrast* between the two facts or ideas.
  *I saw a polar bear **but** he was asleep.*

- We use **or** when there is a *choice* or an alternative fact or idea.
  *You can go to the zoo **or** stay at home.*

- We use **because** to say *why* things happen.
  *I gave the cat some fish **because** it was hungry.*
  ***Because** the cat was hungry, I gave it some fish.*

5 Complete these sentences using *and, but, or* or *because*.

1 Dogs like going for long walks *and* also playing with balls.
2 My cat is getting old, ... she still climbs walls.
3 I took my dog to the park .... she needed a walk.
4 Elephants in India work in the early morning .... sleep in the afternoon.
5 .... I live in a flat, I can't have a pet.
6 Would you like a cat as a pet .... do you prefer dogs?

Unit 6

Comparative and superlative adjectives

adjective	comparative	superlative
short words		
tall	taller	the tallest
big	bigger	the biggest
easy	easier	the easiest
long words		
expensive	more/less expensive	the most/least expensive
exceptions		
good	better	the best
bad	worse	the worst

*Theme parks in the USA are **bigger than** the ones in the UK.*
*My ticket was **more expensive** this year **than** last.*
*I think Disneyland is **the best** theme park.*

6 Complete these sentences with either the comparative or the superlative form of the adjective in brackets.

1 The park was _____busier_____ (busy) on Saturday than on Sunday.
2 Children's tickets are usually _____ (expensive) than adults' tickets.
3 The ride I went on was _____ (tall) in the park.
4 My uncle is _____ (rich) than I am, so he paid for my trip to Disneyland Paris.
5 It was _____ (sunny) on Tuesday than it was on Monday.
6 _____ (popular) ride was in Japan.
7 The ride was _____ (fast) in the park.
8 The theme park was _____ (expensive) than the one I usually go to.
9 Some theme parks are _____ (good) than others.
10 Our hotel was _____ (bad) in the area.

Unit 7

Simple and continuous tenses

- We use the **present continuous** to talk about **something temporary**, that is true now but not in general. Compare these sentences:
  I'm wearing a skirt today because I've got an interview.
  I usually wear jeans.

- We can use the **past continuous** to talk about a **temporary situation in the past**. Compare this with the **past simple**, which we use for a **completed action**:
  Most people were wearing Roma shirts at last week's match.
  Roma won last week's match 2–0.

- We also use the **past continuous** to talk about **something which continued before or after** another action.
  I was shopping for shoes when my mobile phone rang.

7 Put the verbs in brackets in the correct past tense.

1 Helena _____was looking at_____ (look at) jackets when I _____met_____ (meet) her.
2 I _____ (try on) some new earrings when I _____ (lose) one.
3 John _____ (wait) to pay when he _____ (remember) his wallet was at home.
4 Martina _____ (choose) her meal when the fire alarm _____ (start).
5 Maria _____ (study) in the garden when it _____ (begin) to rain.
6 When my friend _____ (phone), I _____ (have) a shower, so she _____ (leave) me a message.

Unit 8

Modal verbs 1

must and *have to*

- In the present, we use **must** and **have to** to talk about obligation.
  *You **must** finish your homework before you go out.*
  *James **has to** work at the hotel every night this week.*

- In the past, we cannot use **must**. Instead, we use **had to**.
  *I **had to** queue for twenty minutes at the cinema.*

may and *might*

- We use **may** and **might** to talk about possibility.
  *I **may** come with you tonight.*
  *There **might** be some tickets left for the concert.*

can and *could*

- In the present, we use **can** to talk about ability.
  *I **can** ride a bike.* (= I know how to ride a bike.)
  *I **can't** drive.* (= I don't know how to drive.)

- In the past tense, we use **could** and **couldn't**.
  *Sam **could** play the guitar before he was 12.*
  *He **couldn't** read music when he was at school.*

8 Complete the sentences using each modal verb once only.

> can   can't   ~~couldn't~~   has to   had to
> may   might   must

1 Giacomo didn't know how to find the cinema.
  Giacomo _couldn't_ find the cinema.

2 Perhaps I'll borrow that DVD from Jo.
  I .... borrow that DVD from Jo.

3 Don't forget to wear a white shirt and black trousers for tonight's concert.
  You .... remember to wear a white shirt and black trousers for tonight's concert.

4 Sorry, I'm busy next Friday, so it's not possible to go out.
  I .... go out next Friday because I'm busy.

5 The front door of the club was shut.
  We .... use the back door of the club.

6 The singer can't do tonight's show because she's flying home early.
  The singer .... fly home early, so she can't do tonight's show.

7 Does the theatre website have more information, maybe?
  The theatre .... have more information on its website.

8 I know how to play the drums.
  I .... play the drums.

Unit 9

The future with *going to*

- We use *to be going to* to talk about plans and arrangements which are definite.

affirmative

I	am	
He/She/It	is	going to swim every day.
You/We/They	are	

question

Am	I	
Is	he/she/it	going to walk up the hill?
Are	you/we/they	

negative

I	'm not	
He/she/it	isn't	going to sleep in a tent.
We/you/they	aren't	

question

Aren't I/we/you/they	
Isn't he/she	going to book a room?

Note: Am I not becomes Aren't I.

I'm going to stay in Tokyo when I'm in Japan.
He isn't going to spend a lot of money on an expensive hotel.
Sam's going to take one small suitcase with him when he goes on holiday next week.

The future with *will*

- We use *will* to give information about the future or guess what will happen in the future.

affirmative and negative

I/you/he/she/it/we/they will / will not (won't) travel.

question and negative

Will/won't I/you/he/she/it/we/they travel?

One day people will live on the Moon.

- We often use *will* with sentences beginning *I think …* and with adverbs like *certainly* (100%), *definitely* (100%), *probably* (about 70%) and *possibly* (about 40%).
I think I will / I'll get a holiday job next year.
I will / I'll probably work in a hotel.
I don't think I'll earn a lot of money.
I probably won't spend a lot of money.

9 Use *be going to* or *will* in these sentences.

1 I ___am going to___ go to Sicily for my holidays next month – I already have my ticket.
2 Congratulations! I hear you and Theresa _____ get married.
3 What _____ you study when you go to university?
4 I _____ have a party on Saturday – do you want to come?
5 The Lunar Hotel _____ probably be the first hotel in space.
6 Claire thinks she _____ definitely go to Australia next year.
7 Maria _____ fly to South Africa next week and she's very excited.
8 I don't think people _____ enjoy living on the moon very much.
9 I think flying _____ become much cheaper in the future.
10 Maria _____ buy a new camera for her holiday.

Unit 10

The passive

present simple passive	am/is/are (not)	+ past participle painted
past simple passive	was/were (not)	seen built made

The sentence *I painted my bedroom black* is active.

The sentence *My bedroom was painted black* is passive.

- We often use **by** with the passive to tell us who did the action.
  My bedroom was painted by my father.

- The past participle of regular verbs ends in -*ed*, like the past tense.

- See page 159 for a list of past participles of irregular verbs.

10 Make sentences in the passive using A, B and C.

  EXAMPLE: *The song 'Imagine' was sung by John Lennon.*

A	B	C
1 The song 'Imagine'	stop	by J. K. Rowling.
2 Portuguese	give	in sweet shops.
3 The Pyramids	win	to swim by my father.
4 The *Harry Potter* books	sing	by Spain in 2010.
5 Presents	sell	in Brazil.
6 Spaghetti	teach	by John Lennon.
7 I	build	on birthdays.
8 Chocolate	eat	by the Egyptians.
9 The World Cup	speak	all over the world.
10 The car	write	by the police.

Unit 11

Verbs in the -*ing* form

- The -*ing* form is added to the infinitive of the verb:
  play + -ing = playing   *I enjoy **playing** tennis.*

- Different groups of verbs are followed by a verb in the -*ing* form:
  - verbs of liking and disliking:
    enjoy, like*, love*, hate, don't mind
    *Sam hates **losing** tennis matches.*
  - verbs of doing:
    keep, spend time
    *He kept **asking** questions.*
    *We spent the day **fishing**.*
  - verbs of starting and stopping:
    begin*, start*, finish, stop
    *We finished **playing** just before lunchtime.*
    *They stopped **talking** immediately.*

* these verbs can also take an infinitive with no change of meaning:
  *I like **to listen** to the football scores at 5 o'clock.*
  *The team starts **to train** harder two days before a match.*

11 Complete the sentences with the -*ing* form of the verb in brackets.

1 I don't mind __coming__ (come) with you to basketball training.
2 I spent yesterday afternoon .... (swim) – what did you do?
3 Harry likes .... (choose) the team himself.
4 Do you enjoy .... (use) the gym equipment?
5 Kate hates .... (sit) and .... (watch) – she prefers to play in every match.
6 I hope Jenny doesn't mind .... (get) wet – it's going to rain!
7 How about .... (run) in the park before dinner?
8 Dan enjoys .... (ride) his horse every morning.

Unit 12

Pronouns

- There are different forms of personal pronouns:

subject pronouns	object pronouns	reflexive pronouns
I	me	myself
you	you	yourself
he, she, it	him, her, it	himself, herself, itself
we	us	ourselves
you	you	yourselves
they	them	themselves

- These are also pronouns:

things	people
something	somebody / someone
anything	anybody / anyone
everything	everybody / everyone
nothing	nobody / no one

- Remember that you must use a positive verb with *nothing*, *nobody* and *no one*.
  I've got nothing to read on the train.
  (= **I haven't got anything** to read on the train.)

12 Complete the second sentences using suitable pronouns from those above.

1 Jenny came to the party alone.
Jenny didn't come with _____*anyone*_____ .

2 David knows what happened.
I've told David _____ .

3 There's a phone message for you.
_____ from work called you.

4 I'm sure I can help.
There must be _____ I can do.

5 All my family came to the party.
_____ in my family was at the party.

6 The bus was empty.
There was _____ on the bus.

Unit 13

Adverbs of degree: *enough* and *too*

adjective + *enough*
*I don't want to go swimming. It isn't **hot enough**.*
***too* + adjective**
*Can you close the window? It's **too cold** in here.*

- We can also use *to* + infinitive after *too* and *enough* with adjectives or adverbs.
  *It's hot enough **to fry** an egg.*
  *It's too far **to walk**.*

13 Complete the sentences with *too* or *enough* and the adjective in brackets.

1 It's ____*too dangerous*____ (dangerous) to go outside if there's a tornado.

2 It's _____ (dry) here to grow tomatoes.

3 It's _____ (wet) to go for a walk.

4 The sun isn't _____ (hot) to heat the water in the pool.

5 It isn't _____ (cold) to wear a coat.

6 The wind was _____ (strong) to go sailing.

Unit 14

Position of adjectives

- Sometimes we use two or more adjectives together. We put the 'opinion' adjective(s) first, and the 'fact' adjective(s) after.
  The story is about a nice young man.

- If there is more than one fact adjective, there are rules about the order they go in.

1 What's it like? opinion	2 How big? size	3 How old? age	4 What colour?	5 Where's it from? nationality	6 What kind?	NOUN
great		new			electric	guitar
	tall			American		boy
	large		white			house

14 Put the adjectives in brackets in the correct place.

1 a old building (lovely)
   a lovely old building
2 a wooden reading desk (large)
3 a popular American magazine (music)
4 an interesting story (adventure)
5 a friendly detective (young)
6 my French comic book (favourite)

Unit 15

Present perfect

- The present perfect is formed with:
  have ('ve) / has ('s) + past participle
  *I **have worked** as a waiter.*
  *I**'ve seen** an interesting job advert.*
  *The manager **has sent** me an application form.*

- Be careful with the past participle forms of irregular verbs! See the table on page 159.

- We use the present perfect
  - for something that started in the past but is still true:
    *I**'ve broken** my arm.* (= it's still broken)
  - for something that happened recently (but we don't know when):
    *Alan**'s left** for work.*

- The words *for* and *since* show how long something has been true:
  *I've worked here **for** four months.*
  *I've worked here **since** August.*

- The word *just* shows that something happened only a short time ago:
  *The bus has **just** gone.*

15 Rewrite these sentences using the present perfect and *just*.

1 Tyler began working as a chef last week.
   Tyler has just begun working as a chef.
2 Joan took the customer's order five minutes ago.
3 Giorgio recently became a doctor.
4 Someone left a message for you a couple of minutes ago.
5 I saw our dentist crossing the street a few seconds ago.
6 I spoke to the engineer on the phone a few minutes ago.

Unit 16

Modal verbs 2

should

- We can use **should** (and **shouldn't**) to give advice.
  *You **should** walk to school – it's good exercise.*
  *You **shouldn't** come by car – it's better to walk.*

must and have to

- We use **must** and **have to** to talk about obligation.
  *You **must** buy a ticket before you get on the bus.*
  *We **had to** take a taxi because we missed the bus.*
- We use **mustn't** to talk about things that aren't allowed.
  *You **mustn't** get on the bus without a ticket.*

need to

- We use **need to** to talk about something necessary.
  *You **need to** check the train times on Saturdays.*

don't have to and needn't

- We use **don't have to** and **needn't** when something is not necessary (when there is no obligation).
  *You **don't have to** show your ticket to the driver.*
  *You **needn't** wait for me on the platform. I'll see you on the train.*

16 **Find the pairs of sentences that have the same meaning.**

1 You don't have to book a seat on the flight. *6*
2 You mustn't make any phone calls during the flight.
3 You should take something to read on the flight.
4 You need to arrive early for the flight.
5 You cannot use your mobile during the flight.
6 You needn't book a place on the flight. *1*
7 You shouldn't arrive just before the flight leaves.
8 Why not bring a book for the flight?

Unit 17

Infinitive of purpose

- We often use the infinitive (**to** + **verb**) to say *why* we do things.
  Liz needed a new bed.
  She went to a large department store.
  *Liz went to a large department store **to buy** a new bed.*

17 **Make one sentence using a phrase from A and a phrase from B.**

EXAMPLE: *I went to the bus stop to catch a bus to town.*

A	B
1 I went to the bus stop	to pass the exam.
2 I turned on the radio	to buy a computer game.
3 I went to the museum	to take to the party.
4 I borrowed some money	to see an exhibition.
5 I worked hard	to listen to the news.
6 I bought a cake	to catch a bus to town.

Unit 18

First conditional

- The first conditional is formed with:
  If + present tense + *will* + infinitive
- We use this structure to express a possible condition.
  If he **goes** swimming every day, he**'ll get fit**.
  (comma after the 'if' clause)
  We can also say:
  He**'ll get fit if** he **goes** swimming every day.
  (no comma)

18 Complete these sentences.

1 If you (sleep) ___*sleep*___ with the window open, you (sleep much better) ___*you'll sleep much better*___ .

2 If you (eat) .... an apple a day, you (not get ill) ....

3 If you (not eat) .... too many sweets, you (not get fat) ....

4 You (lose) .... weight if you (stop eating snacks) ....

5 Your teeth (stay) .... healthy if you (visit the dentist) .... once a year.

6 You (have) .... bad dreams if you (eat cheese in the evening) ....

Unit 19

Prepositions of place

- We use **at** to talk about a specific place:
  *We're meeting **at** the stadium.*
  *Who's that **at** the bus stop?*
- We also use **at** to talk about places where you study or work:
  *Jane's studying Greek **at** university.*
- We use **on** to talk about where something is:
  *My bag is **on** the table.*
  *There's another bottle of lemonade **on** the shelf.*
- We can use **in** or **on** with street names (but not for addresses):
  *The bookshop's **in** Bridge Street.*
  *I live **on** Madison Avenue.*
  *I live **at** 495 Madison Avenue.*
- We use **in** to talk about where something is:
  *There's a present for you **in** this box.*
  *Carrie's **in** the garden if you want to speak to her.*
- We use **in** with cities and countries:
  *I studied French **in** Paris.*
  *Uppsala is **in** Sweden.*

19A Complete the sentences with *at*, *in* or *on*.

1 I left my coat ___*on*___ the chair. Could you get it?

2 Where's Punta Arenas? – It's .... Chile.

3 I'm meeting Sam .... the college gates.

4 Robert is living .... London.

5 How long will you be .... work?
  – I won't be free before six.

6 There's a new jazz club .... Hilton Road.

7 We're living .... 16 Pinewood Road until April.

8 Is that your pen .... the floor?

9 Nick is studying Biology .... Leeds University.

10 How much is the red guitar .... the window?

Prepositions of time

- We use **at** with exact times, periods of time, meals and festivals:
  *Come round **at** five o'clock.*
  *We'll be free **at** the weekend.*
  *Kelly sat with John **at** breakfast.*
  *I'm doing a French course **at** Easter.*

- We use **in** with centuries, years, months, seasons and parts of the day:
  *Cornish was spoken **in** the 18th century.*
  *The book first came out **in** 2003.*
  *I went to Milan **in** January.*
  *It gets very busy here **in** summer.*
  *Shall we meet **in** the morning?*

- We use **on** with days of the week, dates and special days:
  *I have Spanish classes **on** Tuesday and Thursday.*
  *The concert will be **on** 27th June.*
  *I always have a party **on** my birthday.*

19B Complete the sentences with *at, in* or *on*.

1 Will I see you __*in*__ March?
2 My birthday's .... September 30th.
3 Dani's going to visit us .... Christmas.
4 What do you like to do .... the evening?
5 I can't go to the theatre .... Saturday.
6 This house was built .... 1872.
7 Your appointment is .... 3.15.
8 You can't swim here .... winter.

Unit 20
Review of tenses

Present simple
I like Daniel Radcliffe.
Most people wear jeans.
→ **See Unit 3**

Present continuous
I'm reading an adventure story.
→ **See Unit 7**

Past simple
Leonardo da Vinci designed a helicopter.
→ **See Unit 4**

Past continuous
We were having a picnic when it started to rain.
→ **See Unit 7**

Present perfect
I've just had a text message from my brother.
→ **See Unit 15**

Future with *will*
We'll meet in London for your birthday.
→ **See Unit 9**

Future with *going to*
I'm going to have a bath and go to bed.
→ **See Unit 9**

20 Complete the sentences in the correct tense, using a verb from the box.

ask	drive	eat	go out	make	sing
stop	win				

1 Before she was famous, Pink ......*sang*...... in an all-girl band called *Choice*.
2 Adele .... a new album – it'll go on sale next month.
3 Do you think Zac Efron .... with Lily Collins at the moment?
4 Barack Obama and the President of Russia .... a burger after their meeting.
5 The police .... Justin Timberlake when he .... too fast.
6 Meryl Streep .... an Oscar as Best Actress in 2012 for the film *The Iron Lady*.
7 While she is on tour, Katy Perry .... for white and purple flowers to welcome her in every dressing room.

Vocabulary folder

Here is a list of words and phrases from each unit of Objective Key. Try to learn their spelling and how you can use them. Some words are in more than one unit, to help you remember them.

Unit 1

Things you do with friends
borrow a DVD/money, etc. from someone
chat about football, make-up, etc.
forget/remember a birthday, etc.
get/send a text message
go on the PlayStation
go shopping
lend someone a DVD/ magazine, etc.
tell someone a lie

Asking and answering
OK …
Right …
So …
And …
Well …
That's easy.
That's difficult.
That's right.

Adjectives
amazing
angry
boring
free
funny
great
happy
horrible
ill
lucky
pleased
popular
sad
sick
special
true
worried
wrong

Unit 2

Places to go shopping
bookshop
chemist
department store
market
sports shop
supermarket

Things to buy – uncountable nouns
bread
cheese
chocolate
fish
ice cream
leather
make-up
medicine
money
pasta
shampoo
soap

Things to buy – countable nouns
apple
ball
birthday card
book
box (boxes)
DVD
camera
carrot
dish (dishes)
ice cream
magazine
map
potato (potatoes)
sandwich
shoes
sweets
T-shirt
tennis racket
tomato (tomatoes)
toy
trainers

Short phrases
No problem
Of course
OK
You're welcome

Unit 3

Food
apple
banana
beans
biscuits
bread
burger
cake
carrot
cheese
chicken
chilli
chips
chocolate
curry
egg
fish
fruit
grape
ice cream
meat
mushroom
onion
orange
pasta
pizza
potato
rice
salad
sandwich
soup
steak
tomato
yogurt

Drink
coffee
juice
lemonade
milk
tea
water

Meals
breakfast
lunch
dinner
snack

Verbs
drink
eat

Verb + noun
have a drink
have (a) pizza
make a meal

Unit 4

Regular verbs
(Irregular verbs see p151)
arrive
carry
decide
email
help
like
listen
look

open
pick up
play
return
show
stay
stop
study
travel
use
visit
want
work

Unit 5

Animals
bear
bird
cat
chicken
cow
dog
duck
elephant
fish
horse
lion
monkey

Verb + noun
do homework
do nothing
do the cooking
do the shopping
make an appointment
make a cake
make a phone call
spend money
spend time
take a photograph
take an exam
take the dog for a walk

Unit 6

Adjectives
angry
attractive
bad
beautiful
big
boring
bright
cheap
closed
comfortable
easy
expensive
fast
good
happy
high
horrible
large
long
modern
new
old
open
popular
short
small
tall
thin
tidy

Adverbs
badly
carefully
cheaply
early
fast
hard
late
later
long
near
quietly
soon
well

Things you do in your free time
go to the cinema
go cycling
go dancing
go shopping
go skateboarding
go swimming

have a party
listen to music
play chess
play computer games
play table tennis
read comics
see friends
watch TV

Unit 7

Clothes
baseball cap
belt
boots (a pair of boots)
button
coat
dress
hat
jacket
jeans
pocket
shirt
shoes (a pair of shoes)
shorts (a pair of shorts)
size
skirt
socks
suit
sweater
T-shirt
trainers (a pair of trainers)
trousers (a pair of trousers)

Jewellery
earring (a pair of earrings)
necklace
ring

Adjectives
cheap
clean
cotton
dirty
expensive
gold
heavy

large
leather
light
long
new
old
silver
short
small
unfashionable
wool

Unit 8

Talking about films
actor
film
movie
music
scene
sound effects
story

Adjectives
amazing
awesome
excellent
exciting
famous
well-known

Music
album
band
bass
concert
drums
festival
guitar
lights
piano
singer
speakers

Short phrases
☹
Never mind.
That's bad.
That's a shame.
What a pity.

☺
Cool!
Fantastic!
Thanks a lot.
That's great!

Unit 9

Kinds of holiday
a beach/camping/
  cycling/sightseeing/
  walking holiday

Places
campsite
holiday home
holiday centre
hotel

Verbs
book a hotel, holiday
catch a plane, bus,
  train
go/travel by plane,
  by car, by boat
go sightseeing

Nouns
guidebook
journey
luggage
map
passport
suitcase
ticket
tour

Unit 10

The home
bathroom
bedroom
dining room
garage
hall
kitchen
living room

Things in a room
bed
bookshelf
carpet
chair

computer
curtains
desk
DVD player
floor
lamp
light
mirror
pillow
poster
sofa
TV
wardrobe

Materials
cotton
glass
gold
leather
metal
paper
plastic
silver
wood
wool

Adjectives
big
double
expensive
hard
high
little
long
low
narrow
new
quiet
short
single
soft
wide

Colours
black
blue
brown
green
grey
orange

pink
purple
red
white
yellow

Unit 11

Sports
baseball
basketball
football
horse-riding
sailing
skiing
snowboarding
surfing
swimming
volleyball

More sports words
ball
basket
bat
board
boots
competition
court
exercise
glove(s)
goal
match
net
racket
stadium
team

Unit 12

Family
aunt
brother
cousin
dad
daughter
father
grandchild
granddaughter
grandfather
(granddad)

grandmother
(grandma)
grandson
mother
mum
parent
sister
son
uncle

Unit 13

Weather
cloud(y)
cold
dry
fog(gy)
hot
ice/icy
rain(y)/raining
snow(y)
storm(y)
sun(ny)
tornado
warm
wet
wind(y)

Unit 14

Kinds of reading
material
adventure story
book
comic
detective story
funny story
love story
picture book
science fiction book

Saying what you think
I think it's awesome,
  brilliant, cool, great.
It's horrible, terrible,
  boring, crazy, strange.
It isn't very exciting,
  interesting.
It's OK / all right.
It isn't boring.

Subjects
art
geography
history
languages
maths
music
science
sport

Unit 15

Jobs
actor
chef
cleaner
dentist
doctor
engineer
farmer
footballer
journalist
nurse
photographer
police officer
receptionist
secretary
shop assistant
teacher
tennis player
tour guide
waiter

People at work
boss
colleague
manager
staff

Unit 16

Transport – nouns
airport
bicycle (bike)
boat
bus
car
coach
helicopter
horse

plane
ship
taxi
train

Transport – verbs
board
catch
drive
fly
get (on/off)
park
ride
sail
take off

Free-time activities –
verb + noun
climb a hill
fly a kite
have a picnic
kick a football
throw a Frisbee
visit a museum

Unit 17

Technology
battery
calculator
computer
email address
gadget
internet
laptop
mobile phone
program
robot
smartphone
text (message)
video
web page
website

Verbs
be/go online
call
chat
check email
download
email

text
turn on

Verb + noun
get a bus
get a job
give a party
give someone a call
have a good time
have a job
have a party
have friends
make a film
make a noise
make friends
see a film
see friends
watch a film
watch TV

Unit 18

Parts of the body
arm
back
ear
eye
foot
hair
hand
head
leg
mouth
neck
nose

Health
ambulance
chemist
doctor
hospital
medicine
nurse
sick
temperature

Verb + noun
have a broken arm
      a cold
      a cut
      a headache

a sore throat
stomach ache
toothache

Other verb phrases
be/feel sick
break a leg, arm, etc.
get better
get fit
go on a diet
go to sleep
have an accident
have a bad dream
hurt your arm
keep healthy
sleep well
wake up

Unit 19

Communication
email
envelope
Facebook
letter
mobile phone
note
phone message
postcard
stamp
telephone
text message

Languages
Arabic
Chinese
Cornish
Danish
Dutch
French
Gaelic
German
Greek
Italian
Japanese
Norwegian
Polish
Portuguese
Russian
Spanish

Swedish
Turkish
Welsh

Unit 20

Winning – nouns
competition
luck
prize

Adjectives
angry
awesome
broken
clever
famous
happy
kind
lucky
married
positive
single
special
worried

Practice for *Key* Writing Part 6

Unit 1

Read the descriptions of some adjectives about people and things.

What is the word for each one?

The first letter is already there. There is one space for each other letter in the word.

Example:

0 You can use this word to describe someone with lots of friends. p _ _ _ _ _ _

Answer: | **0** | *popular*

1 This is what you are if you aren't busy and you are available to see friends. f _ _ _

2 If you are pleased about something, you feel this. h _ _ _ _

3 When something is not correct, it is this. w _ _ _ _

4 This is another way of saying someone is ill. s _ _ _

5 When something makes you laugh, it is this. f _ _ _ _

Unit 2

Read the descriptions of some things you can buy in a department store.

What is the word for each one?

The first letter is already there. There is one space for each other letter in the word.

Example:

0 When you wash your hands, you use some of this. s _ _ _

Answer: | **0** | *soap*

1 You can take pictures of your friends with this. c _ _ _ _ _

2 Young children like playing with these. t _ _ _

3 You can wash your hair with this. s _ _ _ _ _ _

4 You hold this above your head when it is raining. u _ _ _ _ _ _ _

5 This has a picture on the front and may have a birthday message inside. c _ _ _

Unit 3

Read the descriptions of some things you can have for lunch.

What is the word for each one?

The first letter is already there. There is one space for each other letter in the word.

Example:

0 This is round and has cheese and tomatoes on it. p _ _ _ _

Answer: | **0** | *pizza*

1 Oranges, apples and bananas are examples of this. f _ _ _ _

2 This usually has green vegetables in it and is very healthy. s _ _ _ _

3 You can have a slice of this sweet food for dessert. c _ _ _

4 This Italian food can be long or short and often comes with a tomato or meat sauce. p _ _ _ _

5 You eat this from a bowl with a spoon and it is good on a cold day. s _ _ _

Unit 4

Read the descriptions of some verbs.

What is the word for each one?

The first letter is already there. There is one space for each other letter in the word.

Example:

0 You use your ears to do this. l _ _ _ _ _

Answer: | **0** | *listen*

1 This is what you do at the end of a journey when you get to a place. a _ _ _ _ _

2 You do this when you go or come back to a place. r _ _ _ _ _

3 When you hold something and take it somewhere else, you do this. c _ _ _ _

4 If you choose to do something, you do this. d _ _ _ _ _

5 This means to go to a place and spend some time there. v _ _ _ _

Unit 5

Read the descriptions of some animals.

What is the word for each one?

The first letter is already there. There is one space for each other letter in the word.

Example:

0 You can take this animal for a walk in the park.

d _ _

Answer: | **0** | *dog*

1 This is a large animal with four legs and you can ride it. h _ _ _ _

2 You can drink the milk of this large farm animal. c _ _

3 You can see this bird on rivers and lakes. d _ _ _

4 This very large animal is grey and has big ears. e _ _ _ _ _ _ _

5 This bird lives on a farm and its eggs are good to eat. c _ _ _ _ _ _

Unit 6

Read the descriptions of some adjectives to describe places and things.

What is the word for each one?

The first letter is already there. There is one space for each other letter in the word.

Example:

0 You can use this word to describe a mountain or a tall building. h _ _ _

Answer: | **0** | *high*

1 Something that costs a lot of money is this. e _ _ _ _ _ _ _ _

2 This is a way of saying that something uses the newest ideas. m _ _ _ _ _

3 You can use this to describe something with a strong colour. b _ _ _ _ _

4 If a shop or a club is not open, it is this. c _ _ _ _ _

5 You can use this word to describe a beautiful place. a _ _ _ _ _ _ _ _ _

Unit 7

Read the descriptions of clothes or parts of clothes.

What is the word for each one?

The first letter is already there. There is one space for each other letter in the word.

Example:

0 You wear this on your head. h _ _

Answer: | **0** | *hat*

1 This is a short coat that is sometimes made of leather. j _ _ _ _ _

2 You wear these on your feet inside your shoes. s _ _ _ _

3 Most coats have two of these for you to carry small things in. p _ _ _ _ _ _

4 If you buy a pair of these, make sure they are long enough for your legs. t _ _ _ _ _ _ _

5 This will keep the top half of your body warm in cold weather. s _ _ _ _ _ _

Unit 8

Read the descriptions of some things you might see at a music festival.

What is the word for each one?

The first letter is already there. There is one space for each other letter in the word.

Example:

0 This is a group of people playing rock music.

b _ _ _

Answer: | **0** | *band*

1 This instrument is round and you hit it to make a sound. d _ _ _

2 This instrument is often made of wood and is played with the hands. g _ _ _ _ _

3 You can buy this after a concert and listen to your favourite songs again. a _ _ _ _

4 When it gets dark, people turn these on so you can see the stage. l _ _ _ _ _

5 This large instrument makes different sounds when you play its black and white keyboard. p _ _ _ _

Unit 9

Read the descriptions of some things to take on holiday.

What is the word for each one?

The first letter is already there. There is one space for each other letter in the word.

Example:

0 You can wear these to look through on a bright day.   s _ _ _ _ _ _ _ _

Answer: | 0 | sunglasses |

1 Suitcases and other kinds of bags are examples of this.   l _ _ _ _ _ _
2 You need to show this when you arrive in another country.   p _ _ _ _ _ _ _
3 This will give you lots of information about things to see in a place.   g _ _ _ _ _ _ _ _
4 You need this to travel on a bus or a train.   t _ _ _ _ _
5 This is a picture of all the roads and rivers in a city or area.   m _ _

Unit 10

Read the descriptions of some things in a bedroom.

What is the word for each one?

The first letter is already there. There is one space for each other letter in the word.

Example:

0 You can put this on the wall to look at.   p _ _ _ _ _

Answer: | 0 | poster |

1 This is a piece of glass and you can see yourself in it.   m _ _ _ _ _
2 These are sometimes made of cotton and cover a window at night.   c _ _ _ _ _ _ _
3 You need to use this when it is dark outside and you want to study.   l _ _ _
4 This is soft and is under your head when you sleep.   p _ _ _ _ _
5 You put this on the floor so your feet aren't cold.   c _ _ _ _ _

Unit 11

Read the descriptions of some sports.

What is the word for each one?

The first letter is already there. There is one space for each other letter in the word.

Example:

0 This is a winter sport where you move quickly over snow with something on each foot.   s _ _ _ _ _

Answer: | 0 | skiing |

1 You need a bat and a glove to play this American sport on a field.   b _ _ _ _ _ _ _
2 In this sport, two teams of eleven players try to score goals during a 90-minute match.   f _ _ _ _ _ _ _
3 You do this sport on the sea using a special board.   s _ _ _ _ _ _ _
4 You can play this sport on the beach if there is a net.   v _ _ _ _ _ _ _ _ _
5 Each player of this sport uses a racket to hit a ball over a net.   t _ _ _ _ _

Unit 12

Read the descriptions of some family members.

What is the word for each one?

The first letter is already there. There is one space for each other letter in the word.

Example:

0 This is the word for someone's child if it is a girl.   d _ _ _ _ _ _ _

Answer: | 0 | daughter |

1 This is the word for your father and mother.   p _ _ _ _ _ _
2 This is the child of your aunt.   c _ _ _ _ _
3 This man is married to your aunt.   u _ _ _ _
4 This is your name for your mother or father's father.   g _ _ _ _ _ _ _
5 This girl has the same mother and father as you.   s _ _ _ _ _

Unit 13

Read the descriptions of some weather words.

What is the word for each one?

The first letter is already there. There is one space for each other letter in the word.

Example:

0 In this weather, it is very difficult to see anything.

f _ _

Answer: | **0** | *fog* |

1 This is when the air moves very fast.   w _ _ _
2 People use umbrellas when this falls from dark clouds.   r _ _ _
3 This is soft and white, and falls from the sky in winter.   s _ _ _
4 You need to be careful if this is on the road during cold weather as it is dangerous.   i _ _
5 In this very bad weather you may hear thunder and it will be wet.   s _ _ _ _

Unit 14

Read the descriptions of school subjects.

What is the word for each one?

The first letter is already there. There is one space for each other letter in the word.

Example:

0 In this subject you paint or draw pictures.

a _ _

Answer: | **0** | *art* |

1 This subject is about the world and its seas, mountains and rivers.   g _ _ _ _ _ _ _ _
2 You need to understand numbers and add them together in this subject.   m _ _ _ _
3 In this subject you can study nature and find out how plants grow.   s _ _ _ _ _ _
4 For this subject, you learn dates and facts about what happened centuries ago.   h _ _ _ _ _ _
5 If you study this subject, you might be able to play an instrument.   m _ _ _ _

Unit 15

Read the descriptions of some jobs.

What is the word for each one?

The first letter is already there. There is one space for each other letter in the word.

Example:

0 This person repairs the engines of cars and buses.

m _ _ _ _ _ _ _

Answer: | **0** | *mechanic* |

1 This person works outside and often has animals such as cows or sheep.   f _ _ _ _ _
2 This person works in a hospital and helps sick people.   n _ _ _ _
3 This person brings food and drinks to customers in a restaurant.   w _ _ _ _ _
4 This person looks after your teeth.   d _ _ _ _ _ _
5 This person plans and cooks meals in a restaurant kitchen.   c _ _ _

Unit 16

Read the descriptions of things you can travel in.

What is the word for each one?

The first letter is already there. There is one space for each other letter in the word.

Example:

0 This has an engine, four wheels and seats for four or five people.   c _ _

Answer: | **0** | *car* |

1 A pilot flies this from one airport to another.   p _ _ _ _
2 This large boat carries people or things across the sea.   s _ _ _
3 You catch this at a station with lots of other people.   t _ _ _ _
4 This is a comfortable bus that can take groups of people on long journeys.   c _ _ _ _
5 This has two wheels but no engine.   b _ _ _ _ _ _

Unit 17

Read the descriptions of computer things.

What is the word for each one?

The first letter is already there. There is one space for each other letter in the word.

Example:

0 You might need this to make your keyboard work and there is one in a mobile phone too.

b _ _ _ _ _ _

Answer: | **0** | *battery* |

1 You can watch lots of these on the internet.

v _ _ _ _ _

2 This gives information about something and is read online.

w _ _ _ _ _ _

3 This is a message you send from your computer.

e _ _ _ _

4 You can carry this small computer around with you easily.

l _ _ _ _ _

5 This is the instructions that make a computer do something.

p _ _ _ _ _ _

Unit 18

Read the descriptions of things about health.

What is the word for each one?

The first letter is already there. There is one space for each other letter in the word.

Example:

0 Sick people are driven to hospital quickly in this.

a _ _ _ _ _ _ _ _

Answer: | **0** | *ambulance* |

1 If you are ill, you may need to take this to feel better.

m _ _ _ _ _ _ _

2 This person finds out what is wrong with you and decides how to help you get better.

d _ _ _ _ _

3 A nurse takes this to find out how hot or cold your body is.

t _ _ _ _ _ _ _ _ _

4 At this shop you can buy things to make you better.

c _ _ _ _ _ _

5 If you have this, you should go to a dentist immediately.

t _ _ _ _ _ _ _ _

Unit 19

Read the descriptions of different ways of contacting people.

What is the word for each one?

The first letter is already there. There is one space for each other letter in the word.

Example:

0 This is a phone that you have with you all the time.

m _ _ _ _ _

Answer: | **0** | *mobile* |

1 You put a letter inside this when you post it.

e _ _ _ _ _ _ _

2 If you want to leave a message on your friend's desk, you may write this.

n _ _ _

3 You buy this to put on a letter that you want to send by post.

s _ _ _ _

4 This has a picture on one side and you can send it to your family from another place.

p _ _ _ _ _ _ _

5 You receive this type of message on your phone.

t _ _ _

Unit 20

Read the descriptions of some adjectives about people.

What is the word for each one?

The first letter is already there. There is one space for each other letter in the word.

Example:

0 If you are this, good things often happen to you.

l _ _ _ _

Answer: | **0** | *lucky* |

1 This describes a person who is not married.

s _ _ _ _ _ _

2 A big movie star or a popular singer will be this.

f _ _ _ _ _

3 Someone who helps you a lot when you have problems is this.

k _ _ _

4 If you think someone's clothes are amazing, you might describe them as this.

a _ _ _ _ _ _

5 Someone with problems may feel like this.

w _ _ _ _ _ _

Irregular verbs

Here is a list of the irregular verbs you need to know at A2 level.

Infinitive	Past simple	Past participle
be	was/were	been
become	became	become
begin	began	begun
break	broke	broken
bring	brought	brought
build	built	built
burn	burnt/burned	burnt/burned
buy	bought	bought
catch	caught	caught
choose	chose	chosen
come	came	come
cost	cost	cost
cut	cut	cut
do	did	done
draw	drew	drawn
dream	dreamt/dreamed	dreamt/dreamed
drink	drank	drunk
drive	drove	driven
eat	ate	eaten
fall	fell	fallen
feel	felt	felt
find	found	found
fly	flew	flown
forget	forgot	forgotten
get	got	got
give	gave	given
go	went	gone/been
grow	grew	grown
have	had	had
hear	heard	heard
hit	hit	hit
hold	held	held
hurt	hurt	hurt
keep	kept	kept
know	knew	known
learn	learnt/learned	learnt/learned
leave	left	left
lend	lent	lent
lie	lay	lain
lose	lost	lost
make	made	made

Infinitive	Past simple	Past participle
mean	meant	meant
meet	met	met
pay	paid	paid
put	put	put
read	read	read
ride	rode	ridden
ring	rang	rung
run	ran	run
say	said	said
see	saw	seen
sell	sold	sold
send	sent	sent
show	showed	shown
shut	shut	shut
sing	sang	sung
sit	sat	sat
sleep	slept	slept
speak	spoke	spoken
spell	spelt/spelled	spelt/spelled
spend	spent	spent
stand	stood	stood
steal	stole	stolen
swim	swam	swum
take	took	taken
teach	taught	taught
tell	told	told
think	thought	thought
throw	threw	thrown
understand	understood	understood
wake	woke	woken
wear	wore	worn
win	won	won
write	wrote	written

Answers and recording scripts

Unit 1

1.1 pages 8–9

Grammar extra

2 The full negative form *I am not, I have not*, etc. is also correct, although this is not practised here.

The verb *be*	The verb *have*
I am, I'm, I'm not	I have, I've, I haven't
you are, you're, you aren't	you have, you've, you haven't
he/she/it is, he's, she isn't	he/she/it has, he's, she hasn't
we are, we're, we aren't	we have, we've, we haven't
they are, they're, they aren't	they have, they've, they haven't

Pronunciation

3 In Part 1 of the Speaking test you often have to spell something, for example your surname. In Parts 4 and 5 of the Listening test you often have to write down a word that is spelled out. Remember: if there are two letters, for example *BB*, we say *double B*.

1 NOVAK DJOKOVIC **2** PENELOPE CRUZ **3** BART SIMPSON **4** TAYE TAIWO **5** THE HOBBIT **6** THE FOO FIGHTERS

Listening

4

1 13; play football
2 Raquel; every day
3 Vicky; her sister; 13
4 Lucky / his dog; to the river

Recording script 1 03

1

Maria: OK, Matt, let's start with you. What's your best friend called?

Matt: Er, Jonny, and <u>he's thirteen</u>, the same as me.

Maria: Right, and what do you do together, you know, in your free time?

Matt: That's easy to answer. We <u>play football</u>, as much as possible. We're in the same team, you see.

2

Maria: And Elena, what can you tell me about your best friend?

Elena: Well, her name's Raquel. Shall I spell that? It's <u>R-A-Q-U-E-L</u>.

Maria: Uh huh. And when do you get together? Like, just at weekends?

Elena: Oh no, we're best friends, Maria! I see Raquel <u>every day</u> … in school Monday to Friday, and then we go out at weekends.

3

Maria: Kelly-Anne, I know your best friend is Vicky. Do you spell that <u>V-I-C-K-Y</u>?

Kelly-Anne: That's right.

Maria: And do you see her every day?

Kelly-Anne: Yes, because Vicky's my <u>sister</u>.

Maria: Mmm, that's a really special friend. So how old are you, Kelly-Anne?

Kelly-Anne: It's my birthday next week. I'll be fourteen … so I'm <u>thirteen</u> now.

4

Maria: Hi, Tom! Come here so I can ask you some questions. Who's your best friend?

Tom: My best friend … huh, that's difficult. I mean, I've got lots of friends, but a best friend? I'd say it's Lucky, my dog. You spell that <u>L-U-C-K-Y</u>.

Maria: Ah, that's sweet. So where do you go with Lucky? Do you take him for walks?

Tom: Of course, every day! We go <u>to the river</u>. Lucky likes the water!

Maria: Hope he can swim. OK, thanks, all you guys. See you.

All: Bye!

6 The *Key speaking* and *Key Words* boxes have useful words for the exam. Learn them!

1.2 pages 10–11

2

Sam is angry at the beginning because Gary's got his DVDs.
Sam isn't angry at the end because he hears that Gary is having problems at school.

Grammar

3

Yes/No questions:
Do you know about Gary's problems?
Is he OK?
Has Gary got your *Avatar* DVD?
Are you free tonight, Sam?
Can you text him about my DVDs?
Wh- questions:
When do you want them back?
What can we see?

4

1. When *do* you want to come here?
2. Where *are you* now?
3. How about *meeting* me at 7 o'clock?
4. (correct)
5. Why do you think it is interesting?
6. (correct)
7. Who *does* he like?

5 This gives more practice of *Wh-* questions.

Questions
2. Where do you live?
3. What's your dad's first name?
4. When does this lesson finish?
5. Who is your special friend?
6. How about lending me your bike tomorrow?

Vocabulary

6

1 lucky 2 sick 3 free 4 horrible 5 pleased 6 worried
7 amazing 8 popular
Three more adjectives are: different (4), angry (6), boring (8)
The extra adjective in the box is *true*.

Exam folder 1 pages 12–13

Listening Part 1 Short conversations

Example: The answer is A.

Part 1

1 C   2 A   3 A   4 B   5 C

Recording script 1 05
You will hear five short conversations.
You will hear each conversation twice.
There is one question for each conversation.
For questions 1–5, put a tick under the right answer.

1 *What is the man buying for his lunch?*
Woman: Can I help you, Mr Stoker? Some soup, as usual?
Man: Not today, thanks. But I'd like something hot – <u>a slice of that pizza</u>, please.
Woman: OK. Anything else?
Man: Just some egg sandwiches for Sally. I'm taking them back to her desk. She's very busy.

Now listen again.

(The recording is repeated.)

2 *When is Maria's party?*
Woman: David, you know it's my birthday on Friday. Are you free to come to my party?
Man: Oh dear, Maria, I'm in London that day. Can I take you to a restaurant on Saturday instead?

Woman: That's a great idea, and you can still come to my party because <u>it's on Wednesday</u>. It starts at eight thirty.
Man: Great!

Now listen again.

(The recording is repeated.)

3 *Which postcard does the woman choose?*
Man: Are you getting a postcard for your sister? Here's a beautiful one of the lake.
Woman: But we didn't go there. I only send cards of places I know. This one of the city at night looks good.
Man: I agree, but your sister doesn't like cities!
Woman: You're right, <u>I'll get her the forest one</u>. We went there two days ago, remember?

Now listen again.

(The recording is repeated.)

4 *How much does the woman pay for the DVD?*
Woman: I want to buy an *Avatar* film on DVD. Have you got any under ten pounds?
Man: I'm sorry, no. The new one's nineteen pounds fifty, and that's not a bad price. How about buying the one before that? <u>That's only ten pounds fifty.</u>
Woman: <u>OK, I'll take that one.</u> Here's twenty pounds.
Man: Thank you, and that's nine pounds fifty back. Enjoy it.

Now listen again.

(The recording is repeated.)

5 *What did the girl leave at Ben's flat?*
Girl: Hello, Ben. Thanks for the coffee this afternoon. <u>I think the lights for my bike are on your kitchen table.</u> I put them down there when you gave me my jacket, remember?
Ben: They are. I found them next to my books just now.
Girl: Sorry. Can you bring them to college tomorrow, please?
Ben: No problem.

Now listen again.

(The recording is repeated.)

Unit 2

2.1 pages 14–15

Vocabulary

1

1 *market:* carrots, fish, tomatoes, cheese, apples, potatoes
2 *bookshop:* books, DVD, map, magazine, birthday card
3 *chemist:* (cough) medicine, shampoo, soap
4 *department store:* belt, camera, sunglasses, sweater, umbrella, wallet
5 *sports shop:* tennis racket, tennis balls, trainers, football

Grammar extra

4

> How many books ...
> How many clothes ...
> How many DVDs ...
> How much ice cream ...
> How much make-up ...
> How much shampoo ...
> How many shoes ...

Reading

5

> **A** on (wool or silk) clothing, e.g. a sweater or dress
> **B** in a supermarket car park
> **C** on a shoe box
> **D** on a menu / at a restaurant
> **E** on a market stall / in a shop
> **F** on a poster/wall/door
> **G** in a shop window
> **H** in a newspaper

6 This is a training activity for Reading Part 1.

> **A** HA **B** PA **C** MA **D** PA; SA **E** CA **F** SA; TI **G** CA; SA
> **H** AD; GA; ON; PH

7

> **1** G **2** D **3** H **4** B **5** A

Pronunciation

8 Be careful with the letter 'a'. It can make three different sounds.

/ɑː/	/eɪ/	/æ/
<u>car</u>	f<u>a</u>ce	<u>a</u>pple
superm<u>a</u>rket	s<u>a</u>le	m<u>a</u>p
<u>a</u>rtist	Pl<u>a</u>yStation	c<u>a</u>rrot
dep<u>a</u>rtment store	em<u>ai</u>l	<u>a</u>dvert

9 Some of the words are words with missing letters from the texts.

> /ɑː/ half, parking
> /eɪ/ made, games, eight (8)
> /æ/ hand, cameras, pasta, and (&), salad, Saturday

2.2 pages 16–17

1

> The pictures show two different ways of shopping:
> ordering from a catalogue and buying on the internet.

Listening

2

> The conversation is about ordering goods from a
> sportswear catalogue.
> **1** 14   **2** (£)26.40   **3** 57   **4** (£)18.95   **5** 38

Recording script 🔊 **1 07**

Kevin: Good morning. Sportswear, Kevin speaking. How can I help you?

Sally: Hi. I've got your catalogue here, but I can't find the price list. Can you give me some prices?

Kevin: Of course. Please tell me the page number you're looking at.

Sally: OK. The first thing is on page <u>14</u> and it's the football shirt, the blue and red one.

Kevin: OK, the small and medium sizes are £22.65 and large and extra-large are <u>£26.40</u>.

Sally: Right. I'd like to order one, please, size small.

Kevin: Fine. Have you got any more things to order?

Sally: Yes, I'd like some trainers. They're on page <u>57</u>. How much are the black and purple ones at the top of the page?

Kevin: Well, they *were* £49.50 but they're in the sale now so they're only <u>£18.95</u>. But we don't have any left in small sizes. What shoe size are you?

Sally: I'm a <u>38</u>.

Kevin: Let me check. Wow, you're lucky! We've got one pair in that size.

Sally: Great. Well, that's all I need. My name and address is …

Grammar

4

> **a** some – sentence 2
> **b** any – sentence 4
> **c** some – sentence 1
> **d** some – sentence 5
> **e** any – sentence 3

5

> **2** some   **3** any   **4** some   **5** some   **6** some   **7** any
> **8** some   **9** any; some

6

> baby – babies   group **e**
> coach – coaches   group **b**
> dress – dresses   group **b**
> monkey – monkeys   group **d**
> potato – potatoes   group **c**
> tooth – teeth   group **f**
> window – windows   group **a**

Activity

This practises plural spellings.

1 map – maps   2 camera – cameras   3 bus – buses
4 dress – dresses   5 book – books   6 bicycle – bicycles
7 fly – flies   8 rice – rice   9 box – boxes   10 – bananas
11 arm – arms   12 glass – glasses   13 tomato – tomatoes
14 potato – potatoes   15 lion – lions
The four words say PASS KEY EXAM SOON.

Exam folder 2 pages 18–19

Reading Part 1 Notices

1

Possible answers
1 you should   2 bigger   3 Keep quiet   4 at 6.30; on Sunday
5 in the field

2

1 (modal verbs)
  Question 4: you can
  Question 5: you may
2 (comparison)
  Question 1: later
  Question 2: cheaper
  Question 3: lower
  Question 5: younger
  Notice H: longer
3 (imperatives)
  Example 0: Do not leave
  Notice A: Buy
  Notice D: Please put
  Notice G: Spend
4 (prepositions with times/days)
  Notice C: from 7 pm
  Notice E: until then (next Tuesday)
5 (prepositions with places)
  Example 0: on the floor
  Notice A: at machine
  Notice D: above your seat

Part 1

Try to complete the task in six minutes.

1 H   2 B   3 E   4 A   5 F

Unit 3

3.1   pages 20–21

Vocabulary

1   The photos show …

  Photo 1: potatoes, rice, pasta, bread
  Photo 2: pizza, sandwich, burger, soup
  Photo 3: tomatoes, carrots, onions, salad

Photo 4: apples, grapes, bananas, oranges
Photo 5: lemonade, orange juice, mineral water, coffee
Photo 6: steak, chicken, fish, cheese
Photo 7: ice cream, cake, biscuits, chocolate

1 grapes   2 apple   3 fish   4 tomato   5 chocolate
6 burger   7 orange   8 salad   9 sandwich   10 steak
The word in the yellow squares is *restaurant*.

Pronunciation

2   Here you are practising the sounds /ɪ/ as in *chicken* and /iː/ as in *cheese*.

group 1 /ɪ/ chicken	group 2 /iː/ cheese
bin	beans
biscuit	eat
chips	feel
dinner	leave
fill	meal
fish	meat
live	seat
sit	tea

Listening

4

1 J   2 K   3 K   4 J   5 J   6 K   7 J and K   8 K

Recording script 1 10

Katie: Hi, Jack! It's twelve-thirty. Come and have lunch with me! I'm really hungry today.

Jack: Hi, Katie! So am I. I eat lots for breakfast every morning but I still eat a lot for lunch too. What about you, what do you usually have for breakfast?

Katie: Nothing much. My mum makes breakfast at seven o'clock and that's too early for me! I always get a cake or something on my way to school so I don't feel hungry during lessons.

Jack: And then you have chips or pizza for lunch?

Katie: Yes, nearly every day. I love them!

Jack: They're not very good for you, are they? I try to eat a lot of salad. It's healthy. And I drink lots of water. It's better for you than juice.

Katie: I don't like salad very much, and I don't like water. And I think tea and coffee taste horrible. I prefer cola or lemonade.

Jack: I guess you like chocolate as well, don't you? I love chocolate.

Katie: Mmm, I love it too, and sweets and biscuits. But I don't like ice cream very much. It makes my teeth too cold!

Grammar

6   Look at the Grammar folder if you need more help.

affirmative	I/You/We/They like
	He/She/It likes
negative	I/You/We/They don't like
	He/She/It doesn't like
question	Do I/you/we/they like
	Does he/she/it like

Spelling spot

7

do + not = don't
has + not = hasn't
have + not = haven't
is + not = isn't
are + not = aren't

8   Reading Part 3 in the exam sometimes tests telling the time.

1 c   2 f   3 a   4 d   5 e   6 b

9

1 orange juice   2 1.15 / one fifteen / a quarter past one
3 water   4 6.30 / six thirty / half past six   5 fish
6 (a cup of) coffee

Recording script 1 11

Harry: What do I usually eat and drink? Well, I get up about seven thirty, have a shower and then have breakfast about eight o'clock. I make a cup of tea, and then I have toast and <u>orange juice</u>. Then, I go to my office – I work in advertising. I don't eat snacks, so I'm quite hungry by lunchtime. I have lunch at <u>one fifteen</u>. I have about an hour for lunch, and I often go to a café near my office. I have salad and I sometimes have a cake – the café does fantastic chocolate cakes. And to drink? Well, <u>water</u>. I don't like to have too much tea or coffee in the day.
I get home from work about five thirty. I have my evening meal at about <u>six thirty</u> and I like cooking so I try to make something healthy and interesting – usually chicken or <u>fish</u> with rice or pasta. I never have a dessert, but I do have <u>a cup of coffee</u> then. Then I often go out – maybe to the cinema or with friends. I'm usually in bed by ten thirty during the week.

3.2 pages 22–23

Reading

2   This exercise is practice for Reading Part 4, but here you only choose between 'Right' and 'Wrong'. Don't worry about words you don't know.

1 Wrong   2 Wrong   3 Right   4 Wrong   5 Wrong
6 Wrong   7 Wrong   8 Right

Grammar extra

3

2   My mother *usually* makes cakes on Tuesdays.
3   I am *always* hungry at lunch time.
4   I am *often* late for dinner.
5   Pete *always* has a party on his birthday.
6   We *sometimes* have fireworks on New Year's Eve.
7   Sam *usually* meets his friends on New Year's Eve.
8   You *never* eat spaghetti with a knife.

4

1 have   2 wear   3 carry   4 wears   5 wakes   6 help
7 often ask   8 aren't   9 don't wear   10 choose
11 sing   12 like   13 always closes

6   This is practice for Writing Part 9. You must write about all three parts of the message.

Sample answer
Dear Maria,
We have a special festival in our town on 14th July for Independence Day. We have fireworks in the evening and we have wonderful cakes and sweet biscuits.
Love,
Paula

Writing folder 1 pages 24–25

Writing Part 6 Spelling words

1

2 butter   3 waitress   4 dish   5 juice   6 market
7 pasta   8 tomato   9 carrot   10 apple

2   You can use an English–English dictionary to help you with this exercise.

2 pilot   3 yellow   4 mirror   5 uncle   6 beautiful
7 telephone   8 sunny   9 which   10 interesting
11 believe   12 apartment   13 motorbike   14 because
15 address   16 bicycle

3

Possible answers
2   This food is very popular in Italy.
3   I will bring you your food in a restaurant.
4   This is where you can go to eat lunch.
5   This is the first meal of the day.
6   This is something small you can eat between meals.
7   This is where you cook food.
8   This keeps food cold.
9   An apple is an example of this.
10   This is good to eat on a hot day.

Part 6

1 lemonade   2 tomatoes   3 orange   4 sugar
5 sandwiches

Unit 4

4.1 pages 26–27

1

1 Right – It is often used to decorate cakes.
2 Wrong – They are mainly made from silver and covered with gold.
3 Wrong – Most gold comes from China today.
4 Right – They have gold in the engines.
5 Right – the photo shows a wedding dress made from gold thread, designed by Yumi Katsura.

Reading

2

1 Wrong   2 Right   3 Wrong   4 Doesn't say   5 Wrong
6 Doesn't say   7 Right

Grammar

3

1 wanted   2 worked   3 found   4 became   5 was; were
Where **did** the Canadian Skookum Jim **find** gold?
But some people **didn't** (did not) **go** for the gold, they went for the adventure too.

Spelling spot

4

1 arrived   2 stopped   3 helped   4 looked   5 used
6 returned   7 liked   8 played   9 studied   10 opened

Pronunciation

5

Recording script and answers		
/t/	/d/	/ɪd/
worked	carried	wanted
picked	showed	decided
	travelled	needed
	stayed	

6

1 found   2 saw   3 knew   4 sold   5 left   6 built
7 went   8 became   9 spent

Activity

The famous person is Leonardo da Vinci.

Recording script 1 13

Boy: Are you ready to play?
Girl: Yes, I'm ready.
Boy: Were you a man?
Girl: Yes, I was.
Boy: Were you American?
Girl: No, I wasn't.
Boy: Were you European?
Girl: Yes, I was.
Boy: So, dead, man and European. Did you live more than a hundred years ago?
Girl: Yes, I did.
Boy: Were you Italian?
Girl: Yes, I was.
Boy: Did you play music?
Girl: No, I didn't.
Boy: Were you a writer?
Girl: No, I wasn't.
Boy: Did you paint pictures?
Girl: Yes, I did.
Boy: Were you …?

4.2 pages 28–29

1

Where did you go / stay?
When did you go / come home?
How much did it cost?
How did you travel / feel?
What did you do / see / buy?
What did you see?
Who did you go with?
How long did you stay?

Listening

2   This is practice for Listening Part 5.

1 5   2 5.30   3 £340   4 BERRI   5 boat trip

Recording script 1 14

Melanie: About two years ago I went with my class on our first school trip – five days in Paris! There were about thirty of us and four teachers. We all went in one big coach from our school in London. The teachers told us to be at school at four thirty in the morning. Everyone was there on time, but the coach didn't arrive until five o'clock and we didn't leave until five thirty! We were very cold and tired.

Anyway, the coach was very comfortable and we watched a DVD and listened to some music on the journey. We had some sandwiches and drinks with us, so we went straight to Paris without stopping. The trip was quite expensive. <u>It cost £340</u> and we wanted to save money, so we didn't stop at motorway cafés. It only took us eight hours to reach Paris.

The name of the hotel in Paris was <u>the Hotel Berri – that's B-E-double R-I</u>. It was very old, but our room was nice and the bed was great – really soft! I shared the room with three other girls.

When we went shopping I tried to practise my French a few times but sometimes I didn't know the right words and spoke in English instead! The shops were great – I bought lots of presents, even a T-shirt for my little sister!

I think <u>what I enjoyed most was the boat trip</u>. I took lots of photos of my friends and also of Notre Dame cathedral, and the wonderful art galleries.

I was sad to leave Paris. I had a lovely time there. We came home by coach and this time the journey was much shorter – we even arrived back half an hour early!

3

2 Yes, she did.	**5** No, she didn't.
3 Yes, it did.	**6** Yes, she did.
4 No, they didn't.	**7** No, they didn't.

Grammar extra

4

Possible questions and answers
1 When did you last eat some chocolate?
   I ate some chocolate three hours ago.
2 When did you last email a friend?
   I emailed a friend two days ago.
3 When did you last read a magazine?
   I read a magazine last night.
4 When did you last listen to music?
   I listened to music twelve hours ago.
5 When did you last go to the cinema?
   I went to the cinema two weeks ago.
6 When did you last play football?
   I played football yesterday. / I don't play football.
7 When did you last do some homework?
   I did some homework at breakfast time.
8 When did you last go to an art gallery?
   I went to an art gallery last weekend.
9 When did you last buy some clothes?
   I bought some clothes on Saturday.
10 When did you last eat pizza?
   I ate pizza at lunchtime.

5

1 You didn't *come* home at six o'clock.
2 Who *did you go* to London with?
3 I *laughed* a lot during the game.
4 I *danced* with Louise last night.
5 I *played* football with my brother on Saturday.
6 I *stayed* with my friend yesterday.
7 I *bought* it because I love green.
8 (correct)
9 How much *did the trip* cost?
10 Last Monday, the school *told* us about the new holiday.

Activity

Across
went   ate   began   travelled
Down
liked   had   took   arrived   saw   stayed

Units 1–4 Revision

pages 30–31

Vocabulary

2 Other answers may also be correct.

1 green – not a feeling
2 small – not a character adjective
3 friend – not an adjective
4 house – you can't buy things there
5 coffee – you drink it not eat it
6 onion – not a fruit
7 chemist – not a geographical feature
8 clothes – something you wear, not something you use

3

1 tomato   2 snack   3 meat   4 milk   5 juice   6 grape
7 fish   8 carrot   9 burger   10 chocolate   11 potato
12 chicken

Writing

4

1 market   2 department store   3 chemist
4 supermarket   5 sports shop

Grammar

5

1 some   2 much   3 is   4 any   5 Does   6 Sometimes
7 doesn't   8 go   9 Did   10 return

6

1 starts   2 a   3 make   4 their   5 eat   6 some
7 at   8 Many   9 wear   10 is

7

1 knew 2 came 3 found 4 sold 5 took 6 told
7 became 8 left 9 went 10 built

8

2 am/'m 3 telephoned 4 were 5 needed 6 went
7 Did you get 8 do you think 9 'm/am not 10 like
11 Are 12 are / 're 13 looked 14 took 15 saw 16 were
17 Were 18 look 19 got 20 were

Unit 5

5.1 pages 32–33

Vocabulary

1

1 bear 2 cat 3 dog 4 elephant 5 horse 6 fish
7 monkey 8 lion

Listening

3 All the words are on the recording. They are *in italics* in the recording script below.

Recording script 1 15

Mark: Natalie, what about going to the *zoo* at the weekend?

Natalie: Oh, sorry, Mark, but I'm going shopping on Saturday and I'm going to see my grandparents on *Sunday*, but I'm free in the week.

Mark: OK, then <u>let's say Thursday</u>.

Natalie: Fine. It's cheaper then too. At the weekend it's £18.50 for adults and £17.50 for *students*! But in the week student tickets are £3 cheaper.

Mark: Mm, <u>£14.50</u> – not bad! At the zoo, I've got to take some photographs of the animals for *homework*. My <u>art teacher</u> asked me and a friend to take as many as possible. It's lucky my mum bought me a *camera* for my birthday!

Natalie: Well, there are lots of different animals. My favourites are the lions, bears and monkeys. The <u>monkeys</u> always make me *laugh*.

Mark: Let's visit them first then. <u>I need some photos of them.</u>

Natalie: OK, so how are we going to get there, Mark? Can your mum *drive* us there?

Mark: She'll be at work then. I think <u>the bus is best,</u> as the *train* is too expensive. I don't want to spend too much money.

Natalie: Fine, but I need to be home by six thirty.

Mark: Well, that's no problem because <u>it shuts at five thirty</u>. We'll be tired anyway, so why don't we leave at half past *four*?

Natalie: That's *great*! See you soon, then.

Mark: Bye!

4 You hear all three days on the recording but the answer to the question is C: Thursday.

5

1 A 2 C 3 B 4 A 5 B

Grammar extra

7

1 I saw a nice, colourful parrot at the zoo.
2 Yesterday we went to the zoo and the museum.
3 Susanna went out yesterday and took her dog for a walk.
4 There are many cats, dogs and horses at the farm.
5 Some sheep and cows were at the farm.

Vocabulary

8

do – homework, the shopping, nothing, the cooking
make – a phone call, an appointment, a cake
take – the dog for a walk, an exam
spend – time, nothing

9

1 spent 2 did 3 did 4 make 5 took

5.2 pages 34–35

Reading

2

Answers to the quiz in exercise 1
1 a 2 b 3 a 4 a 5 a 6 b 7 b 8 b 9 a

Grammar

3

We use *because*, *and*, *but* and *or* to make one long sentence.
1 because 2 or 3 and 4 but

4 This is practice for Reading Part 5.

1 B because		5 A or
2 A and		6 C but
3 A or		7 A because
4 B because		

5

1 and/but 2 because 3 but 4 or/and/but 5 because

Spelling spot

6 Exam candidates often make mistakes with these words.

1 They're 2 there 3 their 4 Their 5 They're 6 there

7

Sample answer
Dear Lucia,
I went to a great zoo in London last weekend with my friend Caroline and her family. We saw lots of animals but I liked the lions best. We had ice cream and juice and took lots of photographs.
Love from
Sandro

Exam folder 3 pages 36–37

Reading Part 2 Multiple choice

1

a verb – *go, made, carry, horse*
an adjective – *happy, sun, nice, friendly*
a noun – *left, house, dog, teacher*
an adverb – *hard, slowly, want, carefully*
words which go together – *have breakfast, make your homework, take a trip*

Part 2

6 A   7 B   8 C   9 B   10 A

Reading Part 5 Multiple-choice cloze

2

1 c   2 d   3 e   4 f   5 g   6 a   7 b

Part 5

28 C   29 A   30 B   31 A   32 B   33 A   34 C   35 A

Unit 6

6.1 pages 38–39

Speaking

3   This is practice for Part 2 of the Speaking test.

Possible questions
1   How many rides does Magic Land / Space Adventure have?
2   Which dates is Magic Land / Space Adventure open on?
3   What are the opening hours of Magic Land / Space Adventure?
4   How many visitors does Magic Land / Space Adventure have a year?
5   How many hotel rooms does Magic Land / Space Adventure have?
6   How much does Magic Land / Space Adventure cost?

4

1 newer   2 shorter   3 smaller   4 more   5 more
6 better   7 less

Grammar

5

1/2 older, newer, longer, shorter, bigger, smaller
3 more/less expensive   4 better   5 worse   6 than
7 more   8 fewer

7

1   the oldest amusement park
2   the tallest roller coaster
3   the fastest roller coaster

Spelling spot

8

adjective	comparative	superlative
modern	more modern	the most modern
comfortable	more comfortable	the most comfortable
fit	fitter	the fittest
horrible	more horrible	the most horrible
angry	angrier	the angriest
attractive	more attractive	the most attractive
bright	brighter	the brightest
tidy	tidier	the tidiest

6.2 pages 40–41

Speaking

1

Possible answers
I go shopping every Saturday with my friends.
I like to listen to music when I do my homework.
I see my friends after school and at the weekend.
I don't go swimming very often but I go to the cinema about once a month.
I like to play football and also to read books.

Listening

2   In the exam it will help you if you read the questions and think about what type of word the answer will be. For example: Is the answer to 1 a number or a word? Is it a price or a time? What do you think the missing word is in 4? What do cafés sell? If you do this, it will help you to understand what you are listening for.

1 10 (p.m.)   2 (£)55   3 Glendennan   4 ice cream   5 books

Recording script ① 19

Man: Hello, Aqua Park. Can I help you?

Girl: Yes, please. I'd like some information. Are you open on Saturdays?

Man: We're open every day. From nine in the morning until six, but on Saturdays we close much later, <u>at ten</u>.

Girl: OK. And how much does it cost?

Man: Adults are £20 and children £15, but families can get in more cheaply with a family ticket – <u>only £55</u>.

Girl: And do you have a large car park? I'm coming from London.

Man: We have four car parks. From London it's much easier for you to park in the one in Glendennan Road.

Girl: I'll write that down. Can you spell the name of the road for me?

Man: It's <u>G-L-E-N-D-E-double N-A-N</u>.

Girl: And is there anywhere to get food and drink?

Man: Yes, there's a restaurant for hot food. There's also a café for <u>ice cream</u> and drinks.

Girl: Is there anything else I need to know? Do you have a shop?

Man: Yes. It sells sweets, newspapers, and you can get <u>books</u> there, too.

Girl: That's great. Thank you.

Grammar extra

3

| 1 sooner | 2 harder | 3 more quietly | 4 earlier | 5 longer |
| 6 better | 7 more carefully |

4

| friend | beautiful | because | interesting | there | which |

Reading

5

| 1 C | 2 B | 3 C | 4 B | 5 A |

Pronunciation

7

Across
1 alone   6 computer   9 interesting   10 America
Down
2 listen   3 camera   4 longer   5 father   7 cinema
8 letter

Exam folder 4 pages 42–43

Listening Parts 4 and 5 Gap-fill

Part 4

16 eleven/11   **17** £300
18 Kensal – this must be spelled correctly
19 eighteen/18   **20** nine-thirty / 9.30 / half past nine

Recording script ① 21

Questions 16 to 20. You will hear a woman asking about a guitar for sale. Listen and complete questions 16 to 20.

You will hear the conversation twice.

Man: 669872.

Woman: Oh, hello. I'm ringing about the guitar you have for sale. Can you tell me what make it is?

Man: It's a <u>Fender</u>.

Woman: And how old is it?

Man: Well, I bought it from a friend about six months ago, and he was given it for his birthday, so it's about <u>eleven</u> months old now.

Woman: How much are you selling it for?

Man: Umm, I think I'd like <u>three hundred</u> pounds for it. I bought it for six hundred.

Woman: Sounds good. Can I come and see it?

Man: Sure. I live at 60, Kensal Road. That's <u>K-E-N-S-A-L</u> Road.

Woman: Can I walk there from the High Street?

Man: It's probably best if you get a bus. The number <u>eighteen</u> bus stops in my road outside number seventy.

Woman: I'm free tonight. Would about eight o'clock be OK?

Man: A bit later? After <u>nine thirty</u> is better for me as I don't get back from work until eight.

Woman: My name is Jenny Levine and you are …?

Man: Josh Bentley.

Woman: See you tonight then.

Now listen again.

(The recording is repeated.)

Part 5

21 tennis   **22** £425   **23** 18   **24** Wright – *this must be spelled correctly*   **25** 8775980

Recording script ◀1 22

Questions 21 to 25. You will hear some information about an activity centre. Listen and complete questions 21 to 25. You will hear the information twice.

Woman: Thank you for calling High Cross Activity Centre. The Centre is open from <u>March to October</u> and we have things to do for all ages. At High Cross you can play football or try our new climbing wall, and you can also learn to play <u>tennis</u>. It costs £35 to come for a day and for this you get your classes and lunch in our restaurant. One week's stay is <u>£425</u> for a room and all meals. It is cheaper if you come here as part of a group. We are happy to accept group bookings, especially from companies and schools. Group sizes can be from five to <u>eighteen</u> people. If you would like to talk about what we do here, then ring our Manager, Pete Wright, that's <u>W-R-I-G-H-T</u>. Office hours are nine o'clock until five thirty and the number to ring is <u>8775980</u>. After five thirty you can ring Pete's mobile on 0770 5566328.

Now listen again.

(The recording is repeated.)

Unit 7
7.1 pages 44–45
Reading
2

> **Answer**
> Converse boots are the oldest:
> T-shirts – 1940s   Converse boots – 1917
> baseball cap – 1954

3   This is practice for Reading Part 4. See Exam folder 10 on page 116 for help with Part 4.

> 1 A   2 C   3 B   4 C   5 B   6 A   7 B

Grammar
4

> 1 1954   2 1955   3 1959

5

> 1   the present continuous (temporary)
> 2   the present simple (habitual)
> 3   the past continuous (*was wearing* = temporary in the past) and past simple (*fell* = completed action)

7   Ask students to fill in the missing verbs in the timeline in pairs and then complete the story.

> *Timeline*
> 10.20 – 10.45   was looking at
> 10.35   saw
> 10.45   started
> 10.46   left
> *Story*
> 2 saw   3 was trying on   4 decided   5 said   6 went
> 7 found   8 was waiting   9 started   10 left

8

> 1 were selling   2 bought   3 was watching; rang
> 4 was wearing; stopped; changed
> 5 was waiting; drove; gave   6 was living; heard

Spelling spot
9

> | break | breaking |
> |-------|----------|
> | leave | leaving |
> | make | making |
> | throw | throwing |
> | stay | staying |
> | lend | lending |
> | sit | sitting |
> | win | winning |

7.2 pages 46–47
Vocabulary
1

> 1 boots   2 hat(s)   3 belt(s)   4 sweater   5 tights
> 6 suit   7 baseball cap(s)   8 jacket   9 jeans   10 shirt
> 11 trainers   12 skirt   13 shoes   14 shorts   15 socks
> 16 trousers   17 ring   18 scarf   19 earrings   20 necklace

2

> *A pair of* describes things that are used together (e.g. *socks, shoes*), sometimes it is used with a noun that only has a plural form (e.g. *scissors, trousers*). *A couple of* means two of something, not necessarily identical things.
>
> Pictures 1, 5, 9, 11, 13, 14, 15, 16 and 20 show pairs of things.

Listening
4

> *Speaker 1, Ben:*   shorts and (two) T-shirts
> *Speaker 2, Louisa:*   jacket
> *Speaker 3, Chris:*   trousers and cap

Recording script ◀1 23

Speaker 1: Ben I work as a waiter on Wednesday evenings and I save most of the money I earn. My dad said I should buy some new trousers for work, but yesterday I saw this pair of <u>yellow cotton shorts</u>, with lots of

pockets. They looked wonderful, and I decided to get them for the summer, with a couple of extra T-shirts. Dad still thinks I need some trousers, but my boss doesn't mind what I wear!

Speaker 2: Louisa There was this beautiful Italian leather jacket in the sale. It was soft black leather, with a pocket on each side. I tried it on over a red shirt I was wearing at the time, and it looked so cool. But the thing was that it cost well over £200, even in the sale! In the end, my mum lent me half the money. I'm really pleased I got it. It'll stay in fashion for years, I'm sure.

Speaker 3: Chris I don't buy many clothes. Until last Saturday, I had two pairs of jeans and some T-shirts and that was about it. But I saw a great pair of trousers in town, dark green and really well made. My girlfriend was with me when I tried them on. She hated them. She prefers me in jeans, you see. Anyway, I decided to get them. I bought this cap in the same colour, too. Nice, isn't it?

Pronunciation

5 Don't forget the last letters of the alphabet – W, X, Y, Z. Note that the letter Z is pronounced /zed/ in British English and /ziː/ in American English. The pictures have the sounds /w/ as in *waiter*, /ks/ as in *taxi*, /j/ as in *yellow* and /z/ as in *zebra*.

> 1 work; waiter; Wednesday   2 yesterday; yellow
> 3 wonderful   4 extra

6   ◖1 25◗

> **Recording script and answers**
> 1 zoo   2 wool   3 young   4 excellent   5 zero   6 water
> 7 year   8 expensive   9 yogurt   10 women   11 exam
> 12 worry

Reading

7 This is practice for Reading Part 3.

> 1 B   2 C   3 A   4 C   5 B

Writing folder 2 pages 48–49

Writing Part 7 Open cloze

1

> **Possible answers**
> *articles:*   an, the
> *pronouns:*   me, they
> *prepositions:*   on, in
> *quantifiers:*   any, every
> *auxiliary verbs:* has, had
> *modal verbs:*   must, should

2

> 1 pronoun: *you*
> 2 auxiliary verb: *did/do*
> 3 preposition: *to*
> 4 modal verb: *should*
> 5 quantifier: *any*
> 6 article: *a*

3   The photo shows Quartier 206 shopping centre, Berlin.

> 1 in   2 some   3 for   4 must   5 our   6 from   7 much
> 8 Do   9 because   10 the

Part 7

> 41 some   42 me   43 There   44 for   45 because/where
> 46 it   47 much   48 on   49 are   50 my

Unit 8
8.1 pages 50–51

1 The photos show stills from *Avatar*, *Pirates of the Caribbean (On Stranger Tides)* and *The Adventures of Tintin*.

Grammar

3

> 1 I can understand most films in French.
> 2 Jenny may buy that DVD, but she's not sure.
> 3 You must book in advance for the 3D film.
> 4 I had to take my passport to the cinema to show my age.
> 5 When he was in New York, Roberto could see a different movie every night.
> 6 Cinema staff sometimes have to work very long hours.
> 7 My brother might have an extra ticket for tonight's film – I'll ask him.

4

> a 3, 6   b 4   c 2, 7   d 1   e 5

5

> **Completed notes**
> • We cannot use the word *must* in the past. Instead, we use *had to*.
>   Example: *Last night, I had to do my homework.*
> • When we are talking about something we are unable to do, we use the word *cannot* or the contracted form *can't*.
>   Example: *I can't ride a horse, but I'd like to be able to.*
> • If we are talking about something we were unable to do in the past, we use *could not* or the contracted form *couldn't*.
>   Example: *Before I was five, I couldn't read, but now I can.*

6

> 1 can't   2 had to   3 couldn't   4 could   5 Can   6 must
> 7 may   8 have to

Reading

8 The photo shows a still from *Transformers 3*.

> **1** B **2** B **3** C **4** A **5** B **6** A **7** C **8** C

8.2 pages 52–53

Vocabulary

2 The band in the photo is Kasabian.

> play, dance, guitar, album, speakers, singer, lights, festival, drums, piano, concert, band

s	l	q	f	b	s	p	l	a	y
i	d	w	e	a	t	i	t	e	t
n	d	w	s	t	d	a	n	c	e
g	u	i	t	a	r	n	j	o	x
e	l	n	i	o	u	o	w	n	e
r	i	t	v	k	m	v	s	c	i
p	g	x	a	e	s	u	a	e	b
b	h	a	l	b	u	m	r	r	a
o	t	a	m	p	d	a	t	t	n
l	s	p	e	a	k	e	r	s	d

> **Possible answers**
> There's a band with a singer. A man is playing the guitar. He is singing too.
> The singer might be dancing.
> We can see some drums and a big speaker.
> There are lights. It looks like a concert. They could be at a music festival.

Listening

3 This is practice for Listening Part 1.

> **1** A **2** B **3** C **4** B **5** A

Recording script 🔊 **1 26**

1 *How much did Craig earn from the concert?*

Boy: The band earned a hundred and fifty pounds last night. That's the best yet!

Girl: But what did they pay you, Craig? You booked the concert, so you should earn more than the other two.

Boy: I don't agree. We took <u>fifty pounds</u> each and that's fine.

Girl: Well, they must give you half next time. Seventy-five pounds sounds right to me!

Now listen again.

(The recording is repeated.)

2 *Which band did the girl see?*

Girl: I saw a good band at last Saturday's rock festival. The singer was great!

Boy: The band with the piano player? He sang well, didn't he?

Girl: I didn't see anything with a piano. This singer was called Queen Cat. She could really dance too.

Boy: Oh, I know who you mean – <u>the band had three guitars</u>. Yes, excellent.

Now listen again.

(The recording is repeated.)

3 *Where is the next band from?*

Boy: Who's on next, Kate? Is it that Brazilian band? They're great!

Girl: Yeah, they are, but they're not on until this evening. It's a new <u>band from Iceland now</u> … you know, where the singer Bjork is from.

Boy: Sounds interesting. I enjoyed that last band from Australia. Did you?

Girl: No, they were boring.

Now listen again.

(The recording is repeated.)

4 *What does Ben play?*

Boy: Hi, Anna. Tell me, is your brother <u>Ben still playing the drums</u>? We want someone tonight because Ray's ill.

Girl: Is he? Ben still plays, but he's away this week. I'm learning the keyboards you know.

Boy: Great. Perhaps you can play in our band one day then!

Girl: Can I? Ben says the guitar's a better choice because all bands have guitar players.

Now listen again.

(The recording is repeated.)

5 *What must Kim bring to the party?*

Girl: Hello, Kim. Listen, I want some special lights for my party tonight. Can you bring some?

Boy: Sorry, Tracey, I can't. Try the music shop in town. Do you want to borrow my guitar tonight?

Girl: No thanks, but <u>don't forget your new albums</u>. I'll phone the shop about the lights now.

Boy: OK. See you later.

Now listen again.

(The recording is repeated.)

Pronunciation

4

> **1** Did I? **2** Have you? **3** Aren't they? **4** Can't you? **5** Isn't it? **6** Did they?

Recording script ① 28

(NB The sentences are recorded twice: the first time you will hear sentences 1 to 6 with Speaker 1 only, with a pause for you to write your answers; the second time you will also hear Speaker 2, so that you can check your answers.)

1

Speaker 1: Here's your scarf. You left it at my house after the party.

(pause)

Speaker 2: Did I?

2

Speaker 1: I've got tickets for *Adele's* next concert.

(pause)

Speaker 2: Have you?

3

Speaker 1: Jon and Alice aren't coming to see the band now.

(pause)

Speaker 2: Aren't they?

4

Speaker 1: We went to Glastonbury last summer but we can't this year.

(pause)

Speaker 2: Can't you?

5

Speaker 1: The next band's not on until midnight.

(pause)

Speaker 2: Isn't it?

6

Speaker 1: *Casio Kids* played six songs from their new album.

(pause)

Speaker 2: Did they?

5

> **Possible answers**
> 1 Did I? Thanks a lot.
> 2 Have you? That's great! / Fantastic!
> 3 Aren't they? What a pity. / That's a shame.
> 4 Can't you? That's a shame. / What a pity.
> 5 Isn't it? That's too bad. / That's a shame.
> 6 Did they? Fantastic! / That's great!

6 The questions not used in exercise 4 are *Must I?*, *Don't you?* and *Couldn't she?*

Spelling spot

7 *Key* candidates often make these spelling mistakes.

> 1 Yesterday I was at a *beautiful* rock concert.
> 2 It's my *favourite* cinema.
> 3 I'm selling my piano *because* I don't want it any more.
> 4 A lot of *tourists* visit my town.
> 5 I went to a nightclub with my *friends*.
> 6 There are two *museums* in the town.

Activity

The photo is of Jay-Z.

Units 5–8 Revision

pages 54–55

Grammar

2

> 1 C   2 B   3 C   4 A

3

> 1 B   2 C   3 A   4 B   5 C   6 C   7 B   8 A

Vocabulary

4

> 1 tall   2 hot   3 dirty   4 boring   5 old   6 fast   7 thin
> 8 small

5

> *Animals:* bear, elephant, fish, horse, lion, monkey
> *Clothes:* button, jacket, jeans, pocket, shorts, socks, sweater, trainers
> *Music:* album, concert, drums, guitar, piano
> *Activities:* chess, climbing, cycling, skateboarding, table tennis

Writing

6

> 1 to   2 It   3 were   4 more   5 at/in/inside
> 6 best/greatest/coolest   7 because/as   8 his
> 9 may/might/could   10 why

Unit 9

9.1 pages 56–57

Listening

2

> 1 Julia   Australia   beach
> 2 Daniel   Switzerland   walking
> 3 Simon   France   camping
> 4 Natalie   Greece   sailing
> 5 Julia – by plane and car
> 6 Daniel – by motorbike
> 7 Simon – by train
> 8 Natalie – by boat

Recording script ① 30

Daniel: Hi, Julia!

Julia: Daniel! Hi, how are you?

Daniel: I'm fine. I hear you're on holiday next week – are you going to go to Florida again with your parents?

Julia: No, <u>Australia</u> this time. My father's friend has a flat by a beautiful <u>beach</u>. We're going <u>to fly</u> to Sydney and then <u>drive</u> along the coast to the flat. What about you?

Daniel: I'm going to do some <u>walking</u> in <u>Switzerland</u> with my older brother. I did ask a friend to come with me but he's decided to stay at home this year – he wants to save enough money to buy a car. We're going to go on my brother's <u>motorbike</u>. Oh, there's Natalie and Simon. We're just talking about holidays. Are you planning anything, Simon?

Simon: Hi! I'm going to go <u>camping</u> with my family again. We're catching a <u>train</u> down to the south of <u>France</u>, which will be great. Some of my friends are driving to Italy, so they're going to visit us on the way.

Daniel: What about you, Natalie?

Natalie: My cousin has asked me to go with her to <u>Greece</u>. We're going to hire a <u>boat</u> and then <u>sail</u> around the Greek islands for three whole weeks! I can't wait!

Daniel, Simon and Julia: That sounds really good! Wow! Amazing.

Grammar

3

> **Suggested answers**
> 2 He's going (to go) swimming / dive into the pool.
> 3 They're going to play tennis.
> 4 He's going to buy/have/eat an ice cream.
> 5 They're going to have a pizza.
> 6 She's going (to go) cycling.

4

> 2 is going to telephone
> 3 are going to do
> 4 am/'m going to book
> 5 is going to visit
> 6 is/are going to close
> 7 are going to meet
> 8 are/'re going to have

Pronunciation

5

> The words which contain the sound /h/ are: hand, holiday, home, hill, how, happy, hotel
> The words which don't include the sound /h/ are: why, when, honest, hour, school

6

> **Recording script and answers**
> 1 He has a holiday home in the hills.
> 2 Helena hopes she'll get a horse for her birthday.
> 3 Help him with his homework.
> 4 Have a happy holiday!
> 5 I'm going to hire a boat and have fun.
> 6 Help me into the helicopter!

7

> **Recording script and answers**
> 1 high 2 hold 3 it 4 and 5 air 6 hall 7 art

Reading

8 This exercise is practice for Reading Part 3.

> 1 C 2 A 3 G 4 E 5 B

9.2 pages 58–59

Vocabulary

1

> 1 d 2 j 3 b 4 a 5 h 6 f 7 i 8 c 9 e 10 g

Reading

3

> **Suggested answers**
> 2 Where will we/people have holidays?
> 3 How will we/people travel?
> 4 Where will the mirrors be?
> 5 What will the mirrors tell you?
> 6 Why won't there be (any) curtains? / Why will there be no curtains?
> 7 Where will the food come from?

Grammar

5 This is practice for Writing Part 7.

> 1 on 2 a 3 going 4 is 5 but 6 its 7 can 8 there
> 9 some 10 will

Spelling spot

6

> 2 plays 3 happier 4 key(s) 5 monkeys 6 batteries
> 7 enjoyed 8 stays 9 families 10 buys

Exam folder 5 pages 60–61

Speaking Parts 1 and 2

Part 1

Name:	Pilar Martinez
Town/country:	Madrid, Spain
Favourite subject:	English
Countries visited:	England, France, Portugal
Free-time activities:	shopping, going out with friends, cinema

Recording script `1` `34`

Examiner: Good morning.
Candidate: Good morning.
Examiner: What's your name?
Candidate: My name is Pilar Martinez.
Examiner: How do you spell your surname?
Candidate: It's M-A-R-T-I-N-E-Z.
Examiner: And where do you come from?
Candidate: I come from Madrid, in Spain.
Examiner: Where do you study?
Candidate: I study at a school here in Madrid.
Examiner: And which subjects do you study?
Candidate: I ... I study English... and History and Geography.
Examiner: Which subject do you like best?
Candidate: Oh ... English, of course!
Examiner: Why do you like it?
Candidate: Mmm ... I enjoy learning languages, and I think ... I need English – you know, for a job later.
Examiner: Have you ever been to other countries?
Candidate: Yes, as well as England, I have been to France.
Examiner: What are you going to do next weekend?
Candidate: Next weekend it's ... it's my friend's birthday and she is having a big party.
Examiner: Tell me something about what you do in your free time.
Candidate: Erm ... In my free time I play tennis. I like tennis because it keeps me fit. I feel great! Um, I also go shopping, I ... I like doing that with my friends and ... and I go to the cinema.
Examiner: Thank you.

2

> **Possible questions and answers**
> How do you spell your surname?
> – It's R-O-S-S-I-N-I.
> Where do you come from?
> – I come from Milan.
> Where do you study?
> – At a college.
> What subjects do you study?
> – I study English, Maths, Italian, Art and History.
> Which subject do you like best?
> – I like English best / I prefer English.
> What are you doing / going to do next weekend?
> – Next weekend, I'm going shopping with some friends.

3 Try to use longer sentences here, with conjunctions such as *because, but, so*.

Part 2

4

> **Holiday Centre – possible questions and answers**
> B: Where is it?
> A: It's in/at Westcliffe on Sea.
> B: What can I do there?
> A: You can go swimming and play tennis.
> B: How much is it for an adult? / How much does it cost for an adult? / What's the price for an adult?
> A: It's £400 for a week in July.
> B: Is it open all year?
> A: No, only from March to November
> B: Is there a place to eat? / Can I eat there?
> A: Yes, there's an excellent restaurant.

5

> **Burford Arts Cinema – possible questions and answers**
> A: What can I see at the cinema?
> B: You can see/watch an adventure film. / You can see *The Return of the Martians*.
> A: What time does the film start? / When does the film start?
> B: It starts at two o'clock.
> A: Can I eat there?
> B: Yes, you can eat at the Riverside Café.
> A: What is the address? / Where is it?
> B: It's 68 Helman Street, Burford.
> A: How much is a student ticket? / How much does a student ticket cost?
> B: It's £5.00.

Unit 10

10.1 pages 62–63

Vocabulary

1

> 1d 2j 3g 4l 5m 6i 7n 8o 9k 10c 11h
> 12b 13e 14f 15a

Spelling spot

3

> 2 I have *some bookshelves* in my room.
> 3 *The knives are* on the table.
> 4 *The roofs are* red.
> 5 *Their wives are* in the kitchen.
> 6 I found *some leaves* on the floor.

Listening

5 This is practice for Listening Part 2.

> 1D 2F 3H 4A 5B

Recording script 🔊1 35

Lisa: Hi, Tom!

Tom: Oh hi, Lisa! How's the new flat?

Lisa: It's great! But we haven't finished moving all our furniture yet. The <u>metal desk</u> from my old room is still <u>in the garage</u> with lots of other things!

Tom: Did you have any problems when you moved?

Lisa: A few. The <u>leather sofa</u> was too big for the living room so <u>it's in the dining room</u> for now.

Tom: What's your new <u>bedroom</u> like?

Lisa: It's bigger than my old one and I can have the <u>computer in there</u> now. We had it in the corner of the kitchen before. My parents have put the <u>small TV in their room</u>, but they said I could have one for my birthday!

Tom: Great! What about that large <u>mirror</u> you had in the kitchen? Have you still got it?

Lisa: Yes, and it looks really good <u>in the new bathroom</u>. And do you remember my mum's books? Well, she now has <u>new bookshelves in the hall</u> – it's much better than the books being in their bedroom! Why don't you come and see us this evening?

Tom: That'd be great. I'll do that.

Vocabulary

6

the bag – leather or plastic	
the book – paper	
the bowl – wood	
the credit card – plastic	
the curtains – cotton	
the necklace – gold	
the sweater – wool	
the TV – glass, metal and plastic	
the vase – glass	
the watch – silver, metal, glass	
the window – glass and wood/plastic	

7

big	little/small
cold	hot
double	single
expensive	cheap
high	low
large	small
long	short
narrow	wide
new	old
noisy	quiet
soft	hard

8   This is practice for Reading Part 2.

1 B   **2** C   **3** A   **4** A   **5** B

10.2 pages 64–65

1

1	Empire State Building	New York, USA	1931	designed by Tom Wright
2	Opera House	Sydney, Australia	1959–73	designed by Jørn Utzon
3	Taj Mahal	Agra, India	1653	built by Shah Jehan
4	Burj al Arab	Dubai, UAE	1999	built by the government of UAE
5	Forbidden City	Beijing, China	1420	built by the Ming Emperors
6	Great Pyramid	Cairo, Egypt	2500BC	built by King Khufu

Pronunciation

2

Recording script and answers
1   twelve ninety-two
2   fifteen sixty-nine
3   seventeen eighteen
4   eighteen ninety
5   nineteen sixty-three

3

Recording script and answers
1 1340   **2** 1519   **3** 1630   **4** 1780   **5** 1870

Grammar

4

2 was/is made   **3** are borrowed   **4** was painted
5 was sold   **6** were built   **7** are taught   **8** was bought

5

1 was designed   **2** was organised   **3** wanted
4 are carried   **5** designed   **6** was built   **7** worked
8 was built   **9** was developed   **10** made   **11** were made
12 was produced

6

2 When was the competition organised?
   It was organised in 1994.
3 How many people are carried on it / can be carried on it / does it carry?
   800 people can be carried on it.
4 Where was the wheel developed?
   It was developed in the Netherlands.
5 Where were the capsules made?
   They were made in the French Alps.
6 Who produced the glass?
   It was produced by an Italian company.

Exam folder 6 pages 66–67

Reading Part 4 Right, Wrong, Doesn't say

1

> **1** *The castle is bigger than other houses in California.*
> You might think this is true or you might know for a fact that it is true, but it doesn't actually say so in the text. The answer you should give according to the text is C Doesn't say.
>
> **2** *Hearst Castle is one very large building.*
> Usually, a castle is one large building, but if you read the text you will see that Hearst Castle is made up of four houses. The answer you should give is B Wrong.
>
> **3** *Very famous American singers went to parties at Hearst Castle.*
> You might think that this is true. But the text only says 'Hollywood film stars' often came to the parties. It doesn't say singers. The answer you should give is C Doesn't say.

Part 4

21 B	22 B	23 A	24 C	25 A	26 C	27 B

Unit 11

11.1 pages 68–69

Vocabulary

2

> *surfing:* board
> *tennis:* ball, court, net, racket
> *baseball:* ball, bat, boots, glove
> *basketball:* ball, basket, boots, court, net, stadium
> *snowboarding:* board, boots, gloves
> *volleyball:* ball, court, net

3

	sport	play/do or watch?
Speaker 1	tennis	play
Speaker 2	basketball	watch
Speaker 3	baseball	watch
Speaker 4	snowboarding	do
Speaker 5	surfing	do
Speaker 6	volleyball	watch

Recording script 2 02

Speaker 1: I'm doing really well this year. I bought a new racket, perhaps that's why! The main thing is I can hit the ball much harder now. I've won my last three matches.

Speaker 2: They have matches on television here every week and I sometimes go to support the college team. Last time I went, they scored twenty-nine baskets, but they still lost!

Speaker 3: Last year, I stayed in New York with my uncle and he got tickets for the Yankees. I loved every minute of the game, it was so exciting. He gave me a bat to bring home. I haven't used it. It's on my bedroom shelf!

Speaker 4: It's much more fun than skiing. I tried it for the first time last month, when the snow was very good. I'm saving for my own board now. There are some awesome videos on the Internet – I want to be as good as those guys!

Speaker 5: I had a week of lessons in Portugal. The sea was very warm there. Back in England, I have to wear a wetsuit because it's very cold and I spend a lot of time in the water!

Speaker 6: My friends and I usually go to the beach for the Saturday matches because we're big fans of one of the women's teams there. It's a really exciting game and those girls can run and jump! They're amazing.

Reading

6 This is practice for Reading Part 4.

1 B	2 C	3 A	4 C	5 B	6 A

7

> **Possible answers**
> She's got a brother.
> She plays football in different American cities.
> She prefers playing in the USA. (11.2 focuses on the gerund/-ing form)
> She often eats pasta before a match.
> She doesn't play in goal.

Grammar extra

8

> **2** Which team does Lionel Messi play for?
> **3** Have you got a snowboard?
> **4** When is the next World Cup?
> **5** Why didn't you go to the match?
> **6** Which is your favourite sport? / Which sport is your favourite?
> **7** Where does the referee come from?
> **8** Do you want to swim in the competition?

9 In Part 2 of the Speaking test you will have to form questions from a card like this.

> **Possible questions**
> When is the sports competition?
> Which sports will there be?
> Will the sports competition be at the college or somewhere else?
> What clothes should I wear?
> Are there any prizes in the competition?

11.2 pages 70–71

Grammar

3

> spend more time <u>playing</u> computer games
> <u>going</u> out with your friends
> <u>winning</u>
> keep <u>taking</u> the lift
> <u>walking</u> to school
> <u>relaxing</u>
> <u>exercising</u>
> <u>sleeping</u> in a maths lesson
> start <u>playing</u> some sport
> stop <u>exercising</u>

4

1 sitting	**4** getting	**7** running
2 making	**5** driving	**8** throwing
3 swimming	**6** playing	**9** carrying

5 Ask students to complete the exercise and then compare answers.

> **2** hitting **3** going **4** moving **5** walking **6** winning
> **7** playing; scoring **8** practising

Listening

7 This is practice for Listening Part 5.

> **1** 11.15 (p.m.) / quarter past eleven **2** 88679
> **3** 25 / twenty-five **4** Colville **5** Tuesday

Recording script 2 04

This is the 24-hour information line for the Solway Sports Centre. Our opening hours are from six thirty in the morning until <u>eleven fifteen</u> at night, seven days a week. If you love exercising, you'll love our club! It has all the latest equipment. To book an introduction to the gym, please phone Jack Bergman on 01453 <u>88679</u> now.

There are two pools at the club. We have a ten-metre pool just for diving and a <u>twenty-five</u> metre swimming pool. Why not try relaxing in our steam room before you swim? It's fantastic!

If you'd like to become a member of Solway Sports Centre, please phone us again during working hours and ask to speak to Mrs <u>Colville</u>, that's C-O-L-V-I-double L-E.

We also give guided tours of the centre once a week. These tours are at two fifteen every <u>Tuesday</u> afternoon. You don't have to book a place, but don't be late!

We hope you enjoy getting fit at Solway Sports Centre!

8

> **1** quickly **2** quarter **3** guitar **4** guest **5** quiet **6** guess

9 This is practice for Writing Part 6.

> **1** skiing **2** cycling **3** fishing **4** climbing **5** sailing

Writing folder 3 pages 72–73

Writing Part 9 Short message

1

> **Corrected answers**
> **1**
> I'm going to visit your town next Friday. I'd like to visit the sports club near your house. I think it's a very nice place. Meet me at 7 p.m.
> Yours,
> **2**
> I think that the most interesting place near my town is a little lake, because it's not noisy there and there are a lot of animals. You can drive to it.
> Love,
> **3**
> Let's meet in front of the football ground at 17.00. I want to buy a camera and a computer game. See you on Saturday.
> **4**
> Hello,
> I have a basketball, a football, a computer and a television to sell. The basketball and football are almost new. I've only played with them once. I've had the computer and television for six months but I want to sell them.
> Bye,

2

> All four answers need to be signed (see introduction).

3

> **Answer**
> 1 information about the pool
> 2 how to get there
> 3 the best time to swim

4

> **Answer**
> Answer B is better, because it has the right number of words and includes all the necessary information.
>
> With only 20 words, answer A would lose one mark out of five. It also doesn't give information about how to get to the pool from the town centre, so it would only score three marks out of five.

5

> **Possible answer**
> Hi Alex,
> There's a swimming pool near the motorway. It's really big and has a nice café, too. Why not go at lunchtime or on Saturday? You can take tram 14 from the town centre. It stops outside the pool.
> See you,
> Mario

6

> **B** 1　**C** 2　**D** 3　**E** 1　**F** 1　**G** 3　**H** 2

7

> **Sample answer**
> Dear Alex,
> Our pool is lovely! It's big and very deep at one end. Why not go in the afternoon, when it's not as busy? You can catch a bus or walk there. It's not too far. Have fun!
> Love,
> Ellie

Unit 12

12.1 pages 74–75

Vocabulary

1

> **1** grandfather　**2** father　**3** mother　**4** (older) brother
> **5** sister

2

> **1** uncle　**2** aunt　**3** cousin　**4** grandmother　**5** grandson
> **6** granddaughter　**7** grandchild

Listening

4 This is practice for Listening Part 3.

> **1** C　**2** B　**3** C　**4** A　**5** B

Recording script 2 05

Nick: Hello, Nick speaking.

Helen: Hi, it's your cousin, Helen.

Nick: How are you?

Helen: Fine. I'm ringing about Granddad's 70th birthday party. Will it be on Friday 26th, or Saturday 27th September?

Nick: Actually, Mum and Uncle Jack decided on Sunday 28th because several people couldn't do Friday or Saturday.

Helen: OK. Are you going to have the party at your house?

Nick: It's too small! There's a nice room at his golf club, so we'll have it there. There's lunch before the party, at

Mario's restaurant.

Helen: Great. Will the party still start at three thirty?

Nick: No, four. We'll finish eating around two forty-five and it's an hour's drive.

Helen: Mm. I can take you there in my car.

Nick: Thanks, but I'll have mine. Why don't you take Aunt Rose, Uncle Jack's sister from Australia?

Helen: Fine. Now, what about presents? My brother's going to buy Granddad a box set of three DVDs, and there's a beautiful mirror I'd like to get for him. What do you think?

Nick: Sounds excellent. I've bought him a leather suitcase.

Helen: He'll love that. Well, see you on the day then, Nick.

Nick: Yes. Bye, Helen.

Pronunciation

5

> **Recording script and answers**
>
> | group 1 /aʊ/ cow | group 2 /ɔː/ draw |
> | --- | --- |
> | house | all |
> | mouth | August |
> | now | draw |
> | out | or |
> | shout | order |
> | town | saw |

Spelling spot

6

> **1** castle　**2** bicycle　**3** apple　**4** single　**5** little　**6** people

12.2 pages 76–77

2

> **Possible answers**
> being by yourself
> having a low supermarket bill
> keeping the place tidy
> travelling cheaply

Reading

3 This is practice for Reading Part 4.

> **Answer**
> Sam is close to Michael. (*get on quite well … because he is kind and helps me*)

4

> **Answer**
> Joe gets on well with Michael and David.

5

> **2** B **3** C **4** B **5** C **6** A **7** C

6

subject pronouns	object pronouns	reflexive pronouns
I	me	myself
you	you	yourself
he, she, it	him, her, it	himself, herself, itself
we	us	ourselves
you	you	yourselves
they	them	themselves

7

> **2** myself **3** them **4** himself **5** It **6** herself
> **7** themselves

8 *Everybody* has the same meaning as *everyone*, and the same is true for *anybody – anyone* and *nobody – no one*.

things	people
something	somebody / someone
anything	anybody / anyone
everything	everybody / everyone
nothing	nobody / no one

9

> **2** Somebody/Someone **3** anything **4** something
> **5** nobody / no one **6** everything **7** everybody/everyone
> **8** anybody/anyone

Units 9–12 Revision

pages 78–79

Speaking

1

> **1** G **2** E **3** H **4** F **5** C **6** D **7** B **8** A

Grammar

2

> **1** I enjoyed *seeing* your family.
> **2** I will *wait for you* at the station.
> **3** This is the best book for *learning* English.
> **4** I think *it* will cost £30.
> **5** You don't need to ask *anybody*.
> **6** I don't mind *getting* the bus to your place.
> **7** We can ride horses and we can *fish / go fishing* in the lake.
> **8** If anybody *is* interested, call this number.
> **9** You can *come* to London by train.
> **10** The village is famous because it *was* built *by* three Roman emperors.

3

> **2** was taken **3** was shown **4** was worn **5** was written
> **6** is known **7** was given **8** was built

Vocabulary

4

> **1** racket **2** net **3** gloves **4** bat **5** snowboard

5 There may be more than one correct answer.

> **Possible answers**
> **1** cousin (because a cousin could be male or female)
> **2** desk (because everything else can go on the wall)
> **3** curtains (because the other three are items of furniture)
> **4** grey (because it has no red in it)
> **5** golf (because it is not played on the water)
> **6** silver (because it is not a kind of material, but an example of a metal)

6

> **1** C **2** B **3** B **4** A **5** B

Writing

7

> **Corrected emails**
> **A**
> I'd love to come sailing with you and your family, Andrea. I go sailing about ten times a year, so I've got something to wear. Can I borrow a life jacket?
> **B**
> You asked me about my room. Well, it's quite big, with two windows. From one, I can only see the street, but from the other, there's a lovely park with trees. I want some new curtains for my room.
> **C**
> I'm going to Sicily with my brother at Easter. We're going to spend a week by the sea and then we'll go walking near Etna. It's beautiful there.

> **Questions**
> Email A answers questions 3, 8 and 10.
> Email B answers questions 1, 6 and 9.
> Email C answers questions 2, 5 and 7.
> Question 4 does not match any of the emails.

Unit 13

13.1 pages 80–81

Vocabulary

1 The photos show: (1) *fog*, (2) *cloud*, (3) *storm*, (4) *sun*, (5) *snow*, (6) *wind*, (7) *rain*. You should also know the adjectives *foggy, cloudy, stormy, windy* and *sunny*. When we talk about today's weather, if it is raining we usually say *It's raining* and not *It's rainy*. We use *rainy* to describe a period of time when it rained often. *Snowy* and *It's snowing* are also used in that way. We can use *wet* and *dry* to talk about the weather. For example: *It's dry and sunny. It's cold and wet.*

2

1 windy	**2** raining	**3** sunny	**4** cloudy	**5** wet	**6** foggy
7 storms	**8** dry	**9** snow			

Listening

5 This is practice for Listening Part 2.

1 A	**2** H	**3** F	**4** G	**5** B

Recording script 2 ⟨07⟩

Girl: How was your trip, Dan? I'd love to go round the world.

Dan: It was great. First we went to London, but only for a few days as it rained all the time. Both of us got really wet.

Girl: You went to Paris next, didn't you?

Dan: Well, Paris wasn't at all sunny but it was better than London – a bit cloudy.

Girl: Did you go up the Eiffel Tower?

Dan: Yes, we both had a great time!

Girl: Where did you go after Paris?

Dan: To Cairo. We saw the Pyramids.

Girl: Was it very hot?

Dan: It wasn't as hot as in summer. It was quite windy actually.

Girl: I'd love to go there.

Dan: Yes, you'd like it. We went to Sydney next. We didn't get to the famous Bondi Beach as there were a lot of storms. We did lots of shopping there.

Girl: That sounds expensive!

Dan: It wasn't as expensive as Tokyo. It was hot and sunny there – no rain at all for the whole five days we were there!

Girl: And then you went to the USA, didn't you?

Dan: Yes, to San Francisco, which is famous for its fog. It was so thick we couldn't even see the Golden Gate Bridge! But it was warmer than some of the other places!

Grammar extra

6

Possible answers
The weather in Beijing was cloudy yesterday, the same as in Rome.
Vancouver was not as cold as Moscow.
Mexico City was hotter than Sydney.
Athens was as warm as Madrid.

Pronunciation

7

Recording script and answers
1 You went *to* Paris.
2 Paris was *a* bit cloudy.
3 We had *a* great time.
4 I'd love *to* go there.
5 We stayed in *a* hotel.
6 We did *some* shopping there.
7 There was no rain *at* all.
8 It was warmer *than* some of the other places.
The missing words are all unstressed, weak forms with the sound /ə/.

8

1 Bob went camping with <u>a</u> friend.
2 Both <u>of</u> them like camping.
3 They got <u>to</u> <u>the</u> campsite late.
4 They slept <u>for</u> ten hours.
5 There <u>was</u> <u>a</u> good view <u>from</u> their tent.
6 They had hot chocolate <u>to</u> drink.
7 Bob took <u>some</u> great photos.

13.2 pages 82–83

1

1 True
2 True
3 False – The Atacama Desert has an average rainfall of 0.5 mm, although there are some parts of it where rainfall hasn't been recorded for 400 years!
4 True

Grammar

2

Suggested answers
1 It's too cold to go swimming. / It isn't warm enough to go swimming.
2 It's too windy to use an umbrella.
3 It's too difficult to do.
4 It's too far to walk. / I'm too tired.
5 It's too expensive to buy. / I'm not rich enough to buy it.
6 It's too heavy to carry very far. / I'm not strong enough to carry it very far.

3 Some adjectives can be used more than once.

Reading

4 This is practice for Reading Part 5.

1 B 2 B 3 A 4 B 5 C 6 B 7 A 8 C

Spelling spot

5

1 I went *to* Tokyo last year for *two* weeks.
2 My cousin went *too*.
3 We took taxis *to* places because it was *too* difficult for us *to* use the subway.
4 When I got home I tried *to* cook some Japanese food.
5 I made some sushi and invited *two* friends for a meal.
6 They wanted *to* know how *to* make it so they could cook it *too*.

6

1 The weather *is* very sunny.
2 This year the weather *is* colder than last year.
3 What *is* the weather like in Australia?
4 The weather in Caracas is hotter *than* in Santiago.
5 It was not *hot enough* to go swimming.
6 I like sunny weather *very* much.

Exam folder 7 pages 84–85

Listening Part 2 Multiple matching

1

Possible answers
2 *Months of the year:* January, February, March, April, May, June, July, August, September, October, November, December.
3 *Sports:* football, swimming, rugby, baseball, basketball, volleyball, tennis, golf, hockey, skiing, skating, surfing, snowboarding, table tennis, skateboarding
4 *Colours:* blue, red, green, yellow, purple, pink, black, brown, white, orange, grey
5 *Clothes:* dress, jacket, trousers, jeans, blouse, T-shirt, pants, socks, coat, skirt, shorts, jumper, sweater
6 *Family:* aunt, sister, uncle, cousin, grandmother, grandfather, daughter, niece, nephew, son, father, mother
7 *Food:* apple, soup, burger, bread, salad, fish, chicken, cheese, rice, spaghetti, tomato, toast, chips

Part 2

6 A 7 G 8 B 9 F 10 C

Recording script 2 [10]

Listen to Penny talking to her cousin about the presents she bought on holiday for her friends. Which friend got each present? For questions 6 to 10 write a letter, A to H, next to each friend. You will hear the conversation twice.

Penny: Hi, Nick.

Nick: Hi, Penny. How was your holiday in Switzerland?

Penny: It was great – hot and sunny every day and some nice shops! Look, <u>Nick</u>, I bought you <u>a mug</u>. See, it's got 'Switzerland' written on it.

Nick: Oh thanks! Did you get <u>James</u> a pen? He's always taking mine.

Penny: I got him <u>an album</u> of a local band – he likes anything to do with music.

Nick: True. What about <u>Becky</u>? Did you get her a watch? It might help her to be on time!

Penny: She's actually getting one for her birthday, so I got her some <u>nice soap</u> – look, it's in a really lovely box.

Nick: Mm. She'll like that.

Penny: And for <u>Alice</u> – well Alice is difficult to buy for, but in the end I bought her <u>a book</u> about skiing.

Nick: Good idea! Now, what about <u>Tom</u>?

Penny: He's got lots of books about Switzerland, so I bought him <u>a picture</u> to put on his wall.

Nick: That leaves <u>Lucy</u>. You didn't get *her* a watch, did you?

Penny: No, I just got her <u>a comb</u>. I couldn't think of anything else.

Nick: OK. Anyway, I must go. Thanks for the mug!

Now listen again.

(The recording is repeated.)

Unit 14

14.1 pages 86–87

Reading

2 This is practice for Reading Part 4.

1 C 2 B 3 A 4 A 5 C 6 A 7 B

Grammar

4

1	2	3	4	5	6	NOUN
What's it like?	How big?	How old?	What colour?	Where's it from?	What kind?	
opinion	size	age		nationality		
	deep		blue			lake
good-looking				Australian		guitar player
great		new			computer	games

5

1 a boring old book
2 a colourful new magazine
3 a modern Japanese computer
4 the excellent new school library
5 the long adventure book
6 the expensive little leather bag
7 a beautiful white dress
8 a clever young writer

6

Possible answers
1 I am reading a great new thriller. It is about this brilliant American scientist who finds a way of making people invisible.
2 My favourite item of clothing is a short, blue cotton skirt which I wear to parties.
3 My best friend is a fifteen-year-old French girl. She's tall and slim and I think she's very pretty.
4 My favourite film is the last *Harry Potter*. It's a really fast, exciting film.
5 I like Justin Bieber because he sings such brilliant, new songs.

7

The silent letters are underlined.
1 light 2 knows 3 guitar 4 what 5 who 6 often

8

Recording script and answers
1 island 2 castle 3 half 4 climb 5 autumn 6 knife
7 Wednesday 8 hour

Spelling spot

9 Candidates often confuse these words in the Writing part of the exam.

1 *Then* Suzy ran into the sea, but it was colder *than* it looked.
2 The weather was really *bad* when I was on holiday.
3 You don't *want* to stay in *bed* all day, do you?
4 She said, '*Bye*' and went out to *buy* a book.
5 We are going to get some *things* from town.
6 I *won't* be home late tonight.

14.2 pages 88–89

Listening

3 This is practice for Listening Part 4.

1 November 2 (£)240
3 9.15 / a quarter past nine / nine fifteen
4 Marylebone (High Street) 5 189

Recording script 2 13
Man: Hello. Can I help you?
Sylvia: Yes, please. I'd like some information about Saturday classes at the school.
Man: I'm afraid the classes are full until the end of October. The new classes begin on 3rd November. Which classes are you interested in?
Sylvia: Singing and dance.
Man: OK. Can you send me a cheque and I'll keep a place for you? It's £120 for each class, so that'll be £240 then.
Sylvia: And what time do the classes begin? I'm free all morning.
Man: The school opens at nine o'clock on Saturdays and classes start at nine fifteen.
Sylvia: Could I visit the school to see what it's like?
Man: Of course. We're in Marylebone High Street – that's M-A-R-Y-L-E-B-O-N-E.
Sylvia: Thanks. Can I get a bus? I prefer buses to the underground.
Man: Yes, there's the 139 or the 189. The 189 stops right outside the school.
Sylvia: That's great. When can I come and visit?
Man: Any time. What about next week?
Sylvia: OK, I'll do that. Thank you very much.
Man: You're welcome. Goodbye.
Sylvia: Goodbye.

Reading

4 This is practice for Reading Part 3.

1 C 2 D 3 B 4 A

5

1 G 2 E 3 I 4 H 5 F 6 J 7 A 8 D 9 C 10 B

Recording script 2 14
1
Girl: I can't come on the school trip.
Woman: What a pity.
2
Boy: What are you doing?
Girl: Chemistry homework.
3
Girl: I've got an exam tomorrow.
Man: Good luck!

4

Boy: I've passed all my exams.
Girl: Congratulations!

5

Woman: Would you mind opening the classroom window?
Boy: Sure, I can do that.

6

Girl: Where's the library?
Man: On the first floor.

7

Boy: Hi! How are you?
Girl: Fine, thanks.

8

Man: Is that your teacher?
Girl: No, it's not.

9

Man: Can I sit here?
Woman: I'm afraid it's taken.

10

Boy: Let's study together tonight.
Girl: Sorry, I can't – I'm going swimming.

6

Across		Down	
3	language	1	pen
4	library	2	study
6	board	5	bookshelf
7	listen	8	desk
9	teacher	10	cupboard
11	history	12	saw
13	homework		

Grammar extra

7

> 2 Would you like to marry someone famous or someone who isn't famous?
> 3 Do you prefer eating in restaurants or going on a picnic?
> 4 Would you like to meet Angelina Jolie and Brad Pitt?
> 5 On your next holiday would you like to go to New York?
> 6 Do you prefer getting up early or staying in bed?
> 7 Where would you like to live?

Exam folder 8 pages 90–91

Reading Part 3 Multiple choice

The answer to the example is B. In English people usually answer with 'It's' rather than 'I'm' on the phone. You shouldn't choose A just because you see the word 'Sally' in the possible answers.

Part 3

11 C	12 B	13 A	14 B	15 A	16 D	17 A	18 H	19 C	20 F

Unit 15
15.1 pages 92–93
Vocabulary

1 The chef is Jamie Oliver.

> 1 nurse   2 photographer   3 chef   4 actor   5 farmer

2

> 1 A dentist looks after people's teeth.
> 2 A receptionist helps people when they arrive at a hotel or office.
> 3 A tour guide shows visitors a place or area.
> 4 An engineer designs and builds roads and bridges.
> 5 A journalist writes articles for newspapers and magazines.

Reading

4 This is practice for Reading Part 4.

> 1 B   2 A   3 A   4 B   5 C   6 A   7 C

Grammar

5

> **Answer**
> The present perfect is formed with *has/have* and the past participle.

6

> 1 B   2 A   3 A   4 B
> You must use the past simple with *ago* because it refers to a completed action in definite past time.
> 5 A   6 incorrect   7 A

7

> Sentences 3, 5 and 7 are incorrect:
> 3 The supermarket *advertised* for more staff last week.
> 5 Marion *became* a doctor in 2011.
> 7 Lee *arrived* for his meeting an hour ago.

8

> 2 moved   3 have made   4 has travelled   5 began
> 6 decided   7 meant / has meant   8 wasn't   9 found
> 10 has taken

Spelling spot

10 This is also useful practice for Writing Part 6.

> 1 photographer   2 painter   3 journalist   4 actor
> 5 doctor
> The job in the yellow box is *pilot*.

15.2 pages 94–95

1 In Britain many teenagers work delivering newspapers to people's homes, either before or after school, or do part-time jobs in the evening or at weekends.

The photos show a girl delivering newspapers, a boy helping in a stable and a girl working in a cake shop.

2

1 B 2 A 3 C

Grammar extra

4

> 1 The receptionist at the sports centre has just left a message for you.
> 2 Tom hasn't met his new boss yet.
> 3 They haven't sent me any information about the job yet.
> 4 Nick's dad has just stopped working at the hospital.
> 5 My uncle has just given me a job in his café.
> 6 Charlotte and Andy haven't found a photographer for their wedding yet.
> 7 I have just chosen a computer course to go on.
> 8 The supermarket manager hasn't paid Mike for his extra hours yet.

Listening

5 This is practice for Listening Part 3.

1 B 2 C 3 B 4 A 5 B

Recording script 2 15

Sam: Melody Music Shop?

Kate: Yes, this is Kate Richards. How can I help?

Sam: My name's Sam Bennett. I've just seen your advertisement for a Saturday job. What are the hours?

Kate: The shop's open from ten to six but I need someone to start at nine and stay until seven. I'm always here from eight till eight on Saturdays so I really need some help then!

Sam: I see. What kind of help?

Kate: Well, the most important thing is helping customers, being a shop assistant. I also want someone to do a bit of cleaning at the end of the day, so I can do the money.

Sam: Fine. How much do you pay?

Kate: If you aren't 18 yet, it's £ 5.25 an hour.

Sam: Actually, I am 18.

Kate: Then it's £6.30, and after nine months I'll pay £7.00 an hour.

Sam: Sounds great! Er … where is the shop? I've never been there!

Kate: It's not in the town centre. If you know the university, it's about three minutes' walk from there.

Sam: I live in Weston, but I can cycle along the river to get there.

Kate: That's true. Well, any other questions?

Sam: When can I come and see you about the job? I'm free on Wednesday afternoon.

Kate: Sorry, I've got a meeting then. Um, how about Thursday or Friday?

Sam: I can come early on Thursday, at nine?

Kate: Fine. See you then.

Sam: Great!

Pronunciation

6 The focus is on the sounds /ð/ as in *clothes* and /θ/ as in *thirsty*.

group 1 /ð/	group 2 /θ/
than	thunder
those	theatre
leather	thirty
	month
	nothing

Recording script 2 17

leather month nothing than theatre thirty those thunder

7

> 1 I've worked for the last two months in my father's shop.
> 2 Let's look at all these job adverts together.
> 3 I thought you were working at the museum. Have you finished there?
> 4 Jenny, thanks for looking through my article.
> 5 That footballer earns a hundred and thirty thousand pounds a month!
> 6 My brother's just got a job in the north of Sweden.

Writing folder 4 pages 96–97

Writing Part 8 Information transfer

All the information that you need for the answers is on the question paper. In Part 8, candidates often lose marks because they copy a word or number wrongly.

1

1 ticket 2 poster 3 email

2

1 07765 912448 2 *Animal Farm* 3 August 29 / 29.08 4 Juan Romero 5 £12.30 6 8.00 (pm) / 20.00 7 Brenton College (gardens) 8 £5.75

Part 8

51 lauratou@free.fr 52 18 53 23 June / June 23 / 23.06 54 Eastbourne 55 (£)60

Unit 16
16.1 pages 98–99

1

> 1 False – The world's largest airport in land area is King Fahd International Airport in Dammam, Saudi Arabia, at 790 sq km.
> 2 True
> 3 True
> 4 Partly false – It was a sheep, a duck and a chicken!

Vocabulary

2

> 1 train   2 coach   3 bicycle   4 boat   5 plane
> 6 motorbike   7 helicopter   8 horse

3

> a 7   b 1   c 8   d 6   e 2   f 3   g 4   h 5

4

> *catch* – a coach, a train, a plane
> *drive* – a train, a coach
> *fly* – a plane, a helicopter
> *get* – a coach, a train, a plane, a helicopter, a boat
> *get off/on* – a train, a coach, a bicycle, a boat, a plane, a helicopter, a horse
> *park* – a coach, a motorbike
> *ride* – a bicycle, a motorbike, a horse
> *sail* – a boat
> *take off* – a plane, a helicopter

Grammar

5

> 1–2 *Should* gives advice here (and the girl doesn't have to act on it); *must* holds an obligation – it is essential that this girl is at Gate 43 by six o'clock or she won't be allowed to board the plane.
> 3–4 *Mustn't* is a prohibition (i.e. you must go earlier than six o'clock); *don't have to* means it isn't necessary to go there before six o'clock, but you can if you want to.

6

> 1 should   2 don't have to   3 must   4 mustn't

7 Remember that there is no *to* after *needn't* (*needn't to* is a common error at this level).

> 1 *need to* – The closest verb is *must*.
> 2 *needn't* – The closest verb is *don't have to*.

8

> 1 need to   2 needn't   3 should   4 need to   5 mustn't

9

> **Possible answer**
> You need to fly to Paris first. You should change planes there and fly to Ajaccio. You needn't hire a car at the airport. You should take a taxi to the station. Then you can take a train to Vizzavona.

16.2 pages 100–101

Vocabulary

1

> **Possible answers**
> Visiting a big city – go shopping, go sightseeing, take photos of old buildings
> Hiking in the countryside – walk around a lake, look for wild animals, go swimming in a river
> Spending a day at the beach – play volleyball, go fishing, go surfing

2

> build a sand castle   kick a football
> climb a hill   throw a Frisbee
> fly a kite   visit a museum
> have a picnic

Speaking

3 This is practice for Speaking Part 2.

> 1 Right – Each candidate has a turn at asking the five questions.
> 2 Wrong – You must base your answers on the information given on the card.
> 3 Right – You should talk only to the other candidate.
> 4 Wrong – You should use some other words and expressions, to make the conversation sound as natural as possible and to show your language range.
> 5 Right!

Listening

6 This is practice for Listening Part 1.

> 1 B   2 B   3 C   4 B   5 A

Recording script 2 19

1 *Which train is leaving first?*
Man: Excuse me, is this the Bristol train?
Woman: No, this one's leaving for Oxford in five minutes. There's been a change to the Bristol train. You need to go over the bridge to platform 4.
Man: Oh dear, have I got enough time to get there?
Woman: Plenty, <u>that's the London train that's ready to leave now</u>. Yours will be the next train after that one.

Now listen again.

(The recording is repeated.)

2 *How will the girl get to the cinema?*

Girl: Can you tell me where the ABC cinema is, please?

Man: Certainly. Turn left at the next traffic lights and then take the second on the right.

Girl: Is that Green Street?

Man: That's the turning after. It's Robertson Road you need. Go nearly to the end and you'll see the cinema on your left.

Now listen again.

(The recording is repeated.)

3 *Where is Kate's boat now?*

Adam: Hi, Kate! We've just sailed past that little island. How far have you got?

Kate: Well, Adam, I can't describe anything because there's water all around. We went under a bridge about a quarter of an hour ago, if that means anything?

Adam: Sounds like you'll get to our meeting place in about an hour then.

Kate: Sorry it's taking so long. Bye.

Now listen again.

(The recording is repeated.)

4 *How will the woman get to work today?*

Anne: Mike, it's Anne. Listen, there are no trains this morning because of last night's winds. Is it OK if I get a taxi in to work? Will the company pay?

Mike: Can't you use your car? It's much cheaper.

Anne: I'm afraid it's at the garage.

Mike: OK, then, but make sure you ask for a receipt. See you later.

Now listen again.

(The recording is repeated.)

5 *Where is the nearest petrol station?*

Woman: Can you tell me where I can get some petrol?

Man: Well, the cheapest place is on the motorway. It's not far. You can get on at the next roundabout.

Woman: I really need a nearer one. I haven't got much left.

Man: I see. Turn left by the lights, then, and you'll find one on the right next to a bank, about 200 metres down that road.

Now listen again.

(The recording is repeated.)

Pronunciation

7

2 W	3 S	4 W	5 W	6 W	7 S	8 W

Spelling spot

5

1 museum	2 airport	3 hospital	4 (correct)	5 university

Units 13–16 Revision

pages 102–103

Speaking

1

Possible questions
2 Shall we go swimming at the beach later?
3 Do you want to go for a pizza after class?
4 What does your favourite jacket look like?
5 What's the weather going to be like at the weekend?
6 How much does it cost to get in to the club?
7 Have you visited any other countries?
8 Have you read any good books recently?

Grammar

2

The correct sentences are:
1 B 2 A 3 C 4 B

3

1 C	2 B	3 B	4 A	5 C	6 B	7 A	8 C

Vocabulary

4

Jobs
Nouns: actor, chef, dentist, farmer, journalist, photographer, receptionist, tour guide
Verbs: build, grow, phone, write
Weather
Nouns: cloud, fog, rain, snow, storm, wind
Verbs: rain, snow
Transport
Nouns: boat, car, helicopter, motorbike, plane
Verbs: catch, drive, fly, get off, park, sail, take off

5

1 C	2 B	3 B	4 A	5 A	6 B	7 B	8 C

Writing

6

1 any 2 one/magazine 3 ago 4 lots/plenty
5 every/each/this/next 6 most 7 something 8 by
9 were 10 never

Unit 17

17.1 pages 104–105

Grammar

2 Remember that not all the infinitives with *to* are infinitives of purpose.

> You use your computer <u>to play</u> games until late every night.
> You don't like using Facebook <u>to chat</u> to friends.
> You hate using the computer <u>to do</u> your homework.
> You could use it <u>to help</u> your social life

3

> 2 to download   3 to turn on   4 to call   5 to keep
> 6 to listen   7 to study   8 to buy

4

> **Possible answers**
> 2 People use Google to search for information.
> 3 People buy electric cars to be green.
> 4 People go to other countries to learn a language and to find out about different cultures.
> 5 People play computer games to have fun.
> 6 People use a laptop computer to work outside or to work on the train.
> 7 People read magazines to find out about one of their interests.
> 8 People play team sports to get fit / have fun / keep healthy.
> 9 People learn English to get a good job or to travel.
> 10 People buy the latest technology to be cool.

6 This is practice for Reading Part 5. It is important to try to understand the text before you start to do the exam task. It is a very bad idea to try to answer the multiple-choice questions without reading the text first.

> 1 A   2 C   3 A   4 B   5 B   6 A   7 C   8 B

17.2 pages 106–107

Listening

2 This is practice for Listening Part 3.

> 1 C   2 A   3 B   4 C   5 C

Recording script 2 22

Edward: Hi, Vanessa! Did you have a good weekend?

Vanessa: Great! I had a fun weekend. I went to see a special gadget show in London.

Edward: Sounds interesting, but I think shows like that are too expensive – I paid £15 last time I went.

Vanessa: This was only <u>£9.50.</u> I did buy a guidebook as well – that was an extra £5.95.

Edward: How did you get there?

Vanessa: You can take the underground, but <u>I got the bus</u>. It stops just outside. I got very tired walking around all day though.

Edward: What did you see?

Vanessa: Well, the <u>Games Hall was my favourite</u>, but there was an interesting 3D Theatre and also a large Test Space.

Edward: It sounds great! How early can you go in? At nine?

Vanessa: <u>You can't go in until ten</u>, and we didn't get there until eleven thirty, so there wasn't enough time to see everything.

Edward: Can you eat there?

Vanessa: Yes. You can even take a picnic! I had a <u>sandwich at a café</u> but you can get a hot meal at the restaurant.

Edward: I'd really like to go. I'm free next Saturday – that's 23rd April.

Vanessa: The show's only on until the <u>27th</u>, so the Saturday may be busy.

Edward: Well, I'll go on the 24th then.

Pronunciation

3

> You *cannot* go in until ten.
> We *did not* get there until eleven thirty.
> There *was not* enough time to see everything.
> I *would* really like to go.
> I *am* free next Saturday – *that is* 23rd April.
> I *will* go on the 24th.

4

> **Recording script and answers**
> 1 *I'm* going to buy a new calculator.
> 2 *Aren't* you coming to my house tonight?
> 3 *Who's* playing with my PlayStation?
> 4 *I'd* like a new phone for my birthday.
> 5 (can't be contracted)
> 6 *Dan's* borrowed my laptop again.
> 7 They *can't* get any batteries because the *shop's* closed.
> 8 (can't be contracted)

Vocabulary

5

> | get | a job; a bus |
> |---|---|
> | give | a party; someone a call |
> | have | a party; a good time; a job; friends |
> | make | friends; a noise; a film |
> | see | a film; friends |
> | watch | a film; TV |
>
> We normally say *watch TV* and *see a film*, though *watch a film* is sometimes also possible.

6

1 make	2 get	3 make	4 watch	5 see	6 given	7 give

Spelling spot

7 This has typical errors made by *Key* candidates.

> Hi everyone
> *I want* to sell my phone *because* my girlfriend *bought* me a new *one* last *weekend. It is two months* old. *The price* was about $100 and *I'm selling* it for $50. *Does anyone* want to *buy* it?

Grammar extra

8

> 1 I'd like *to see* you next weekend.
> 2 I must *arrive* home at 10.00.
> 3 I would like *to sell* my books.
> 4 I want *to buy* it.
> 5 You can *go* to a museum there.
> 6 I have decided *to study* chemistry.
> 7 She should *visit* London.
> 8 I hope *to see* you soon.
> 9 We need *to do* our homework tonight.
> 10 We went to London *to see* the London Eye.

Exam folder 9 pages 108–109

Listening Part 3 Multiple choice

The answer to Example 2 is C.

Part 3

11 B	12 A	13 C	14 C	15 A

Recording script 2 25

Listen to Ellie talking to Chris about Lynne, his sister.
For questions 11 to 15, tick A, B, or C. You will hear the conversation twice. Look at questions 11 to 15 now. You have 20 seconds.

Ellie: Hi, Chris. I hear Lynne's here. I thought she was coming on Saturday.

Chris: Yeah, well, <u>she came on Wednesday</u> because she has to be at work again on Monday.

Ellie: That's a pity. How is Lynne's new job with that computer company?

Chris: Great. She did a course in London and <u>now she's in New York</u> for a year. Next year she may go to Hong Kong!

Ellie: That's brilliant! I'd like to work with computers.

Chris: Me too, but Lynne didn't study anything to do with computers at school. Dad <u>taught her at home</u> and then she did maths at university.

Ellie: She must work hard.

Chris: Yes, but she gets four weeks' holiday a year. <u>Next year it'll be six</u> – my dad only gets five!

Ellie: Can I see her tomorrow?

Chris: Of course. Come <u>in the afternoon</u>. She'll be in bed all morning.

Ellie: OK, I'll come after lunch. I've bought her a watch for her birthday.

Chris: Wow, Ellie, she'll love that! She really wanted me to get her a camera but I only had enough money <u>for a computer game, so I got that!</u>

Ellie: I'm sure she'll like it. See you tomorrow.

Now listen again.

(The recording is repeated.)

Unit 18
18.1 pages 110–111

Vocabulary

1

1 head d	2 hair b	3 neck k	4 arm f	5 hands j
6 back l	7 leg a	8 foot h	9 ear c	10 mouth i
11 nose e	12 eye g			

2 This is practice for Reading Part 6.

1 sick	2 nurse	3 ambulance	4 medicine
5 temperature	6 chemist		

3 This is practice for Reading Part 3. There may be more than one correct piece of advice.

Suggested answers
1 H	2 J	3 E	4 B	5 C	6 F	7 I	8 A	9 G	10 D

4

> **Possible answers**
> 1 I think I've broken my leg.
>   – Why don't you go to hospital? / You should call an ambulance.
> 2 I've got stomach ache.
>   – Why don't you lie down?
> 3 I've got toothache.
>   – You need to see a dentist.
> 4 I've cut my knee.
>   – You should put a plaster on it.
> 5 I've got a cold.
>   – You need to drink some hot lemon juice and go to bed.
> 6 I've got a headache.
>   – Why don't you take an aspirin?

Listening

5 This is practice for Listening Part 5.

1 6.30 (p.m.)	2 Peters	3 17	4 (the) cinema	5 01921 6582

Thank you for calling for information about the opening hours for chemists in your area. This information is for the week of the 15th to the 21st December. There are two chemists, one in Sandford and one in Dursley. Bridges Chemist in Sandford opens at eight forty-five from Monday to Saturday and closes at <u>six thirty p.m.</u> Monday to Friday and at twelve thirty p.m. on Saturday. The shop is at 53 Green Street, Sandford. There is a small car park next to the shop.

Outside those hours, please go to Peters. That's <u>P-E-T-E-R-S</u>. This is in Dursley at number <u>17</u> The High Street. It's on the other side of the road to <u>the cinema</u> and is open from ten thirty a.m. to four thirty p.m. on Sundays and has late opening to eight p.m. on weekdays. The telephone number is <u>01921 6582</u>. Ring this number if you need to talk to the chemist at night. You can park in The High Street on Sundays.

Grammar extra

6   Where it is possible to place the time phrase at the beginning of the sentence, this is shown in brackets.

1   (Last night) I was at a big party last night.
2   (On Saturday) I'll come shopping on Saturday.
3   We have been to the beach every day.
4   (After work) I went to the chemist after work.
5   They usually sleep well at night.
6   (Today) I bought some new trainers today.

Pronunciation

7

Recording script and answers
1   Can_you call_an_ambulance?
2   Fruit_and vegetables_are very good for you.
3   You should do some_exercise_every day.
4   Watching TV_all weekend_is not good for you.
5   Make sure you get_enough sleep_at night.

18.2 pages 112–113

Reading

2   This is practice for Reading Part 4.

The oldest person mentioned is Shirali Muslimov.
1 A   2 B   3 C   4 B   5 C   6 A   7 A   8 B

Grammar

If you eat a little but often, you will live a long life.

The tenses used are:
If + *eat* (present simple), + *will live* (future simple)

3

Suggested answers
1 E   2 D   3 A   4 F   5 B   6 C

7   This is practice for Writing Part 9.

Sample answer
This answer includes all the key points and is error-free. It would receive full marks.
Dear Tina,
I want to get fit so I can climb a mountain with my father in the summer. I am going to go running every day and I will do this from tomorrow morning!
Love,
Julia

Spelling spot

8

1 ✓   2 ✗ – faster   3 ✓   4 ✗ – stopping   5 ✓   6 ✓
7 ✗ – thinner   8 ✗ – swimming

Exam folder 10 pages 114–117

Reading Part 4 Multiple choice

One long article

1

Answer
1 C

2

21 B   22 C   23 B   24 A   25 C   26 A   27 B

Three short articles

21 C   22 A   23 B   24 A   25 B   26 C   27 B

Unit 19

19.1 pages 118–119

Vocabulary

1

> *Across*
> call envelope facebook text message write telephone
> *Down*
> internet send email receive mobile postcard ring note

c	a	l	l	r	o	m	a	y	i
w	e	n	v	e	l	o	p	e	n
i	t	f	a	c	e	b	o	o	k
n	s	u	f	e	a	i	s	r	n
t	e	x	t	i	l	l	t	i	o
e	n	e	e	v	l	e	c	n	t
r	d	b	m	e	s	s	a	g	e
n	c	k	a	t	o	m	r	i	t
e	w	r	i	t	e	n	d	a	l
t	t	e	l	e	p	h	o	n	e

Listening

3 This is practice for Listening Part 2.

> 1 D 2 F 3 A 4 E 5 G

Recording script 2 28

Paul: Hello, Ruby.

Ruby: Hi, Paul. I've just seen your facebook page. Congratulations on getting the job!

Paul: Thanks. Mario's travelling up to Scotland today so he hasn't been online this morning. I spoke to him on his <u>mobile</u> instead.

Ruby: Good. Have you told <u>Anna</u> yet?

Paul: Well, I left a <u>message</u> on her <u>phone</u>, but I think she's away. If I don't hear from her, I'll send her a text tomorrow.

Ruby: And what about your brother, <u>Jack</u>? He's away too, isn't he?

Paul: Yes, in Argentina. I <u>emailed</u> him from home this morning after I opened the letter about the job. I know he'll be pleased.

Ruby: Was <u>Tessa</u> still in the flat when the post arrived?

Paul: No, but I've left a <u>big note</u> on the kitchen table for her.

Ruby: Remember to phone <u>your professor</u> and tell him.

Paul: I can't, because the number at the university has

changed. Anyway, I've already told him the news on a <u>postcard</u>. I bought one of that Moroccan carpet we saw at the museum.

Ruby: He'll like that.

Pronunciation

4

> 2 Mario's tra|vel|ling up to Scot|land to|day.
> 3 I spoke to him on his mo|bile in|stead.
> 4 I left a mess|age on her phone.
> 5 Yes, in Ar|gen|ti|na.
> 6 Re|mem|ber to phone your pro|fess|or and tell him.
> 7 The num|ber at the u|ni|ver|si|ty has changed.
> 8 I bought one of that Mo|rocc|an car|pet we saw at the mu|se|um.

Grammar

5

> 2 on 3 in 4 in/on 5 at 6 in 7 at

6

> 1 You can call me *on* my cell phone: 22 59 67 81.
> 2 I'll meet you *at/in* the supermarket in West Street.
> 3 I'm *on* holiday now in Istanbul.
> 4 You can stay *at/in* my house.
> 5 The hotel is *in* the centre of the town.
> 6 We live *in* a new house in Magka.
> 7 (correct)
> 8 If you are interested in joining the club, find me *in* room 12.

7

> 1 many 2 because/as/since 3 some 4 on 5 In
> 6 these 7 Which 8 will 9 me 10 everyone/everybody

Spelling spot

8

> 1 received 2 free; each 3 speak 4 field 5 week 6 kilo

19.2 pages 120–121

2

> 1 *Wrong* – Spanish is spoken by about 390 million people, but Mandarin Chinese is spoken by more than 1000 million people (845 million native speakers, 1025 million total – figures from 2000).
> 2 *Wrong* – Japanese is not an official language of the UN. The six languages are: English, French, Spanish, Russian, Arabic, Chinese.
> 3 *Right*
> 4 *Right*
> 5 *Wrong* – The text in exercise 3 explains this.

Reading

3 This is practice for Reading Part 5.

1 C 2 B 3 C 4 B 5 A 6 C 7 B 8 C

Grammar

4

We use *in* with years, etc.
We use *on* with days, etc.
We use *at* with times, etc.

Vocabulary

6

country	nationality	language(s) spoken
Argentina	Argentinian	Spanish
Brazil	Brazilian	Portuguese
Chile	Chilean	Spanish
France	French	French
Greece	Greek	Greek
Italy	Italian	Italian
Mexico	Mexican	Spanish
Morocco	Moroccan	Arabic, French
Switzerland	Swiss	French, German, Italian, Romansch

Writing folder 5 pages 122–123

Writing Part 9 Short message

1

A, C, D

2

Answer 3 is the best and would score 5 marks. It has only one error (*in the bus stop*) and all parts of the message are clearly communicated.

Answer 2 is the worst and would score 1 mark. Only one piece of information is communicated and the answer is short (23 words).

Answer 1 would score 4 marks. It is just long enough at 25 words and contains some errors in spelling and grammar.

Answer 4 would score 3 marks. All three parts of the message are there but the information is not very clear. There are also some errors in grammar and spelling. This answer is very long (53 words). You do not lose marks if your answer is too long, but it is better to write 25–35 words which are correct and give clear information. A better answer is given in 4 below.

3

Corrected answers

1
Dear Pat
I'll be free at 10 a.m. We can meet ~~us~~ at Paul's ~~caffe~~. I'd like to buy a skirt. See you on Saturday.
Love Anya

2
Dear Pat
~~I will go~~ for two hours. ~~I will meet with~~ John and ~~I will want to buy~~ a red bicycle.
Your friend

3
Dear Pat
I think it is a great idea to go shopping together. We could meet ~~at~~ the bus stop at 12 o'clock in the morning. I'd like to buy some pens.
See you soon. Claudia

4
Yes, ~~I coming~~ with you ~~to shopping~~ on Saturday. I'll probably be free ~~at the lunch~~. We'll meet ~~us~~ at the shopping centre in town. I want to buy ~~me~~ ~~two trousers~~ and a top. Perhaps, I ~~want to buy also~~ a ~~robe~~. And you, what do you want to buy? From your best friend Sylvie

4

Corrected answers
Dear Pat,
I'm free to go shopping at lunchtime on Saturday. Let's meet at the shopping centre in town. I want to buy two pairs of trousers, a top and perhaps a dress too.
From your best friend,
Sylvie

Part 9

Sample answer
Hi Jan,
Let's meet at the cinema at 7.30 tomorrow. I really want to see *Hugo*. You'll love it because your favourite actor, Asa Butterfield, is in it. See you inside.
Love,
Kirsten
(33 words)

Unit 20

20.1 pages 124–125

1 The photos show: top left Cesc Fabregas; top right Shakira; bottom Emma Watson.

3

1 B (Shakira was born in 1977 and Emma Watson in 1992.)
2 C 3 A 4 C 5 B

Grammar

4

1. has sold (present perfect with *since*)
2. became (past simple with definite time in the past)
3. won't play (negative future reference – Fabregas transferred to Barcelona in August 2011)
4. was growing up (past continuous for temporary situation in the past)
5. talks (present simple – habitual present)

Reading

7   This is practice for Reading Part 4.

1 B   2 C   3 B   4 A   5 C   6 C   7 A

8

The present continuous isn't included in the article.
present simple:	doesn't want, enjoys, feels, understands, is, says, are
present continuous:	NONE
past simple:	wanted, was, didn't know, missed, had, got, meant, chose, earned, understood, mattered, kept
past continuous:	was learning, were filming
present perfect:	have been, hasn't given, have understood
future with *will*:	will never need

20.2 pages 126–127

2

Possible answer
Sports stars do this to bring them luck.

Listening

5   This is practice for Listening Part 4.

1 train/rail   2 30(th)   3 Leyton   4 Saturday   5 11.15

Recording script 🔊 2 30

Ruth: Hello, this is Ruth Barnes. I've just heard I've won this month's radio competition!
Man: Ah yes. Congratulations.
Ruth: Thanks. What have I won?
Man: You're lucky, it's two return tickets to Venice from anywhere in Britain.
Ruth: I'll go with my mum. But is that by plane? She doesn't really like flying.
Man: No problem, they're train tickets.
Ruth: Great! When do we have to use them by?
Man: Well, you must travel before 30th April, but today's only April 5th, so there's plenty of time.
Ruth: We can go during my school holidays. Will you send me the tickets?

Man: No, you must come to our office and sign for them.
Ruth: Where are you?
Man: The address is 47 Leyton Road. That's L-E-Y-T-O-N. It's near the theatre.
Ruth: When shall I come? I'll be at school tomorrow and Friday.
Man: Saturday morning, then. And you can have a look around the radio station if you'd like to.
Ruth: Great. What time? About ten thirty?
Man: Let's say eleven fifteen, then you can say hello to DJ Richard Rooster. His show finishes at eleven.
Ruth: I've always wanted to meet him. Thanks very much.
Man: No problem. We'll see you soon.

Pronunciation

6

Recording script and answers
1. What have I won?
2. When do we have to use them by?
3. Will you send me the tickets?
4. Where are you?
5. When shall I come?
6. What time?

Vocabulary

8   This is practice for Writing Part 6.

1 special   2 kind   3 single   4 clever   5 happy
The adjective in the yellow squares is *angry*.

Reading

9   This is practice for Reading Part 2.

1 B   2 C   3 B   4 A   5 C   6 A

Spelling spot

10

1 clock   2 jacket   3 booking; tickets   4 lucky   5 chicken

Units 17–20 Revision

pages 128–129

Grammar

2

Possible answers
1. If I buy a new phone, I'll be able to send photos.
2. If I get a Saturday job, I'll earn some money.
3. If I become famous, I'll build a house with a pool.
4. If I eat more healthily, I'll feel better.
5. If I have a party, I'll invite all my friends.
6. If I do all my homework, I'll go out with my friends.
7. If I go on the internet, I'll visit some new websites.
8. If I take a break soon, I'll get a cup of coffee.

3

> Martinique is the largest island *in* the area of the eastern Caribbean. Over 300,000 people live *on* the island – many *in* the capital city, Fort-de-France. People speak French and it is taught *in/at* schools.
>
> The mountains on Martinique are old volcanoes. The highest one is Mount Pelée, which is 1,397 metres high. *In* 1902, Mount Pelée erupted and about 30,000 people were killed.
>
> The weather *in* Martinique is warm and quite wet – perfect for the farmers to grow bananas *on* their land. Bananas from Martinique are sent all over the world, so look at the bananas *in* your fruit bowl. If they are from Martinique, they will have a blue sticker *on* them.

Vocabulary

4   There may be more than one correct answer.

> **Suggested answers**
> 1   robot (not to do with a computer)
> 2   back (not part of the face or head)
> 3   envelope (not a type of written communication)
> 4   Japanese (not European)
> 5   prize (the result, not what is done)
> 6   ready (not necessarily positive)

5

> 1 C   2 A   3 B   4 B   5 A

Writing

6

> A   2, 5, 6
> B   1, 3, 4

Answers to Grammar folder exercises

Unit 1

1A

2 Can your sister come tomorrow?
3 Are Carmen and Maria from Brazil?
4 Do you like dogs?
5 Is it time to go?
6 Does Arturo catch the same bus?

1B

2 How do you get to school?
3 Where is your house?
4 What have you got in your bag?
5 Why are you angry?
6 Who does Ingrid know?

Unit 2

2 any 3 any 4 some 5 some 6 any 7 some 8 any

Unit 3

3A

2 Does (Pete really) hate 3 love 4 doesn't eat 5 goes
6 Do (you usually) go 7 don't sell

3B

2 g 3 d 4 a 5 e 6 h 7 b 8 f

Unit 4

2 Did you enjoy 3 didn't arrive 4 made 5 travelled
6 did Lyn see 7 did Pete go 8 didn't speak
9 did she spend 10 did she buy

Unit 5

2 but 3 because 4 and (but would also be possible)
5 Because 6 or

Unit 6

2 less expensive 3 the tallest 4 richer 5 sunnier
6 The most popular 7 the fastest 8 more expensive
9 better 10 the worst

Unit 7

2 was trying on; lost 3 was waiting; remembered
4 was choosing; went off 5 was studying; began
6 phoned; was having; left

Unit 8

2 may/might 3 must 4 can't 5 had to 6 has to
7 may/might 8 can

Unit 9

2 are going to 3 will 4 am / 'm going to 5 will 6 will / 'll
7 is / 's going to 8 will 9 will 10 is / 's going to

Unit 10

2 Portuguese is spoken in Brazil.
3 The Pyramids were built by the Egyptians.
4 The *Harry Potter* books were written by J. K. Rowling.
5 Presents are given on birthdays.
6 Spaghetti is eaten all over the world.
7 I was taught to swim by my father.
8 Chocolate is sold in sweet shops.
9 The World Cup was won by Spain in 2010.
10 The car was stopped by the police.

Unit 11

2 swimming 3 choosing 4 using 5 sitting; watching
6 getting 7 running 8 riding

Unit 12

2 everything 3 Somebody/Someone 4 something
5 Everybody/Everyone 6 nobody / no one

Unit 13

2 too dry 3 too wet 4 hot enough 5 cold enough
6 too strong

Unit 14

2 a large wooden reading desk
3 a popular American music magazine
4 an interesting adventure story
5 a friendly young detective
6 my favourite French comic book

Unit 15

2 Joan has just taken the customer's order.
3 Giorgio has just become a doctor.
4 Someone has just left a message for you.
5 I've just seen our dentist crossing the street.
6 I've just spoken to the engineer on the phone.

Unit 16

2 and 5   3 and 8   4 and 7

Unit 17

2 I turned on the radio to listen to the news.
3 I went to the museum to see an exhibition.
4 I borrowed some money to buy a computer game.
5 I worked hard to pass the exam.
6 I bought a cake to take to the party.

Unit 18

2 If you eat an apple a day, you won't get ill.
3 If you don't eat too many sweets, you won't get fat.
4 You will / You'll lose weight if you stop eating snacks.
5 Your teeth will stay healthy if you visit the dentist once a year.
6 You will / You'll have bad dreams if you eat cheese in the evening.

Unit 19

19A

2 in   3 at   4 in   5 at   6 in/on   7 at   8 on   9 at   10 in

19B

2 on   3 at   4 in   5 on   6 in   7 at   8 in

Unit 20

2 has (just) made   3 is going out   4 ate
5 stopped; was driving   6 won   7 asks

Answers to Practice for *Key* Writing Part 6

Unit 1
1 free   2 happy   3 wrong   4 sick   5 funny

Unit 2
1 camera   2 toys   3 shampoo   4 umbrella   5 card

Unit 3
1 fruit   2 salad   3 cake   4 pasta   5 soup

Unit 4
1 arrive   2 return   3 carry   4 decide   5 visit

Unit 5
1 horse   2 cow   3 duck   4 elephant   5 chicken

Unit 6
1 expensive   2 modern   3 bright   4 closed   5 attractive

Unit 7
1 jacket   2 socks   3 pockets   4 trousers   5 sweater

Unit 8
1 drum   2 guitar   3 album   4 lights   5 piano

Unit 9
1 luggage   2 passport   3 guidebook   4 ticket   5 map

Unit 10
1 mirror   2 curtains   3 lamp   4 pillow   5 carpet

Unit 11
1 baseball   2 football   3 surfing   4 volleyball   5 tennis

Unit 12
1 parents   2 cousin   3 uncle   4 granddad   5 sister

Unit 13
1 wind   2 rain   3 snow   4 ice   5 storm

Unit 14
1 geography   2 maths   3 science   4 history   5 music

Unit 15
1 farmer   2 nurse   3 waiter   4 dentist   5 chef

Unit 16
1 plane   2 ship   3 train   4 coach   5 bicycle

Unit 17
1 videos   2 website   3 email   4 laptop   5 program

Unit 18
1 medicine   2 doctor   3 temperature   4 chemist
5 toothache

Unit 19
1 envelope   2 note   3 stamp   4 postcard   5 text

Unit 20
1 single   2 famous   3 kind   4 awesome   5 worried

Acknowledgements

Thanks and Acknowledgements

The authors would like to give their warmest thanks to Alyson Maskell for her many useful suggestions on both editions and her meticulous attention to detail, to Lynn Townsend at Cambridge University Press for her steadfast support and practical help on the second edition, and to Sue Ashcroft for her original editorial input on the first edition. Thanks also go to Stephanie White at Kamae for her creative design solutions.

The authors and publishers would like to thank the teachers who commented on the material for the new edition in the development stage: Andrew Cook, Anna Goy and Jessica Smith, and Annie Broadhead for her comments on the Exam folders.

Development of this publication has made use of the Cambridge English Corpus (CEC). the CEC is a computer database of contemporary spoken and written English, which currently stands at over one billion words. It includes British English, American English and other varieties of English. It also includes the Cambridge Learner Corpus, developed in collaboration with the University of Cambridge ESOL Examinations. Cambridge University Press has built up the CEC to provide evidence about language use that helps to produce better language teaching materials.

This product is informed by the English Vocabulary Profile, developed as part of English Profile, a collaborative programme designed to enhance the learning, teaching and assessment of English worldwide. Its main funding partners are Cambridge University Press and Cambridge ESOL and its aim is to create 'reference level descriptions' for English linked to the Common European Framework (CEF). English Profile outcomes, such as the English Vocabulary Profile, will provide detailed information about the language that learners can be expected to demonstrate at each CEF level, offereing a clear benchmark for learners' proficiency. For more information, please visit www.englishprofile.org

The authors and publishers acknowledge the following sources of copyright material and are grateful for the permissions granted. While every effort has been made, it has not always been possible to identify the sources of all the material used, or to trace all copyright holders. If any omissions are brought to our notice, we will be happy to include the appropriate acknowledgements on reprinting.

Guardian News & Media Ltd for the text on p. 69 adapted from 'Q&A: Eniola Aluko', www.guardian.co.uk 24.05.10. Copyright © Guardian News & Media Ltd 2010; Cambridge University Press for the questionnaire on p. 130 from Activity Box by Joan Greenwood, 1997. Copyright © Cambridge University Press. Reprinted with permission of Cambridge University Press and Joan Greenwood.

The authors and publishers acknowledge the following sources of copyright material and are grateful for the permissions granted. While every effort has been made, it has not always been possible to identify the sources of all the material used, or to trace all copyright holders. If any omissions are brought to our notice, we will be happy to include the appropriate acknowledgements on reprinting.

T = Top, C = Centre, B = Below, L = Left, R = Right, U = Upper, Lo = Lower, B/G = background

p. 8 (TL): Getty Images/Stone/James Darell; p. 8 (CL): Getty Images/Taxi/Antonio Mo; p. 8 (CR): Thinkstock/Photodisc; p. 8 (BL): Thinkstock/Comstock; p. 8 (BR): Superstock/© SOMOS; p. 9 (TR, TL): Thinkstock/Photodisc; p. 9 (CR, BR): Thinkstock/ Digital Vision; p. 9 (BL): Thinkstock/iStockphoto; p. 22: Steve Davey; p. 23 (L): Corbis/Nordicphotos/ © Bertil Hertzberg; p. 23 (R): Thinkstock/iStockphoto; p. 26 (TL): Shutterstock/Jose Ignacio Soto; p. 26 (TR): Getty Images/LOCOG; p. 26 (TC): Getty Images/ AFP/YOSHIKAZU TSUNO; p. 26 (B): Photo: "Skookum Jim" – James Mason, 1898. Source: Library and Archives Canada/ International Harvester Company of Canada collection/C-025640; p. 28 (T): Getty Images/Taxi/Lisa Peardon; p. 28 (UC):

Corbis/©Robert Holmes; p. 28 (LoC): Corbis/©Ed Kash; p. 28 (B): Corbis/©Jose Fuste Raga; p. 31 (BL): Corbis/© Phil Schermeister; p. 31 (R): Topfoto.co.uk/POLFOTO/ Thomas Borberg; p. 32 (TL, TC, BCR, BR): Thinkstock/iStockphoto; p. 32 (TR): Thinkstock/ F1online; p. 32 (CR): Shutterstock/Micimakin; p. 32 (CL): Shutterstock/meunierd; p. 32 (BCL): Shutterstock/Peter Wey; p. 34: Getty Images/Stone/Daniel J Cox; p. 35: Rex Features/James D. Morgan; p. 37: Getty Images/Taxi/Gail Shumway; p. 38 (TL): Shutterstock/Racheal Grazias; p. 38 (TC): Rex Features/Sipa Press; p. 38 (TR): Thinkstock/Hemera; p. 39: ©Ferrari World Abu Dhabi www.ferrariworldabudhabi.com; p. 40: Thinkstock/iStockphoto; p. 43: Thinkstock/Hemera; p. 44 (L): Shutterstock/EML; p. 44 (C): iStockphoto/Kubrak78; p. 44 (R): Shutterstock/Neveshkin Nikolay; p. 48: Corbis/© Jean-Pierre Lescourret; p. 50 (TR): Twentieth Century-Fox Film Corporation/The Kobal Collection; p. 50 (CL): Walt Disney Pictures/The Kobal Collection; p. 50 (BL): Columbia/ Paramount/Wingnut/Amblin/The Kobal Collection; p. 50 (B/G): Alamy/© M.Brodie; p. 51: Paramount Pictures/ The Kobal Collection; p. 52: Getty Images/Samir Hussein; p. 53: Rex Features/Picture Perfect; p. 54: Walt Disney Pictures/The Kobal Collection; p. 55: Rex Features/©SIPA Press; p. 56 (BR): Corbis/© Ocean; p. 56 (BL, TL): Thinkstock/iStockphoto; p. 56 (TR): Getty Images/Taxi/David Nardini; p. 64 (TCL): Superstock/© Hemis.fr; p. 64 (L): SuperStock/Flirt; p. 64 (BR): Rex Features/Action Press/ Uwe Gerig; p. 64 (BCL, TR): Thinkstock/iStockphoto; p. 64 (CR): Shutterstock/Steve Rosset; p. 65: Shutterstock/Zsolt, Biczó; p. 67 (T): Alamy/© Jason O. Watson; p. 67 (B): Alamy/© Robert Martin; p. 68 (TL): Rex Features; p. 68 (TR): Shutterstock/Nurlan Kalchinov; p. 68 (TC): Thinkstock/Hemera; p. 68 (BL): Rex Features/SIPA/Chine Nouvelle; p. 68 (BC): Thinkstock/Brand X Pictures; p. 68 (BR): Getty Images/Cameron Spencer; p. 69: Alamy/Diadem Images /© Jonathan Larsen; p. 74: Getty Images/ WireImage/Steve Granitz; p. 76: ©Bernice Hayden; p. 80 (L): Getty Images/Photographer's Choice/Frank Cezus; p. 80 (TCL, BCR): Thinkstock/iStockphoto; p. 80 (BCL): Getty Images/Stone/Ralph Wetmore; p. 80 (TCR): Getty Images/Taxi/Getty Images; p. 80 (TR): Getty Images/Riser/Color Day Production; p. 80 (BR): Corbis/Reuters/©Richard Chung; p. 83: ©Warren Faidley/ Stormchaser; p. 86 (R): Thinkstock/Photos.com; p. 86 (TL): Thinkstock/Photodisc; p. 86 (BL): Thinkstock/Image Source; p. 88: Getty Images/Stone/Dale Durfee; p. 92 (TL): ©Bubbles/Jennie Woodcock; p. 92 (TC): Shutterstock/Mircea Bezergheanu; p. 92 (TR): ©2002Topham/PA/Topfoto.co.uk; p. 92 (BL): Shutterstock/ Igor Bulgarin; p. 92 (BR): Getty Images/The Image Bank/James Schnepf; p. 94 (L): ©Bubbles; p. 94 (C): Thinkstock/Brand X Pictures; p. 94 (R): Thinkstock/iStockphoto; p. 95: Alamy/© Andrew Michael; p. 102: Getty Images/Taxi/Angela Scott; p. 105 (C): Getty Images/Stone/Javier Pierini; p. 105 (L): Science Museum / SSPL; p. 105 (R): Alamy/© Christopher Stewart; p. 106 (BR): Rex Features/Zuma/KPA; p. 106 (TR): Rex Features/ Jonathan Hordle; p. 106 (C): Getty Images/The Image Bank/Geir Pettersen; p. 106 (R): Rex Features/Marja Airio; p. 110 (a, h, j): Getty Images/Taxi; p. 110 (b, c, e, g, i, k): Superstock/© PhotoAlto; p. 110 (d, f, l): Getty Images/Riser/Sean Justice; p. 112 (T): Topfoto/©2006 Alinari; p. 112 (C): Getty Images/AFP; p. 112 (B): Getty Images/AFP/Oscar Pipkin; p. 115: Corbis/©Robert Garvey; p. 124 (L): Rex Features/Aflo; p. 124 (R): Getty Images/Carlos Alvarez; p. 124 (C), 125: Rex Features; p. 128: Thinkstock/F1online.

Commissioned photography by: Gareth Boden pp. 10, 21, 60.

Illustrations by: James Brown, Kai Chan, Mark Duffin, Joanna Kerr, Francis Fung, Paul Howalt, Janos Jantner, Javier Joaquin, Inigo Montoya, Julian Mosedale, Andrew Painter, David Whittle

Photo research by Hilary Fletcher

Cover concept by Tim Elcock

Produced by Kamae Design, Oxford